ISLAMIC MODERNISM AND THE RE-ENCHANTMENT OF THE SACRED IN THE AGE OF HISTORY

ISLAMIC MODERNISM AND THE RE-ENCHANTMENT OF THE SACRED IN THE AGE OF HISTORY

◆ ◆ ◆

MONICA M. RINGER

EDINBURGH
University Press

For my parents

Edinburgh University Press is one of the leading university presses in the UK. We publish academic books and journals in our selected subject areas across the humanities and social sciences, combining cutting-edge scholarship with high editorial and production values to produce academic works of lasting importance. For more information visit our website: edinburghuniversitypress.com

© Monica M. Ringer, 2020, 2022

Edinburgh University Press Ltd
The Tun – Holyrood Road
12 (2f) Jackson's Entry
Edinburgh EH8 8PJ

First published in hardback by Edinburgh University Press 2020

Typeset in KoufrUni by
Servis Filmsetting Ltd, Stockport, Cheshire,

A CIP record for this book is available from the British Library

ISBN 978 1 4744 7873 1 (hardback)
ISBN 978 1 4744 7874 8 (paperback)
ISBN 978 1 4744 7876 2 (webready PDF)
ISBN 978 1 4744 7875 5 (epub)

The right of Monica M. Ringer to be identified as author of this work has been asserted in accordance with the Copyright, Designs and Patents Act 1988 and the Copyright and Related Rights Regulations 2003 (SI No. 2498).

CONTENTS

Acknowledgements｜vi

Introduction: Historicism, Modernity and Religion｜1
1. Locating Islam｜44
2. Islam in History, Islamic History｜67
3. The Islamic Origins of Modernity｜111
4. The Quest for the Historical Prophet｜140
   Conclusion: God's Intent – The Re-enchantment of the Sacred in the Age of History｜172

Bibliography｜187
Index｜202

ACKNOWLEDGEMENTS

Edward Tylor, in his seminal anthropological work, *Primitive Culture*, notes caustically that 'If in this enquiry we should be obliged to end in the dark, at any rate we need not begin there.' Inversely, historians are notoriously suspicious of origin stories. This project is the product of a long engagement with a series of questions. Can religion be modern? What would modern religion look like? And the elephant in the room: What is modernity? I begin and end the book with Max Weber's notion of 'disenchantment' as a way of emphasising the ways in which these questions matter to us now no less than they mattered in the nineteenth century. It is no coincidence that Weber, even as he characterised the modern project as one necessitating the embrace of disenchantment (*Entzauberung*), literally, the 'de-magicification' of the world, articulated a vision of disenchanted scholarship as an ethical end in and of itself. Weber concluded that in the age of disenchantment, we each must 'find and obey the demon who holds the fibers of his very life'.[1] The project of understanding the role of history in the generation of modernity has certainly been my demon for as long as I can remember. I find myself at the end of this project deeply convinced that history, defined by historicist methodology and epistemology, is the quintessence of modernity.

Amherst College has been a very supportive place for me for the last seventeen years. I have benefitted from the generous support of the Dean of the Faculty and the Senior Sabbatical Fellowship, and have been continually encouraged by the interest and commitment of my students. In particular, in the fall of 2016, I offered an advanced history seminar entitled 'An Era of Translation: The Nineteenth-Century Ottoman Empire' to a very special group of students. Those conversations we held in my office over tea provided a welcome opportunity to think through some of the theories of applying translation to modernity that appear in this book.

---

[1] Max Weber, 'The Disenchantment of Modern Life', lecture given in 1917.

Acknowledgements

Most of all, I am grateful for the collegiality and generosity of my fellow faculty at Amherst, in the Five Colleges, and in the academy more generally. Heartfelt thanks to friends and colleagues who have commented on draft chapters of this book, including: Michael Bessey, Andrew Dole, Tayeb El-Hibri, Yasemin Gencer, Sergey Glebov, Adi Gordon, Margaret Hunt, Melih Levi, Afshin Marashi and Suleiman Mourad. I have also benefitted from conversations with Houri Berberian, Houchang Chehabi, Trent Maxey, Yael Rice, Tariq Jaffer, Amina Steinfels and Mohamad Tavakoli-Targhi. Paul Rockwell and Sanam Nader-Esfahani graciously checked a number of French translations. My research assistants, Shahruz Ghaemi, Yasmeen Saeed and Julia Molin, helped enormously. Nicola Ramsey at Edinburgh University Press has been wonderful, as have Kirsty Woods, Eddie Clark and the entire production team. Thanks to them, and to the anonymous reviewer for their careful read.

I enjoyed two stints away from Amherst at crucial moments, which in some ways marked the beginning and end of this project. In the famously cold winter term of 2014, I had the honour of teaching a graduate seminar at the Divinity School at the University of Chicago. Thank you to my 'home' department of NELC and especially to A. Holly Shissler, Fred Donner, Franklin Lewis and Richard Payne who gave me such a warm welcome. I am forever grateful for the language tutoring of Melih Levi (Turkish) and Ayşe Polat (Ottoman). I have fond memories of the U of C. I remember one morning, as I was trudging to the campus in arctic temperatures wrapped in absolutely every piece of winter clothing I owned, a young man sped by wearing only a sweatshirt. It reminded me of a particularly funny scene at the very end of *A Short Walk in the Hindu-Kush*, as Eric Newby and his travel companion, inadequately outfitted, underprepared and having experienced incredible deprivations, prepare for the night. As Newby recounts, 'the ground was like iron with sharp rocks sticking up out of it'. As they begin to blow up their air-mattresses, they were belittled for their weakness by Wilfred Thesiger, the inveterate traveller, dressed only in 'an old tweed jacket of the sort worn by Eton boys, a pair of thin grey cotton trousers, rope-soled Persian slippers and a woollen cap comforter'.

Several years later, in the fall of 2018, I spent a sabbatical semester as an Academic Visitor at St Antony's College, Oxford University. My hosts, Eugene Rogan and Homa Katouzian, saw little of me as I was determined to complete a first full draft of this manuscript. I will never forget my daily routine that fall in Oxford: walking from Folly Bridge through Christ Church Meadows on my way to Jericho Coffee on High Street; watching the morning bustle against the backdrop of Brasenose College; waiting to be let in to the Radcliffe Library just before it officially opened at 9:00 am in order to get my favorite seat; lunching at the Vault and Gardens and, if I needed a change of scene, spending the afternoon up in the coffee lounge at Turl Street Kitchens. Oxford was an idyllic writing retreat. I am counting the days until I return.

Lastly, thanks to friends and family for your encouragement, and at critical moments, your patience, as this project consumed me. You know who you are. My daughter, Soraya, has always counted herself as 'my biggest fan.' I trust she knows that I am hers as well.

Monica M. Ringer
May 2020

INTRODUCTION:
HISTORICISM, MODERNITY AND RELIGION

The wonderful adaptability of the Islamic precepts for all ages and nations; their entire concordance with the light of Reason; the absence of all mysterious doctrines to cast a shade of sentimental ignorance round the primal truths implanted in the human breast, – all prove that Islam represents the latest development of the religious faculties of our being.[1]

Syed Ameer Ali (1873)

The modern project will not be accomplished until belief in the supernatural, in whatever form it takes, is destroyed, just as belief in magic and sorcery have already been. All of that is of the same order.[2]

Ernest Renan (1848)

Introduction

On Friday, 18 May 1883, the Parisian *Journal des débats politiques et littéraires* published an article by 'Cheik Gemmal Eddine' (Sheikh Jamal al-Din) who, the editors noted by way of introduction, 'has come to Paris to learn our language in order to study sciences and European civilization'.[3] In this article, Jamal al-Din, the peripatetic journalist, intellectual and political activist famous as 'al-Afghani', proposed a corrective to renown French Orientalist Ernest Renan's speech presented fifty days earlier at the Sorbonne entitled

---

[1] Ali, Life and Teachings of Mohammad, 187.
[2] Renan, *L'Avenir de la Science*, 766.
[3] *Journal des débats politiques et littéraires*, 18 May 1883, p. 3. Published precisely fifty days after their publication of Renan's lecture at the Sorbonne entitled 'Islam and Science'.

'Islam and Science', which was subsequently published in the same journal.[4] In it, Renan argued that Islam was a metaphoric 'iron band' crowning the heads of Muslims that prevented rational and scientific thought and which therefore accounted for Islamic societies' backwardness vis-à-vis Europe. Afghani took issue with Renan's characterisation of Islam as uniquely hostile to science. Instead, he proposed that the same held true for all religions:

> Religions, by whatever names they are called, all resemble each other. No agreement and no reconciliation are possible between these religions and philosophy. Religion imposes on man its faith and its belief, whereas philosophy frees him of it totally or in part.[5]

Renan and Afghani, despite important differences, agreed on the same operating assumption, namely, that religion was in conflict with science and thus inhibited progress. Their dispute was symptomatic of the larger debates concerning religion and science that raged throughout the nineteenth century – not only in Christian Europe, but also in Islamic societies. The conflict between religion and science was not, therefore, a specifically Christian conundrum, but also an Islamic one.

Despite their open criticisms of religion, both Renan and Afghani were religious modernists, dedicated to the reconciliation of modernity and religion. Humans, they insisted, were *homo religiosus*; they could not dispense with religion. At the same time, modern civilisation required a rupture with religion as currently understood and practised.

The conflict between religion and science was understood as indicative of the larger question of generating modernity and progress. As Afghani confessed in a rhetorical flourish at the end of his article, 'It is permissible to ask oneself why Arab civilization, after having thrown such a live light on the world, suddenly became extinguished; why this torch has not been relit since; and why the Arab world still remains buried in profound darkness.'[6] For Afghani and Renan alike, Islam was to blame. At the same time, Afghani proposed that Islam was also the solution – the means of relighting the torch of civilisation and progress.

Afghani's 'Response to Renan' was the first, but not the last, of the Muslim refutations of Renan's increasingly infamous lecture. By the turn of the

---

[4] Ernest Renan (1823–92) was one of the most famous nineteenth-century French philologists and Orientalists, and held the renowned Chair of Hebrew at the Collège de France. In his day he was considered one of France's leading intellectuals alongside Baudelaire, Flaubert and Stendhal. His renown stretched from academic and intellectual circles into political and popular circles due both to the controversies surrounding him, as well as to his widely read, and equally widely criticised, *Vie de Jésus* (Life of Jesus), first published in 1863.

[5] *Journal des débats politiques et littéraires*, 18 May 1883, p. 3.

[6] Afghani, 'Answer of Jamal ad-Din to Renan', in Keddie, *An Islamic Response*, 187.

century, at least four other refutations had been penned by Muslim intellectuals, ranging in order of publication from Ataullah Bayezidof (1883), Ali Ferruh (1887), Syed Ameer Ali (1901) and Namık Kemal (1908). Scholars well into the twentieth century continued to write refutations, including Celal Nuri and Mohamed Abduh.[7] As Afghani noted in his article in the *Journal des débats*, Renan was 'the great philosopher of our times ... whose name was renown throughout the entire Occident and had penetrated in the furthest counties of the Orient'.[8]

These refutations demonstrate that debates concerning the relationship of religion and science did not operate in isolation. Islamic modernists were in conversation with each other, even as they were in conversation with religious modernists from other religious traditions. In particular, Islamic modernists engaged in religious reform in an age of European colonialism and attendant claims of ownership of 'modernity' and 'civilization'. So, whereas the editors of *Journal des débats* positioned Afghani as a seeker of 'European civilization', Islamic modernists articulated their own Islamic genealogy of modernity, progress and civilisation. Islamic modernism lies not only at the nexus of the relationship of religion to modernity, but also at the nexus of European and non-European modernities. Understanding Islamic modernism in the context of other nineteenth-century religious modernisms is the project of this book.

Modernity as Disenchantment?

Max Weber's famous articulation of modernity as the 'age of disenchantment'[9] long reigned as an accurate depiction of the irreligion that presumably lay at the heart of modernity. For Weber, 'disenchantment' was an inevitable consequence of progress from savagery to modern civilisation.[10] Disenchantment entailed both triumph and loss – the breaking of the spell of magic, the renunciation of illusions, the shining of the light of truth into the dark corners of ignorance; yet at the same time, the fading of the 'sense

---

[7] For a bibliographical discussion of all the Muslim refutations to Renan's lecture, see Cündioğlu, 'Ernest Renan ve "reddiyeler" bağlamında Islam-bilim tartışmalarına bibliografik birkatke', 1–94.

[8] In the original, al-Afghani describes Renan as 'le grand philosophe de notre temps, l'illustré M. Renan, dont la renommé a rempli tout l'Occident et pénétré dans les pays plus éloignés de l'Orient', *Journal des débats*, 3.

[9] Max Weber described modernity as concomitant with the 'progressive disenchantment of the world' in a lecture given in 1917. Weber, 'The Disenchantment of Modern Life'.

[10] Weber described those people who believed in and practised magic, in other words, people who gave credence to magic as explanatory, as 'savage'. He opposes this worldview with modern 'civilized' man who has abandoned magic and embraced 'the truth of science, which alone seizes not upon illusions and shadows but upon the true being'. See Weber, 'The Disenchantment of Modern Life'.

of mystery' and exile from the 'enchanted' world.[11] Regardless of one's perspective on the (dis)advantages of disenchantment, modernity was understood as necessitating a distancing from, if not open antagonism to, religion. Otherwise put, the emergence of the modern spelled the end of religion, of long-cherished religious accounts of the world, of history, and of humankind's place in history. Natural law replaced miracles; and an evolutionary, geological account of the world, with humankind emerging only towards the very end, replaced older, biblical accounts of Creation. Modernity is closely associated with the secular, the absence if not downright rejection of religion as historically explanatory or philosophically meaningful. This understanding of modernity remains influential. Charles Taylor reiterated Weber's understanding of modernity when he stated:

> Everyone can agree that one of the big differences between us and our ancestors of five hundred years ago is that they lived in an 'enchanted' world and we do not, or at the least much less so. We might think of this as our having 'lost' a number of beliefs and the practices that they made possible. Essentially, we become modern by breaking out of 'superstition' and becoming more scientific and technological in our stance toward our world.[12]

This narrative first emerged in the Enlightenment, long perceived as the crucible of modernity and, with it, secularism. As Jonathan Sheehan explains, 'The old consensus saw an Enlightenment forcing religion into the corners of human experience and destroying the stories it told about nature, society, and mankind.'[13]

Now, almost exactly one hundred years after Weber's impassioned plea to embrace 'disenchantment', scholars acknowledge that the modern has witnessed neither the absence of religion nor the triumph of secularism. Religion has not exited the stage of history. The study of modernity has faltered in accounting for the discrepancy between modernity as it has been claimed, and modernity as it is. Is the persistence of religion evidence of the failure to become modern – the enduring residue of the pre-modern or anti-modern? Or have we not defined modernity in ways that can account for the presence of religion? What is modernity, if not disenchantment?[14]

The problem of understanding modernity has spilled over into our conception of the Enlightenment – the crucible of modernity – long affirmed as a project of disenchantment. Was or was not secularism central to the Enlightenment project of rationalism? If so, then did Enlightenment fail? If not, then what was the Enlightenment? As David Sorkin argues, we need

---

[11] Taylor, *A Secular Age*, 2.
[12] Taylor, 'Afterward: *Apologia pro Libro suo*', 302–3.
[13] Sheehan, 'Enlightenment, Religion, and the Enigma of Secularization', 1065–6.
[14] For a discussion of the scholarship on western modernity as 'enchanted', see Saler, 'Modernity and Enchantment', 692–716.

to completely rethink the Enlightenment project. 'Contrary to the secular master narrative', he argues, 'the Enlightenment was not only compatible with religious belief but conducive to it. The Enlightenment made possible new iterations of faith.'[15]

These questions are further complicated by the ongoing centrality of what I term 'the definitional puzzle'. How, in other words, do we define the Enlightenment and modernity? Which components are essential, and which tangential? Modernity, as a definition, emerged exclusively in a binary relationship – it consistently relies on casting itself as the antithesis of a constructed 'other' – whether this other is 'tradition' and 'traditional', or 'secularism' and 'secular' – modernity sustains itself by claiming a rupture, a rejection. Modernity juxtaposed itself to definitions of tradition that it itself generated. Similarly, 'religion' as a term emerged in the context of the quintessentially phenomenological and comparative enterprise of explaining difference over time and space as a consequence of European travel and exploration in the seventeenth and eighteenth centuries. The utility of 'religion' as a category of analysis is inversely proportional to its specificity. In order to be meaningful, it has to be specific, but to invoke comparison necessarily leads to its flattening out and the impoverishment of meaning. Religion was deployed in the Enlightenment project of constructing secularism as religion's 'other'. Both terms, modernity and religion, therefore, glean meaning from claims of rupture and difference – from their (artificial) construction of their necessary 'other'. Modernity as an age of disenchantment is inherently a modern myth.[16] The powerful binary of modernity versus religion has been carried forward into the study of modernity, which has long evaluated modernity as either present or absent. Societies are, in this reckoning, either modern or not.

The historiography of modernity has been caught up in this definitional quagmire. Scholars have attempted to offer alternative definitions of modernity in order to resolve the discrepancy between modernity defined as antithetical to religion, and the ongoing presence, and relevance, of religion. However, any definition turns out to be empirically unverifiable. It is not enough to propose, for example, that Scottish modernity is fundamentally different from Ottoman modernity; even within a 'national' or local modernity, there are profound variants.[17] The fragmentation of modernity into all of its particular manifestations represents an endless process of definitional Balkanisation.[18] Modernity resists definition; like puzzle pieces assembled from various puzzles, definitions are

---

[15] Sorkin, *The Religious Enlightenment*, 3.

[16] Saler, 'Modernity and Enchantment', 692–3.

[17] For a discussion of the current state of the historiography of the Enlightenment, see Sheehan, 'Enlightenment, Religion' and O'Brien, 'The Return of the Enlightenment', 1426–35.

[18] For a discussion of the heterogeneity and fragmented nature of the Enlightenment's project of modernity, see Conrad, 'Enlightenment in Global History', 999–1027.

repeatedly taken up, but resist piecing together. Nor is the solution to abandon modernity altogether, to suggest that perhaps modernity does not exist or that the Enlightenment did not take place.[19]

Approaching the problem differently, Sheehan suggests that scholars interrogate the definitions themselves. 'What would it mean,' Sheehan wonders,

> for the idea of the Enlightenment if it came to include religion? Can a category defined by its opposition to superstition, faith, and revelation survive when this opposition disappears? What would a reconciliation of the Enlightenment and religion mean to the story of modernity's origins?[20]

Other scholars have also suggested that we move away from struggling with 'the definitional puzzle', to consider the Enlightenment as a process. In other words, putting definitions as truths aside, we ought to focus instead on the 'strategies' or the 'media' of the production of modernity.[21] Secularism, in this vision, Sheehan writes,

> would be an account of how new 'religions' were produced in and through the media of the Enlightenment. It would be an account of how religion was made modern, how it was reconstructed in such a way as to incorporate it into the fabric of modernity.[22]

Along the same lines, Karen O'Brien proposes a refocusing on the Enlightenment as a process, when 'specific ways of knowing and talking about nature were sanctioned or discounted'.[23] Florian Zemmin, too, suggests that scholars focus on the 'epistemic frameworks of Modernity'.[24]

I agree that we need to shift our focus from 'finding the right definition' to exploring the relationship of religion to modernity's epistemic framework. I propose that we push this reconceptualisation of the Enlightenment and modernity further to reimagine both their nature and their relationship to one another. I am convinced that there is a missing link – an intellectual epistemic revolution – which, once properly understood, renders the Enlightenment and modernity comprehensible and accounts for both commonalities and variations of modernities. This missing link is historicism.

We should view the Enlightenment as a process of the digestion and assimilation of ideas and implications of the Scientific Revolution and 'Age of Discovery'. The implications of these ideas gradually, over the course of

---

[19] Sheehan, 'Enlightenment, Religion'.
[20] Sheehan, 'Enlightenment, Religion', 1067.
[21] Sheehan, 'Enlightenment, Religion', 1079–80.
[22] Sheehan, 'Enlightenment, Religion', 1076–7; see also 1079–80.
[23] O'Brien, 'The Return of the Enlightenment', 1429.
[24] Zemmin, *Modernity in Islamic Traditions*, 166.

the eighteenth century, coalesced into a particular constellation – an interrelated cluster of ideas that were mutually constitutive – which ultimately resulted in a fundamental epistemological and methodological shift in landscape. This constellation, which I will call historicism, produced an intellectual revolution.

This new intellectual landscape of historicism necessitated, and enabled, a fundamental reconceptualisation of ideas, a redefinition of definitions, a reconstitution of epistemological and methodological assumptions about humankind and humankind's relationship in the world over time and place. By the end of the eighteenth century, science, history and religion had been fundamentally reconceived and redefined, epistemologically and methodologically.

Historicism gave rise to claims to modernity as a civilisational level. In other words, modernity is the product of the penetration of historicism as a set of assumptions about the nature of history and humankind's place in it. Historicism was the earthquake that fundamentally reshaped the intellectual landscape – and produced new epistemological and methodological 'conditions of possibility'.[25] Definitions of modernity arise as consequences of the passage through the terrain of historicism. As ideas and institutions, intellectual assumptions and practices travelled through this landscape, they were reshaped, reconceived and redefined. Historicism, as epistemology and methodology, both necessitated and allowed for the reconceptualisation of science, of history and of religion. The result was modernity.

The slow digestion of the imperatives of historicism is demonstrated by the famous 'Quarrel of the Ancients and the Moderns' which erupted in the early seventeenth century. The nature of the quarrel ostensibly concerned the relative value of ancient versus contemporary literary and aesthetic models. Yet at a more abstract level, the quarrel was symptomatic of the gradual development and consolidation of historicism. At stake was the nature of history. Was it flat? In other words, could ancient models be emulated, or, as historicist understandings of history would have it, were there fundamental ruptures in history which made precedent as emulation irrelevant. Joseph Levine points to the epistemic implications of historicism when he explains that the quarrel was 'always and everywhere about history, about the meaning and use of the past and about the method of apprehending it'.[26] As Jacques Bos describes: '[moderns] argued that the literary and artistic norms of the ancient world were not necessarily applicable in the cultural context of the present. The present, in other words, is fundamentally different from the past.'[27]

---

[25] De Certeau, *The Practice of Everyday Life*, chapter IX 'Spatial Stories'.
[26] Levine, 'Ancients and Moderns Reconsidered', 84. On the quarrel, see also Leerssen, 'The Rise of Philology', 23–35; and Bos, 'Nineteenth-Century Historicism and its Predecessors', 133.
[27] Bos, 'Nineteenth-Century Historicism', 137.

Arnaldo Momigliano proposed that Edward Gibbon successfully navigated between the two shores of the quarrel and as a consequence, put an end to the squabbling.[28] I see Gibbon differently, as a historian who successfully employed historicism as method and epistemology. Gibbon's *The Decline and Fall of the Roman Empire* thereby marks the petering out of the quarrel, not because Gibbon reconciled, or synthesised, the two 'sides', but because *Decline and Fall* evidenced the successful absorption of historicism. It was his historicist method, I believe, that accounted for Gibbon's enormous standing. *Decline and Fall* was the 'climactic work of eighteenth-century historiography ...'[29] As Henry Hart Milman, an English historian and committed ecclesiastic, observed in his 1838 introduction to Gibbon, 'The great work of Gibbon is indispensable to the student of history ... It has obtained undisputed possession, as rightful occupant, of the vast period which it comprehends.'[30]

Returning to the idea of disenchantment, with the penetration of historicism, older definitions and locations of religion gave way to new definitions and locations in the construction of the modern. Disenchantment spelled the end of certain ways of understanding and practising religion, but simultaneously, gave rise to new concepts and practices. The religion that was abandoned was delegitimised as 'traditional' whereas the religion that was newly embraced was legitimised as 'modern'. We need to relinquish the immutability of the term 'religion' and instead see it as unstable and in a process of continual redefinition. We can read Weber's disenchantment thus as not only signifying the loss of enchantment of tradition as eternal and unconstructed, the breaking of the spell of religious truth, but also of the attendant redefinition and relocation of religion into the modern that resulted. While magic was denounced as false consciousness of the Divine, and while miracles were renounced as primitive ignorance of natural law, this did not mean the end of religion in the modern. Disenchantment facilitated re-enchantment as some definitions of religion were abandoned and others constructed.

This process of translating religion from pre-modern definitions and locations to 'modern' definitions and locations occurred over the course of the eighteenth and nineteenth centuries, as evidenced by the ubiquitous conflict between 'science and religion'. David Sorkin argues that 'religious enlighteners' were deeply engaged in reconciling science and religion throughout the eighteenth century. He notes that they believed that enlightenment and faith were 'compatible if not identical goals'.[31] As Sorkin explains, 'religious enlighteners' advocated for the unity of truth:

---

[28] Momigliano, 'Gibbon's Contribution to Historical Method', 452–4.
[29] Levine, 'Ancients and Moderns Reconsidered', 88.
[30] Henry Hart Milman, Prebendary of St Peter's, and vicar of St Margaret's Westminster, preface to Gibbon, *The Decline and Fall of the Roman Empire*, iii.
[31] Sorkin, *The Religious Enlightenment*, 17.

> Religious enlighteners championed ideas of reasonableness and natural religion, toleration and natural law that aimed to inform, and in some cases reform, established religion. Religious enlighteners were theologians, clergy, and religious thinkers who were fully committed partisans and reformers of their own tradition.[32]

For Sorkin, 'the religious Enlightenment constituted a conscious search for a middle way between extremes',[33] or what, I would suggest, is best understood as a project of translation. According to Sorkin, the French Revolution of 1789 led to the hardening of the binaries of religion and secularism, which 'destroyed the religious Enlightenment'.[34] Nonetheless, the process of marrying religion with modernity via the agency of historicism continued throughout the nineteenth century in many religious traditions, including Protestantism, Catholicism, Hinduism, Judaism and Islam.

Viewing modernity as a product of historicism enables us to disentangle modernity's own claims from empirical reality. We should therefore focus on what modernity claims to be, claims that present themselves as a set of definitions that function to (de)legitimise certain ideas and practices in certain contexts. We need to investigate the stories that modernity tells of itself, as the politics of claims and definitions, rather than being seduced into reifying claims as truths.

This conception of the relationship between modernity and religion also resolves the thorny issue of accounting for the multivalence of modernities. Commonalities are due to this shared historicist landscape – confined to the boundaries of possible routes through this terrain. Disparities are the product of different routes taken – different contexts, be they political, social or religious. This perspective enables us to speak meaningfully of differences between religious traditions – for example, European Christian modernity versus Hindu modernity versus Islamic modernity – but equally, if not more importantly, differences within the same religious tradition. We can understand ways in which definitions and locations of religion proposed by different religious modernists are a function of their position within the larger field of Christian or Hindu or Islamic modernities.

In Europe by the nineteenth century historicism had emerged as normative – it had achieved the status of doxa, an unconscious epistemology, or in Casanova's formulation, 'an unthought'.[35] But the development and

---

[32] Sorkin, *The Religious Enlightenment*, 20.
[33] Sorkin, *The Religious Enlightenment*, 11.
[34] Sorkin notes that 'The French Revolution was "that volcano-crater," in Carlyle's words, that so forcefully jolted Europe as to constitute a seismic shift. Europe's political and cultural terrain was irrevocably altered, and in a manner that virtually eliminated the religious Enlightenment.' See Sorkin, *The Religious Enlightenment*, 21, 311.
[35] Casanova, 'The Secular, Secularizations, Secularisms', 57.

adoption of historicism in Europe, and the resulting claims to modernity, are not uniquely European stories. Historicism penetrated well beyond Europe. Religious modernists, in other words, intellectuals engaged in redefining and relocating religion as a means of claiming the modern, hailed from many different religious traditions.

This book takes up the story of Islamic modernism as a subset of nineteenth-century religious modernisms. A comparative perspective enables us to establish the contours of nineteenth-century religious modernisms and to explore commonalities and differences between them. Moreover, an investigation of Islamic modernism also offers insights into the nature of modernity itself, and its deeply contested relationship to Europe.

To take one example, Europeans typically claimed that the separation of religion from law demonstrated Christianity's superiority to Judaism and Islam. Islamic modernists disagreed with this evaluation. So, whereas Lord Cromer declared that Islam 'crystallises religion and law into one inseparable and immutable whole, with the result that all elasticity is taken away from the social sphere', this was not the only possible interpretation of religion to modernity. Indian lawyer, intellectual and Islamic modernist, Syed Ameer Ali, argued that religion must buttress laws. 'The glory of Islam,' he insisted, 'consists in having embodied the beautiful sentiment of Jesus into definite laws.'[36] 'The compatibility of the laws promulgated by Mohammed with every stage of progress,' he explained, 'shows their founder's wisdom. The elasticity of laws is the great test of their beneficence and usefulness, and this merit is eminently possessed by those of Islam.'[37] The objective of scholarship on religious modernisms should not be to decide which perspective is 'correct'– that is, which is 'modern' and which is not – but to explore possible definitions and locations of religion for ways in which they claimed modernity in particular political, social and religious contexts. As Sorkin persuasively argues in the context of the European Enlightenment, 'We must renounce the temptation, however intellectually seductive or politically expedient, to designate any one version, either in any one place at any one time, or in any one cultural or religious tradition, *the* Enlightenment.'[38] Similarly, we must resist the temptation to assume that particular, European modernities are more 'true' than others.

The Landscape of Historicism

Historicism is often cited as central to nineteenth-century European intellectual history. Johannes Zachuber describes the adoption of historicism as 'a paradigm shift in European thought if ever there was any'.[39] Chakrabarty

---

[36] Ali, *Life and Teachings of Mohammed*, 183.
[37] Ali, *Life and Teachings of Mohammed*, 227.
[38] Sorkin, *The Religious Enlightenment*, 52.
[39] Zachhuber, *Theology as Science*, 4.

emphasises its importance in the development of 'political modernity' yet confesses that historicism 'is not a term that lends itself to easy and precise definitions'.[40] For all that historicism is recognised as constituting a paradigmatic shift, one that denoted the modern, the nature and timing of this shift remains obscure. Rather than assigning one particular moment as its beginning, a 'big bang' origin, historicism has a complex genealogy. Various ideas were emerging in the Enlightenment in the works of Spinoza, Vico, Voltaire, Montesquieu, Hume and others, that would gradually coalesce into a fully developed historicism by the nineteenth century.[41] A detailed exploration of the emergence and development of historicism in the eighteenth century must remain outside the scope of this project. This book takes up the project of articulating the epistemology and attendant methodology of historicism in its fully developed form in the nineteenth century, in order to illuminate ways in which Islamic modernist thought translated Islam into the modern and, in so doing, claimed the torch of progress and civilisation.

Historicism is most accurately described as a constellation of ideas including progress, universalism, comparativism, evolution, civilisation, humanism and science, to name the most salient. These ideas orbited around the central concept of context. Contexts were discreet, bounded and finite – spatially and temporally specific – *sui generis*. Each society in historical time and space was thus embedded in and reflective of its particular context in what Reinhardt Koselleck, following de Certeau, terms 'the conditions of possibility'.[42] Accordingly, ideas and institutions, customs and practices, all belonged to and participated in the same context. They reflected it and were mutually sustaining.

History was comprised of a series of discreet contexts, like beads on a string – linked, yet individually distinct. Indicative of this historicist conception of history was the belief in the fundamental difference, the 'foreignness', of one context to another. In other words, that as discreet and contained, contexts were qualitatively different from one another. By the nineteenth century, frequent allusions appear concerning the rupture between times or 'ages'. For example, Rousseau wrote that 'the Mankind of one age is not the Mankind of another age'.[43] Expressing a similar viewpoint, Indian reformer

[40] Chakrabarty, *Provincializing Europe*, 22.
[41] Baruch Spinoza (1632–77), *Theologico-Political Treatise* (1670); Gianbattista Vico (1668–1744), *Scienza Nuova* (1725); Voltaire (1694–1778), *An Essay on Universal History, the Manners and Spirit of Nations, From the Reign of Charlemagne to the Age of Lewis XIV* (1757); Montesquieu (1689–1755), *Considerations on the Causes of the Grandeur and Decadence of the Romans* (1734); and David Hume (1711–76), *The History of England* (1754–62), are some of the key individuals whose works figure prominently in the genealogy of historicism. See Bod, Maat and Weststeijn (eds), *The Making of the Humanities*.
[42] Koselleck, *The Practice of Conceptual History*, 3.
[43] Jean Jacques Rousseau, *The Discourses*, as quoted in Sheehan, 'When was Disenchantment?', 226.

Syed Ameer Ali frequently referred to what he called the 'circumstances of the age'.[44] Historicism functioned as both a concept and a method – the presumption of and location in historical context. Societies were context-specific, defined by and bound by their historical contexts. To historicise was to reveal and position in context, to understand the internal dynamics, and limits of possibility, of that particular historical moment.

As each historical time was unique contextually, the past also became 'othered' and 'estranged'.[45] The difference between past and present contexts made emulation, imitation and replication of the past an absurd enterprise. The perception of a civilisational rupture between present and past, the 'pastness' of the past,[46] made the past into an object of inquiry. The foreignness of one context to another meant that contexts had to be understood and evaluated on their own terms. Historicism involved the contextualisation of the past and the reconstruction of past contexts. Historical criticism involved the impartial, critical assembling and weighing of 'empirical' historical data about particular cultures, in order to reconstruct the contours of particular contexts. Impartiality and the intellectual freedom to look with fresh eyes were critical components of criticism, which positioned itself as scientific, and vehemently opposed any constraints such as dogma or tradition which constituted 'blind' acceptance.

Alongside historical criticism, the nineteenth-century historian's toolbelt included what I term 'historical empathy'. Whereas historical criticism might fruitfully be understood as the deployment of critical distance, 'historical empathy' involved the deployment of emotional proximity in order to reconstruct and imagine 'foreign' contexts. Historical empathy was understood as transportative – physically and temporally. The historian, through empathy, could be transported to a different context via this methodological 'rabbit hole'. The historian moved virtually into a different space and time, but retained the critical distance that derived from their own context. Emotion and visual experience were both thought to have 'connective' effects that enabled a certain intrinsic connection between the historian and their object of study. Vision and experience created the capacity for empathy – the immersion of 'Self' in a foreign context – and thus provided an enhanced perception of the 'Others' context.

The nineteenth-century historian was trapped between the desire to overcome historical distance, and the recognition of the limitations of this possibility. The deployment of 'historical empathy' was a powerful methodological point of contention in the nineteenth century. Some scholars insisted on the retention of critical, impartial distance, whereas others believed in the value of generating emotional proximity. Thomas Babington Macaulay, in

---

[44] Ali, *Life and Teachings of Mohammed*, 234–5.
[45] Zammito, 'Koselleck's Philosophy of Historical Time(s)', 323.
[46] Bos, citing Auerbach. Bos, 'Nineteenth-Century Historicism and its Predecessors', 8.

his *History of England (1848–1861)*, advocated for the importance of imagination when he wrote:

> To make the past present, to bring the distant near ... to call up our ancestors before us with all their peculiarities of language, manners, and garb, to show us over their houses, to seat us at their tables, to rummage their old-fashioned wardrobes, to explain the uses of their ponderous furniture, these parts of the duty which properly belongs to the historian have been appropriated by the historical novelist.[47]

Other scholars vehemently disagreed. Leopold van Ranke (1795–1886), oft cited as the father of 'modern' historicist method, insisted on 'sticking to facts'.[48] 'I resolve to avoid in my work,' Ranke wrote, 'all imagination and all invention, and to hold myself absolutely to facts.'[49] This is the impetus which lies behind Ranke's famous statement of purpose, to study history 'as it actually happened' (*wie es eigentlich gewesen*).[50]

The perception of history as a series of contexts entailed two possible consequences. The first, that all is constructed and context-specific; the second, that there exists something other than context, something that, by definition, transcends context; something permanent, ahistorical and absolute, an eternal immutable truth – in other words, 'essence'. Twentieth-century relativism committed to the first option; nineteenth-century historical thought to the second. Essence, rather than being inimical to the embrace of historicism, was intimately bound up with it.

The notion of essence was imbued with its genesis – its time and place of origin. Origins were the location of primordial essence akin to the DNA of a culture. Origin as essence contained agency – the inherent potential of future civilisational development. Language and religion were the principal components of essence. Language embodied intellectual and creative possibility; religion embodied both intellectual and moral capacity. Essence was expressed in context, in the 'customs and manners' of a given culture, which included science, arts, religion and literature, as well as gender relations (marital customs, the status of women), freedom/bondage (slavery),

---

[47] Lika, 'Fact and Fancy in Nineteenth-Century Historiography', 152, citing Macaulay, *Critical and Miscellaneous Essays*, vol. 1, 188–9.

[48] Lika, 'Fact and Fancy', 154.

[49] Ranke's original statement reads: 'Je pris la résolution d'éviter, dans mes travaux, toute imagination et toute invention et de m'en tenir sévèrement aux faits.' Cited in Lika, 'Fact and Fancy', 154.

[50] Ranke's sentence in context is as follows: 'To history has been assigned the office of judging the past, of instructing the present for the benefit of future ages. To such high offices this work does not aspire: It wants only to show what actually happened.' Ranke, *History of the Latin and Teutonic Nations from 1494 to 1514*, introduction. For a discussion on the particular translation of Ranke's phrase, see Gilbert, 'Historiography: What Ranke Meant', 393–7.

technology (military triumph, architecture) and religion.[51] Language and religion were thus the most salient markers of the level of civilisation of a particular culture. Max Müller, one of the most important theorists of the discipline of religious studies, in a letter read aloud at the Congress of the History of Religions held in 1900 in Paris, claimed that 'everyone today seems completely familiar with the idea that whomever only knows one religion, knows none, and that one cannot understand a religion if one does not know its origin and history'.[52]

The association of origin with essence explains nineteenth-century scholarly preoccupations with the 'Ur' as origins – the *Ursprache*, the 'Ur' monotheism. The quest for origins was ubiquitous and manifest in attempts to determine the origin of mankind, the origin of Christianity, the origin of language, the origins of government, human inequality, and so on. This idea witnessed it zenith in the quest to identify the language of Paradise.[53] This grail linked the works of Hobbes and Rousseau with Feuerbach and Darwin, and inspired such diverse classificatory disciplines as archaeology, philology and religious studies, as well as anthropology and biology.[54]

Philology, religious studies and history were all animated by this historicist understanding of history as the travelling of essence through different contexts. Human civilisational progress could be charted by these voyages, by the passing of the torch of civilisation from one culture to another. Philology undertook the excavation of essence from context, by attempting to retrieve and reconstitute 'original' and thus 'pure' languages from the vicissitudes of time. Franz Bopp developed the 'family tree' organisation of languages to convey their relationships with one another. Related languages were different parts of the same tree, with common roots even as they gradually diverged from each other along different branches.[55] Charles Darwin was influenced by Bopp's linguistic tree and employed a similar visual idiom to represent evolution.[56]

Jacob and Wilhelm, 'The Brothers Grimm', best known for their collection of fairy tales, were philologists. They believed that language was a carrier of culture and thus indicative of civilisational evolution. Philology was more than the study of grammar – it was the linguistic archaeology of origins – the

[51] Leerssen, 'The Rise of Philology', 24.
[52] Réville (ed.), *Actes du premier Congrès international d'histoire des religions réuni a Paris, du 3 au 8 septembre 1900 à l'occasion de l'Exposition Universelle*, 35.
[53] Olender, *The Languages of Paradise*.
[54] The capaciousness of the quest for origins is evident in Hobbes, *Leviathan* (1651); Jean-Jacques Rousseau, *Discourse on the Origins of Inequality* (1755); Ludwig Feuerbach, *The Essence of Christianity* (1841); Charles Darwin, *The Origin of Species* (1857); and in Protestant biblical criticism and the genre of 'the quest for the historical Jesus' exemplified by David Fredrich Strauss' *Das Leben Jesu* (*The Life of Jesus*) (1835) and Ernest Renan's *Vie de Jésus* (*Life of Jesus*) (1863).
[55] Leerssen, 'The Rise of Philology', 24.
[56] Leerssen, 'The Rise of Philology', 24.

excavation of the trail of human civilisational progress. Philology could take the scholar into prehistory, a place in the past much earlier than the earliest written evidence. Folklore, like language, accumulated new elements as it travelled through different contexts, even as it retained older ones – residual traces of more primitive times – of earlier stages of the civilisational journey. As Orientalist Émile-Louis Bournouf (1821–1907) explained, it permitted the retrieval of 'religious ideas that, in the distant past, were common among an entire race of men, as well as that which their descendants added much later'.[57] The step by step retrieval of original, 'pure' words from their historical distortions, like Hansel and Gretel's trail of breadcrumbs, indicated the path home back through civilisational time to the word in its original, 'pure' form. It is no coincidence that the frontispiece of the Grimm's German Dictionary published in 1854–71 included a vignette with the phrase: 'In the beginning was the word.'[58]

Adopting similar methods as philologists, religious studies scholars worked to identify the essence of particular religions – the pure, inherent, primordial form in which they were 'born'. This methodology underpinned the burgeoning of Semitic studies as fundamental to the establishment of Jesus' Jewish context, and the archaeological pursuit of the 'essence' of Christianity.[59] Only a knowledge of Jesus' context, scholars insisted, could enable the sifting out of that which belonged to his context from that which was transcendent, universal and eternal.[60] Historical time, thus, was the march of human progress from savagery to civilisation, even as it also entailed the gradual accretion of historical detritus. Scholars looked to the future, even as they were preoccupied with discovering the primordial past.

Historical method was propelled by similar imperatives. In order to locate the particular within the universal, historians needed to identify and 'tag' each culture as belonging to one or another civilisational level. As an explicitly comparative enterprise, historians sought to understand each culture's context, and to evaluate and locate it on a civilisational continuum. Religion and language were essential, and thus viewed as the most salient markers of the level of civilisation of a particular culture. Historicism thus embraced the twin projects of locating cultures by dint of their religious 'essence' on a universal taxonomy of progress, as well as explaining change over time within a culture, based on the relationship of religious/linguistic essence to changing context.

---

[57] Burnouf, 'La Science des Religions: sa méthode et ses limites', 2.
[58] The full biblical sentence is: 'In the beginning was the word, and the word was with God, and God was the word.' John 1:1. See Leerssen, 'The Rise of Philology', 30–1. Grimms' fairy tales were first published in 1812.
[59] Thus, the application of historicism to biblical studies also resulted in the attempt to retrieve the 'essence' of Christianity from history in a genre that would be termed the 'quest for the historical Jesus'. See Schweitzer, *The Quest for the Historical Jesus*.
[60] Howard, *Religion and the Rise of Historicism*.

History emerged as the story of universal civilisational progress. Civilisation was imagined as a series of steps, or levels, that displayed particular characteristics. Cultures were assigned to these different levels of civilisation according to their 'civilisational' features. Primitive cultures exhibited primitive features; advanced cultures exhibited advanced features. Writ large, history was the charting of the progress of the torch of civilisation as it progressed from civilisational level to civilisational level, carried forward by one culture before being taken up by another, more advanced culture. At the granular level, history involved the location of specific cultures within the universal civilisational hierarchy, the stringing together of all cultures, past and present, in order of civilisational progress. Each culture needed to be understood on its own terms, as reflective of and bounded by its particular context, even as it could then be located within the larger, comparative framework of human civilisational progress. Historicism, as contextualisation, was thus a tool for understanding contexts in their particulars, as well as the movement from one context to another, the crossing of civilisational thresholds. Historicism was the principle means of locating and retrieving essence from history – only context could reveal its nemesis – that which transcended context.

The explanation of difference in the nineteenth century moved away from a theologically based true/false binary, to a location within a universal evolutionary timeline. Religion, as phenomenological and thus comparable, emerged as a category of analysis. All religions were 'true' in the sense of their impulse to understand the Divine, but this truth was historically contingent.[61] Religious difference was understood as a function of greater or lesser consciousness of the truth of the Divine, determined by the level of civilisation; religious difference was civilisational difference. Primitive religions were characteristic of primitive civilisations, and advanced religions characteristic of advanced, more evolved civilisations. Religions were organised along a civilisational continuum from primitive (savage) to the more 'advanced' level of polytheism (barbarism) and, ultimately, monotheisms. Primitive religions were identified by particular features, such as the emphasis on performative, 'mechanistic' rituals, anthropomorphism and religious explanations of natural law (miracles, weather, and so forth) whereas monotheisms were categorised, and thus claimed, as spiritual, ethical and rational. This universalist, civilisational progress of religions cum civilisations generated a hierarchical taxonomy whereby cultures were located and classified according to their level of religion.

The scholarly investigation of primitive cultures and religions was thus a means of time travel – of the historical recovery of the various strata of human civilisational development. As anthropologist Edward Tylor (1832–1917) explained in his influential book *Primitive Culture*, 'the phenomena of Culture [sic] may be classified and arranged, stage by stage, in a probable

---

[61] Stroumsa, 'History of Religions: The Comparative Moment', 326.

order of evolution'.⁶² Primitive cultures were mined for the light that they shed on human development more generally, not simply for what they might illustrate about a particular society in time. They were viewed as 'relics' of earlier civilizational eras – as pockets of time/space that had not progressed, but that had somehow remained fixed in an earlier civilisational moment, preserved like insects in amber.

Historicism, via the new, scientific disciplines of history, philology and religious studies, permitted both the identification of context and the primordial, unchanging 'essence' of a given culture. Civilisational progress was a function not only of historical development as changing context, but of the interaction in context of essences of religion and language. Languages, like religions, were symptomatic of the 'genius of each people' and thus indicative of their inherent civilisational potential.⁶³ Indo-European languages, European philologists insisted, were by dint of their grammatical structures, conducive to creativity and rational thought, which in turn created the agency that enabled intellectual, religious and scientific progress, the movement from once civilisational level to another. Non-Indo-European languages (and here Semitic languages played the principal role of the dichotomous 'Other') were less flexible, and because of this generated dogmatism, passivity, and what Ernest Renan metaphorically termed an 'iron band' that prevented intellectual and cultural creativity, critical thinking and by extension, scientific advancement.⁶⁴ As I have detailed in another project, Protestant Christianity claimed to exemplify rational and thus 'modern' and progressive religion – characterised by the interiorisation of ethics, individual consciousness of the Divine, spirituality and rationalism – and in so doing, claimed to best reflect progress and civilisation.⁶⁵ European philologists and religious studies scholars thus concurred in claiming European civilisation as inherently creative, rational and capable of generating modernity in ways that other, non-Indo-European and non-Christian peoples, were not.

The adoption of historicism in reshaping the subject and method of history also altered conceptions of time. To chronological and natural conceptions of time were added the idea of civilisational time. The dislocation of historical time from chronological time meant that societies were conceived of in relation to civilisational progress, regardless of their location in chronological time. The equation of historical time with civilisational progress led, as Koselleck noted, to the non-contemporaneity of the contemporaneous, and vice versa.⁶⁶ In other words, cultures, simply because they were

---

⁶² Tylor, *Primitive Culture*, 6.
⁶³ Condillac (1715–80) connected language to the essential character of a 'people'. See Olender, *Languages of Paradise*, 5–6.
⁶⁴ See Ringer and Shissler, 'The Al-Afghani-Renan Debate, Reconsidered', 28–45.
⁶⁵ Ringer, *Pious Citizens: Reforming Zoroastrianism in India and Iran*.
⁶⁶ Here I am following Koselleck's notion of the disconnect between historical time and natural time. I believe that the concept of chronological time, however,

contemporaneous, did not necessarily belong to the same civilisational level. In the same way, cultures might be at a comparable civilisational level with others in the past. Tylor articulated this idea of civilisational comparability when he explained that comparison in the 'same grade of civilization' need have 'little respect for date in history or for place on the map: The ancient Swiss lake-dweller may be set beside the medieval Aztec...'[67]

The language of historicism was from the outset deeply imbued with the interrelatedness of progress and civilisation. The terms 'primitive' and 'backward' became coterminous not only with less advanced levels of civilisation, but also with previous historical time. This explains modernity's claim to be somehow further along in time relative to the non-modern, which was rejected as 'backward' even if it was contemporaneous. The idea of modernity as the speeding up of time, or at least the perception of the speeding up of time, functions as a claim to the increasing frequency of civilisational cum historical ruptures.[68]

Historicism and the Challenge to Religion

There were several, interconnected reasons for the particularly troubled relationship between religion and historicism. First, historicism disabled pretentions of historical transcendence and truth – the ahistorical claims of tradition. Through historicism, religion was embedded in history, and in so doing, became contingent, particular and contextual. Religious dogma and traditions, subject to the dissolvent of historicism, emerged not as transcendent truths, but as human products of particular historical contexts.

Second, continued acceptance of the literal reading of sacred texts themselves became increasingly difficult within a comparative, historicist and universal framework. How could biblical stories be read literally, alongside a contextual interpretation of meaning? Did readers over the span of hundreds of years understand the text similarly? How could one account for more primitive religious understandings of biblical peoples? Similarly, generations of New Testament scholars struggled to reconcile Jesus' miracles within the framework of natural law.[69] Enlightenment philosopher David Hume

---

best describes this phenomenon, since natural time suggests natural, organic earthy rhythms (sunrise, sunset, seasons, and so forth) which I do not believe are disengaged from concepts of historical time the way that chronological time (formerly organising the sequence of dynasties or rulers that was the stuff of much pre-modern history) was. Koselleck, *Futures Past*, 95. Some translators have preferred the terms 'simultaneous' and 'non-simultaneous', but I prefer 'contemporaneous' and 'non-contemporaneous'.

[67] Tylor, *Primitive Culture*, 6.
[68] Zammito, 'Koselleck's Philosophy', 133.
[69] For a history of biblical criticism, see Zachhuber, *Theology as Science*, and Howard, *Religion and the Rise of Historicism*. See also Stroumsa, *A New Science*.

(1711–76) succinctly pronounced that 'A miracle is a violation of the laws of nature.'[70] In the Islamic tradition, scholars were faced with the conundrum of precedent – could the religious practices established by the Prophet in his own historical context be eternally prescriptive?

Last, but not least, the adoption of historicism as a new epistemology and methodology challenged existing Abrahamic historical frameworks. Abrahamic texts (the Old and New Testaments and the Quran) provided powerful historical narratives, from God's creation of the world and humankind, to the expulsion of Adam and Eve from Paradise and the subsequent series of prophets. These historical accounts were destabilised by the universalist, comparativist and contextual epistemology and methodology attendant in historicism. This project of reconciling religious historical accounts with new ideas became even more troubled with the unearthing of archaeological evidence that challenged biblical dating and the narrative of Creation. This, together with the European 'discovery' of new peoples in the Americas, suggested alternative genealogies of human history – accounts that were difficult to reconcile within the Abrahamic historical fabric. Christian apologists stretched the idea of common human ancestry from Adam and Eve and the possibilities of the 'Ten Lost Tribes of Israel' to the breaking point.[71] As Rubiés notes, 'While the history of mankind was illuminated by new types of evidence, it could rarely be conceived without considering at the same time the history of religion.'[72] Evolution also compromised the Abrahamic narrative of Creation by suggesting continuous development, or what Tylor termed 'the progression-theory of civilization'.[73] Primitive peoples were the earliest humans and significantly less civilised than biblical accounts of Adam.

In Europe, by the eighteenth century, historicism had severely undermined the 'truth' of Christian tradition. Indeed, as Zachhuber declared, the eighteenth century witnessed 'the historicization of European intellectual life. In this process, all areas of public discourse and rational enquiry were increasingly inscribed in, and reconstructed as, historical development or evolution.'[74] Historicism imposed new meanings on history which fundamentally threatened the dogmas and truths maintained by religious tradition. As a result, 'religion was and remained a paradigmatic case of a tradition that had lost its unquestioned validity'.[75] By the nineteenth century, the full embrace of historicism in Europe ushered in an era marked by the

---

[70] David Hume (1711–76), *An Enquiry concerning Human Understanding*, Part I 'Of Miracles'.
[71] On the rise of comparative frameworks and their effect on historical thought, see Rubiés, 'Comparing Cultures in the Early Modern World', 116–76.
[72] Rubiés, 'Comparing Cultures', 143.
[73] See Tylor, *Primitive Culture*, 35–6.
[74] Zachhuber, *Theology as Science*, 4.
[75] Zachhuber, *Theology as Science*, 15.

abandonment of formalism, ritual and tradition as inimical to reason and feeble in the face of historical inquiry. Religious history was mapped onto universal civilisational progress; the location of the particular in the universal story of mankind's continuous 'longing after the infinite', to borrow Max Müller's impassioned formulation.[76]

The ubiquitous nineteenth-century debates that raged throughout Europe concerning the (in)compatibility of 'religion and science' should be understood as symptomatic of the ongoing exploration of the relationship between new historicist and scientific methodologies, and the dismantlement of tradition, dogma and Church authority. The emergence of these debates in the eighteenth century and their continuation in the nineteenth century illustrates the ongoing attempts to digest the implications of historicism. They mark the process of the translation of religion into the modern.

While undoubtedly commitments to the unchanging nature of Divine truth gave way to the embrace of historicism as context, it is nonetheless equally true that freedom from tradition opened up new religious possibilities. We should understand modernity as the 'age of disenchantment' – the loss of enchantment with tradition as eternal and unconstructed, the breaking of the spell of religious truth – but equally of the intendent redefinition and relocation of religion that resulted. In other words, while magic was denounced as false consciousness of the Divine, and while miracles were cast as symptomatic of primitive ignorance of natural law, this did not mark the end of religion in the modern. Whereas some abandoned religion as irreconcilable to modern science and historical method, others were committed to their reconciliation – the unification of religion and modernity.

Paradoxically, the premise of context freed essence from history and enabled it to be relocated and recontextualised in the present. Historicism dissolved the fetters of tradition. So, while in the eighteenth century, Hume declared that belief in miracles was 'observed chiefly to abound among ignorant and barbarous nations', by the mid-nineteenth century, David Friedrich Strauss (1808–1974) asserted that 'the supernatural birth of Christ, his miracles, his resurrection and ascension, remain eternal truths, whatever doubts may be cast on their reality as historical facts'.[77] Historicism enabled creative opportunities to reconstruct and reinvigorate religion.

Deliverance from dogma and freedom to reinterpret and relocate religion paradoxically went hand-in-hand. It is here, in this project of re-enchantment, that we need to locate nineteenth-century religious modernisms. Religious modernists, rather than bemoaning the loss of tradition as a fixed and per-

---

[76] Max Müller, asserting the capacity of linguistics to recover religious expressions over time, insisted that 'if we will but listen attentively, we can hear in all religions a groaning of the spirit, a struggle to conceive the unconceivable, to utter the unutterable, a longing after the Infinite, a love of God'. Müller, 'Lectures on the Science of Religion', 113.

[77] Strauss, *The Life of Jesus Critically Examined*.

manent truth, sought instead to rationalise religious practice and ethics and to resuscitate what they believed to be the essence of God's intent from the detritus of historical context. Religious modernists engaged in a profound redefinition and relocation of religion – the re-enchantment of religion in the age of history.

A New Age of Discovery

Historicism was the product of the Scientific Revolution and Enlightenment, capaciously understood as themselves the product of connections and exchanges between Europeans and many other peoples. Throughout the nineteenth century, historicism as a new epistemology and attendant methodology permeated well beyond Europe. By the mid-nineteenth century, the Middle East and South Asia were increasingly connected with Europe, and with each other, through new networks of exchange and travel. Most importantly, these new networks, and the knowledge, experience and possibilities that they offered, both created and demanded new explanatory mechanisms, which contributed to the adoption of historicism.

New possibilities of steam and rail travel allowed both more rapid and less expensive travel between cities, and linked ports in the Middle East to those in South Asia and Europe. These new industrial technologies thus facilitated more extensive travel, and greater numbers of people travelling, than ever before. The travel routes created nodes of connectivity, cities bound by travel itineraries that reorganised the production and diffusion of knowledge. Print capitalism streamed along these arteries, but also flowed through smaller, local capillaries, connecting the local to the trans-local in qualitatively and quantitatively new ways. The routes of intellectual exchange, influence and appropriation were deepened not only across spaces, but within them. New technologies in transportation and print facilitated the development of larger and more complex global networks that enabled the intellectual penetration of new ideas.

The burgeoning of travel, whether experienced directly or disseminated indirectly via the mushrooming press and personal interactions, led to a profound disorientation of identities, space and time for the increasing numbers of Middle Easterners and South Asians who were exposed to the new vistas travel afforded. Nile Green, in his pioneering article on the ways in which steam travel effected notions of Muslim 'Spacetime', noted that the string of port cities that stretched from London to Bombay 'presented confusing medleys of peoples from far and wide, whose ambiguous identities confused the conceptual borders between self and other'.[78] These spaces of interaction and 'entanglement' disrupted boundaries that assumed a firm link between language, religion and place, and instead confronted travellers with European Muslims, Middle Eastern Europeans and people of other complex

---

[78] Green, 'Spacetime and the Muslim Journey West', 406.

and overlapping identities that forced new recalibrations of the criteria of difference between 'self' and 'other'. As T. S. Eliot perceptively remarked, 'we shall not cease from exploration, and the end of all our exploring will be to arrive where we started and know the place for the first time'.[79]

In similar ways, space defied easy mapping onto the binaries of *Dar al-Harb* (the Lands of War) and *Dar al-Islam* (the Lands of Islam).[80] Europe became Islamic space, even as Middle Eastern spaces became Europeanised. According to Green, 'as "European" cities became part of a reconceptualized Muslim geography, "Muslim" cities became correspondingly European in appearance.'[81] This disruption of spatial-identity correlation denoted by the binary distinction of *Dar al-Islam* versus *Dar al-Harb* led to the emergence of the concept of the 'Muslim World' as a global marketplace for the production of Islam.[82] Key to the emerging Muslim world were Muslim intellectuals' renewed acquaintance with sources of knowledge of Islam and Islamic history that they encountered in Europe – whether textual, linguistic or archaeological. Green is right to point out that 'travelers discovered the Muslim past as much as the European present'.[83] Yet while the sources for the 'discovery' of the Muslim past were undoubtedly an important consequence of these interactions, I would further emphasise that it was not simply the 'discovery' of unknown material, but the experience of disruption in this second 'age of discovery' that led Muslim intellectuals to not only encounter, but to find relevant, the conceptual explanatory framework of historicism.

Travel and the experience of the world as interconnected, literally and figuratively, led to comparison, to new ways of framing self/other, to new ways of accounting for difference, and to new ways of understanding the particular in the newly imagined universal. The diversity of times, and means of calculating times, expanded to include not only European time, but a new conception of historical cum civilisational time.[84] Evolutionary explanations of the universal – of mankind's gradual progress through a hierarchy of civilisational levels – explained difference as resulting from 'civilizational factors', themselves calculated and measured with new yardsticks of science,

---

[79] T. S. Eliot, 'Little Gidding'.
[80] These two terms expressed a classic difference between lands in which Islam was the religion of state, and lands in which it was not.
[81] Green, 'Spacetime', 425.
[82] Green, 'Spacetime', 427–8. In conjunction with the discussion of the emergence of the 'Muslim World', see Green's more recent exploration of 'terrains of exchange' and the marketplace for Islam in Green, *Religious Economies of Global Islam*.
[83] Green, 'Spacetime', 403.
[84] The introduction of European clocks into the Ottoman Empire added a further dimension of time measurement to the already diverse systems operating concurrently in the Tanzimat period. See Wishnitzer, *Reading Clocks* 'Alla Turca'. I distinguish between chronological increments of time measured by a variety of clocks (and sun/moon calculations) and 'historical' time, which I argue is measured by assessments of levels of 'civilization'.

religion and language. History as a discipline involved the mapping of the particular context onto universal human civilisational progress.

Just as European explorations in the sixteenth and seventeenth centuries led to concepts of universalism and a phenomenological approach to human difference, so too did this new age of exploration facilitate the adoption of these same explanatory paradigms elsewhere. As Guy Stroumsa notes in the European context, the adoption of concepts of universalism resulted from the experience of comparison; the fluidity of differences and often profound commonalities between peoples and places necessitated more satisfying explanations of difference than binary true/false categories, and led directly to the phenomenological understanding of human societies as particulars in a common universal.[85] The birth of comparativism and historicism led to a 'genuine revolution in knowledge and attitudes ... which in turn allowed a radical transformation in the perception of religious phenomena' within a framework of 'the unity of mankind'.[86] Travel in this new age of discovery gave rise to explicit comparativism and a growing body of analysis concerning 'the secret of European strength', which attempted to account for global power disparities.[87] Historicism offered an explanation for commonalities and difference in time and place within an evolutionary model of human development. History, as civilisation, became the story of this evolution.

This new age of discovery created conditions whereby historicism enjoyed an explanatory capacity for Europeans and Middle Easterners alike. In other words, it is not only that the Islamic past was rediscovered but that it was reconceived and reconstructed. History was adopted as the story of context as it changed over time; time was recalibrated as the progressive development of civilisation. Not surprisingly, the adoption of these new, universalist and historicist conceptions of time, space and history generated a plethora of new history writing in the Middle East and South Asia, just as it did in Europe.

If, as Felicity Nussbaum persuasively argues, we should lengthen and widen the eighteenth century to acknowledge ways in which other peoples and societies participated and contributed to the development of new paradigms and ideas, then I would argue that we should identify the nineteenth century with the bridging of these geographical and intellectual spaces.[88] Historicism was adopted throughout the globe because it provided similar explanatory models. From the beginning, historicism was the product of the age of discovery. It spread through this second age of discovery, and found new soil in which to flourish and become meaningful.

The nineteenth century thus moves us well beyond the concept of 'contacts and encounters' – however reciprocal – into new dimensions of complexity.

---

[85] Stroumsa, *A New Science*, 2.
[86] Stroumsa, *A New Science*, 2, 7.
[87] Ringer, 'The Quest for the Secret of Strength'.
[88] Nussbaum (ed.), *The Global Eighteenth Century*, 1.

We might conceive of this interconnectedness as the existence of many centres and many, deeper edges.[89] The exchange of ideas should not be imagined as linear nor unidirectional, nor even reciprocal, but multi-dimensional and multi-directional. The intellectual networks throughout the Muslim world – a 'world' that now included European capitals, as well as Middle Eastern and South Asian cities – were sites of participation in myriad overlapping conversations.[90]

Thinking Beyond Europe

Christianity was not the only tradition to crack under the weight of historicism. Like their counterparts in other religious traditions, Islamic modernists grappled with the challenge of reforming religion to take into account new epistemological and methodological truths. Islamic modernism was the consequence of these new intellectual commitments – to the intellectual landscape of historicism, to 'modern' values and to the enduring meaning of religion to humankind. Islamic modernists rewrote Islamic history and developed a new historicist epistemology and methodology. In so doing, they constructed 'modern' Islam as the union of modernity and religion – an Islam that they believed could generate progress and civilisation and resolve the disparity between European power and Islamic 'backwardness'. Islamic modernism, currently represented in historiography as primarily (if not uniquely) instrumentalist, was in fact deeply constitutive of modernities in the Islamic societies of the Middle East (largely conceived) and South Asia.

The challenges and opportunities of the adoption of historicism were thus clearly not uniquely European. Insofar as no society was immune to the impact of modern science and insofar as historicism spread throughout the world, they were global challenges and opportunities. Of particular fascination is the way in which different societies grappled with the religious implications of historicism. Christian, Muslim, Jewish, Hindu and Zoroastrian intellectuals, concerned to reserve a place for religion in modernity, developed a variety of strategies in their attempts to subject religion and religious traditions to new scrutiny. Muslim intellectuals engaged in the translation of ideas across and within locales as they re-examined Islamic texts and traditions. Muslim intellectuals were engaged with historicism and its challenge to religious tradition, just as their Catholic, Jewish, Hindu and Zoroastrian counterparts were in Europe, the Middle East, South Asia and beyond. The

---

[89] I take up the concept of centre and edge as articulated by Bulliet, *Islam: A View from the Edge*.

[90] Green, 'Spacetime'. For specific examples of nineteenth-century 'connected' histories, see Berberian, *Roving Revolutionaries*, and Marashi, *Exile and the Nation*. For examples of 'connected' histories in the seventeenth and eighteenth centuries, see Subrahmanyam, *Europe's India*, and Aslanian, *From the Indian Ocean to the Mediterranean*.

challenge for the historian is to 'fold in' the local with the global without at the same time flattening out unique local topographies.[91]

As evidence of the penetration of historicism beyond Europe, Jamal al-Din al-Afghani (whose refutation of Renan inaugurated this introduction), in a letter dating from 1880/81, denounced Darwinism, caustically remarking that 'according to the view of [Darwin], it would be possible that after the passage of centuries a mosquito could become an elephant and an elephant, by degrees, a mosquito'.[92] Yet even as Afghani mistakenly characterised Darwinism as implying transubstantiation, Afghani was profoundly influenced by historicism, evolutionism, comparativism, universalism and the phenomenological view of religion as a category of historical analysis. In other words, while he may have publicly rejected Darwin's ideas as irreligious, he nevertheless operated unconsciously within the very same intellectual landscape that sustained Darwin's ideas and evolutionary thought more generally. More importantly, Afghani's historicist epistemology and methodology led him to insist on Islamic reform – on the redefinition and relocation of religion in order to claim modernity – on the translation of religion into the modern.

The turn to historicism as method and subject re-engaged scholars with their own religious and historical traditions, opening up new avenues of thought, new models and new methodologies. We must therefore reconceive of these conversations as not only occurring between traditions, but more importantly, within them. The adoption of historicism not only entailed an engagement with European ideas and models, but also a re-engagement with Islamic ones. This explains the explosion of discussions in the nineteenth century amongst Islamic liberals and 'fundamentalists' alike regarding the 'opening of the door of *ijtihad*'.[93] It also explains their frequent allusion to pre-modern rationalist and historical traditions, exemplified by al-Ghazzali (d. 1111) and the Rashidun period (AD 632–61), respectively.

---

[91] Nussbaum, *Global Eighteenth Century*, 8.
[92] Afghani, 'The Truth About the Neicheri Sect', 136. Darwin's only observations concerning elephants and mosquitos are as follows: 'Before man inhabited India or Africa, some cause must have checked the continued increase of the existing elephant. A highly capable judge, Dr. Falconer, believes that it is chiefly insects which, from incessantly harassing and weakening the elephant in India, check its increase . . . It is certain that insects and blood-sucking bats determine the existence of the larger naturalized quadrupeds in several parts of South America.' See Darwin, *The Origin of Species*, 97.
[93] On the emergence of debates surrounding *ijtihad* in this period, see Kurzman (ed.), *Modernist Islam*. See also Hallaq, *Authority, Continuity and Change in Islamic Law*; Peters, 'Idjtihad and Taqlid in 18th and 19th Century Islam', 131–45; Watt, 'The Closing of the Door of Ijtihad', 675–8; and van Ess, 'La tradition dans la théologie mu'tazilite', 211–26.

The Historiography of Erasure

Scholars of European history have noted the centrality of the adoption of historicism as an intellectual watershed that not only characterised the nineteenth century, but in many ways defined modernity. European historiography has been less cognisant of the centrality of historicism to the history of religious reform. Indeed, as Zachhuber has argued, it is primarily understood as a 'German story in which Enlightenment historiography is married with romanticism and German idealism to produce an environment in which a particular philosophical and theological understanding of history could appear as the ultimate key unlocking the deepest mysteries of humankind'.[94] The history of biblical criticism, which was an outgrowth of historicism, thus is largely confined to explorations of German Protestant scholars, and only secondarily part of a larger French and British story insofar as individual scholars were influenced by German theological or philosophical thought. Yet as religion was reconsidered and reconceived, it participated in generating the 'theological foundations of modernity'.[95] It is to this period that we must look to understand the religious assumptions lying behind new definitions – of civilisation, of progress – and their complex relationship in the relocation of religion in emerging secularisms.[96]

While not in any way denying that the adoption and subsequent absorption of historicism played a central role in European conceptions of modernity and definitions of 'European-ness', I would argue that this should more accurately be understood as a universal story. The erasure of religion from a participatory role in the development and articulation of modernity in the historiography of the Middle East and South Asia is the result of the intersection and interaction of two powerful forces: first, European claims to ownership of modernity in the context of the broader process of developing new taxonomies of difference in the late eighteenth and nineteenth centuries; and second, the internal dynamics of Middle Eastern reform movements. Together, they disregarded Islamic modernism as participatory in the construction of modernity.

Engagements with religion are part of a continuum of European intellectual history and occupy a central place in the Christian tradition. Their prominence in the historiography of modernity in Europe also lies, I believe, in European efforts, both conscious and unconscious, to make it so. In other words, the origins and definitions themselves – of secularism, of civilisation, of modernity – were claimed by Europe as part of a process of self-definition; a process heavily reliant on the non-European 'other'

---

[94] Zachhuber, 'The Historical Turn', 1.
[95] In the Christian tradition, see Gillespie, *The Theological Origins of Modernity*.
[96] On the theological origins of modernity, see Howard, *Religion and the Rise of Historicism*; Masuzawa, *The Invention of World Religions*; Olender, *Languages of Paradise*; and Stroumsa, *A New Science*.

which deliberately ignored and thus erased the process of interaction and contribution of this constructed 'other'. European definitions, claims of origin and thus the assertion of ownership of modernity were aided and abetted by European political dominance in an age of imperialism and colonialism.

A second set of paradoxically complementary reasons for the absence of religion in the history of modernity in the Middle East and South Asia lie within the particular historical dynamics of the nineteenth-century reform movements themselves. The Ottoman Tanzimat and similar nineteenth-century reforms aimed at secularising and centralising the state in Egypt, and to a lesser extent in Iran, North Africa, Afghanistan and Central Asia, reduced the power and autonomy of religious institutions of law and education and wrested them from the control of the religious establishment. Similar secularising reforms were undertaken in South Asia, alongside determined attempts to minimise religion in public life and combat 'primitive' religious practices and 'superstitions'. Such reforms challenged the *ulama* institutionally, but also socially, culturally and intellectually, as new state schools offered European-inspired curriculums, as newspapers and journals increasingly dominated public discourse, and as reformers called for increased public participation in and/or oversight of government. The gradual shift 'from subject to citizen' created new educational curriculums, new spaces of social and political discourse, and new forms of participation and social leadership that challenged the *ulama*'s standing. The marginalisation of the religious establishment thus extended well beyond the realm of institutional reform, into competition for social, cultural and intellectual capital, particularly with the rise of a reading public and a growing marketplace, literally and figuratively, for competing interpretations of Islamic history, texts and traditions.[97]

As a result, political and social reformers often found themselves in adversarial relationships with the religious establishment. As members of the *ulama* found themselves divided between opponents and supporters of state-backed reforms, opposition to reforms on cultural and religious grounds created tensions between supporters and opponents of such reforms concerning whether or not Islamic tradition and law would support or resist new social and political ideals such as constitutionalism, increased women's rights, and legal equality of non-Muslims. Since the outset of political reforms, advocates found themselves denounced as cultural westernisers and accused of trampling Islamic political traditions and religious sensibilities alike.

The institutional competition between reformers and their *ulama*

---

[97] On the threat that new education and related concepts of authority posed to the Iranian *ulama*, see Ringer, *Education, Religion, and the Discourse of Cultural Reform in Qajar Iran*, 'Negotiating Modernity: Ulama and the Discourse of Modernity' and 'The Discourse on Modernization'. See also Fortna, *Imperial Classroom*.

opponents spilled into the realm of deploying the authority of religious sensibilities, definitions, history, text and traditions. Political reformers, challenged in the name of religion and unable to compete in the battle to shift religious definitions and understandings, often equated religion with religious traditionalism, backwardness and 'superstition'. Although many reformers were interested in rethinking the premises of religious tradition and of integrating religion into many of the reforms, the history of nineteenth-century reform has by and large been cast as one of secular progressive reformers resisted by religious traditionalists. This dynamic, fuelled by the fierce competition over secularisation and the redefinition of religion, led to a historiography of reform as one opposed by the religious establishment. Reform was narrated as a story of progressive social and political ideals aligned versus religious conservatism; of Islam battling the forces of progress and civilisation. The connection of reform to European imperialist and colonial penetration further enabled Islamic rhetoric to be deployed to delegitimise reform as 'inauthentic' and to cast opposition as coterminous with the protection of religious traditions and state sovereignty. This equation reinforced assumptions about the incompatibility of Islam with modernity amongst proponents and opponents of reform alike, both of whom were invested in sustaining this binary to justify their own positions.

The powerful binary association of secularism with modernity and religion with backwardness was reinforced in the post-World War I Middle East, which saw the entire area divided between the rule of European colonial powers and the authoritarian secularising and westernising leaders in Iran and Turkey. This dichotomy permeated the first generation of historical work on the subject of reform, which strongly sided with the secularising reformers and portrayed religion as inimical to efforts to modernise cum westernise. Likewise, South Asian reform movements have only recently emerged from the shadow of colonialist constructions. The pioneers of the history of Middle Eastern and South Asian 'modernization' movements replicated the constructions and legitimisations of westernising reforms, emphasising the purely instrumentalist nature of Islamic language, and defined Islamic religious movements as 'cultural' or 'traditionalist' attempts to temper western ideas and institutions with indigenous, religious-based traditions.[98] The use of Islamic language to oppose reformers and the various attempts to ground reforms in Islamic tradition were certainly present in the pre-World War I period, but not to the exclusion of genuine attempts at reforming religion which occurred simultaneously. The unquestioned assumptions of 'secularizing' reforms'

---

[98] For example, see Hourani, *Arabic Thought in the Liberal Age, 1789–1939*; similarly, Lewis argues that reform was equivalent to the acceptance of European civilisation: Lewis, *The Emergence of Modern Turkey*. For a criticism of Hourani, see Hamzah, 'Introduction', in Hamzah (ed.), *The Making of the Arab Intellectual (1880–1960)*.

own definitions were also, as Michelle Campos recently articulated, buttressed by the triumph of nationalism.[99] The embrace of nationalism as necessary and indeed inevitable permeated assumptions in European, Middle Eastern and South Asian scholarship of modernity, and led to the erasure of alternative possible trajectories and narratives. The teleology of nationalism's triumph and secularism's association with the marginalisation of religion in the post-World War I period further marginalised religion's participatory role in reform, in modernity, and in a variety of nationalisms and secularisms as well.

The assumption that religion is antithetical to modernity is not uniquely an Islamic historiographical phenomenon. Historicism and the construction of modernity did, in fact, erode and destabilise traditions and force long-standing religious certainties into defensive positions. The systematic redefinition and relocation of religion that were fundamental to nineteenth-century religious reform movements in the Middle East and elsewhere, did threaten existing understandings and practices of religion. Efforts at the internalisation of ethics, of the dismantlement of tradition, of the challenge of dogma and the authority of the *ulama* appeared to be and, in some aspects, were attacks on religious truth and pious practice. Religious spheres of practice and authority gave way under state encroachment, as the domain of the profane expanded at the expense of the sacred, even if this process was understood by some religious reformers as a means of preserving religion's centrality in the modern project.

Islamic modernism, since it fundamentally challenged the construction of 'modernity' as anti-religious, was thus misread as a tactical attempt by some reformers to recast religious language and idiom to make reforms more palatable to 'pious' sensibilities. Islamic modernists are primarily characterised as social and political reformers, reformers who successfully instrumentalised Islam as a rhetorical language. Their genuine theological innovations are largely ignored and unappreciated. As I have argued elsewhere in the context of Zoroastrian reform in India and Iran, the 'privatization' of religion and the growth of the secular domain shifted religion into different places, but did not marginalise it.[100]

Islamic modernist engagement with historicism broadly conceived should not be seen simply as a response to European ideas; rather, these ideas had so permeated the global intellectual landscape that all major religious traditions were forced to recalibrate. They all wrestled with similar problems and went through many of the same developmental processes – whether in rationalising administration, constructing national identities and popular sovereignty, or historicising tradition.[101]

---

[99] Campos, *Ottoman Brothers*.
[100] Ringer, *Pious Citizens*.
[101] For Zoroastrian and, to a lesser extent, Hindu modernist religious reform projects, see Ringer, *Pious Citizens*.

We need to follow ways in which religion was redefined, reconceived and relocated, without assuming that secularism is itself antithetical to religion, even if it was an assault on the hegemony of the religious establishment. This historical misconception was facilitated by the historicisation of religion, by the emergence and reinforcement of the dichotomies of modern/traditional, and by the attempt to internalise and rationalise religion, taking it out of the communal, the publicly performed, the publicly visible realm. Even as reformers sought to redefine 'true' religion, they were implicitly drawing new lines between true/false as a way of legitimising/delegitimising a substantive redefinition of religion itself. Religion, as understood and as practised, was denounced and substantiated by profound anti-clericalism. Religious reformers challenged *ulama* authority to interpret and maintain tradition, both in order to permit religious reformulation, but also to assert their own authority in an emerging public sphere of journals and debate.[102] The relocation of religious authority reinforced the idea of the *ulama* as traditionalists opposed to modernity, even as it overlooked the theological dimensions of Islamic modernism.

Embedding Islamic modernism within the narrative of modernising reform also obscured its complex genealogy. Although Islamic modernism was a central, and I argue, largely overlooked component of reform, it emerged not as a result of reforms themselves, but from a more distant and diffuse process of the adoption of the landscape of historicism. In other words, the centrality of political reform in the narrative of Middle Eastern modernisation movements privileges the focus on institutions and political ideals as the sites of reform, with religious reform cast as a by-product, an instrument of legitimation, rather than a site of change in-and-of itself. Religious reform is thus ignored as participatory in the construction of a new intellectual bedrock, cast instead into the role of responding to or of buttressing new hegemonic norms of discourse. Religion moves then from being an agent of modernity, to an unchanging un-modern site requiring dismantlement, dismissal and rejection.

Islamic modernism has become denuded of intellectual and theological content, cast instead as argumentation – a rebranding in the interests of public relations. Yet while it is certainly true that Islamic modernists wrote about the compatibility of Islam with constitutionalism, science and women's rights, their positions were the products of new modes of Islamic thought premised on the epistemology and methodology of historicism. The so-called 'reconciliation of Islam with modernity' was not simply a question of realigning Islam with modern 'values', but a more fundamental shift in ways of thinking, argumentation and the assumptions concerning the nature

---

[102] On the rise of nineteenth-century 'modern' scientists and intellectuals, and their attempts to assert and protect their own authority, see Yalçinkaya, *Learned Patriots*. See also Asil, 'The Tanzimat Novel in the Service of Science'. On the similar phenomena in Iran, see Shayegh, *Who is Knowledgeable is Strong*.

of religion which lay behind them. Historicism was the instrument of the translation of Islam into the modern.

Islamic modernism should not be seen as a belated and ultimately futile attempt to instrumentally craft Islam into a language that legitimised its own marginalisation in an increasingly secular modern world. This would be to accept the myth of the modern as non-religious or even anti-religious, which prevails in the historiography of nineteenth-century secularising reforms in the Middle East and beyond. Rather, I propose that a closer examination of Islamic modernist texts will subject modernity's own narrative to necessary scrutiny, and illuminate distortions in our understanding of the place and role of religious thought in the emergence and development of secularism and the citizen in the Middle East and beyond. Islamic modernism is a valuable window onto wider nineteenth-century attempts to reconcile religious truths and traditions with new conceptions of religion, of humanity, and the new political and social ideals and possibilities that resulted.

One of my primary aims is to emphasise the participation of religious modernism in establishing theological foundations for modernity as modernist scholars responded to and grappled with the theological implications of historicism. Any accurate historical account of reforms must include Islamic modernism as a serious endeavour by those committed to the genuine re-unification of religion and science, alongside new social and political ideals. Modernist scholars believed in the unitary nature of truth, and attempted to reconcile reason and revelation as paths to a single truth. They also were committed to applying new scientific methods to questions of religious authority. The critical reading of texts and the historicising scrutiny of Islamic tradition were corollaries to the commitment to empirical, rational modes of scientific inquiry, and necessitated a serious redevelopment of Islamic epistemological methodology. Islamic modernists were committed to rethinking the nature and function of religion in society, and of the individual's relationship to sacred texts and traditions; yet were equally committed to the revivification of Islam in order to serve the ethical and moral needs of their contemporary Muslim world.

Towards a New Methodology: 'Conversation' and 'Translation'

The history of modernity in the Middle East and South Asia has been trapped in the replication of the ambivalent relationship reformers themselves experienced with Europe. Imagining reform as located somewhere on a linear continuum between imitation and rejection of European 'models' has confined the discussions to questions of transmission, adaptation or rejection. These questions, while certainly productive of greater understandings of absorption and diffusion, have reinforced the importance of origins and causality, circumscribing alternative analysis. In particular, the emphasis on origins organises the exchange around both 'roots and routes', focusing on the 'origin' of ideas and their subsequent transmission, adaptation and/or rejection elsewhere.[103]

Identification of ideas with their 'origins' is based on essentialist claims to agency. Perception of origin affected the perception of capacity for integration and, ultimately, the authenticity of modernity. The ability to claim origins entailed the ability to claim agency and the capacity for the self-generation of modernity – an authentic modern as opposed to one necessarily based on imitation and adaptation. Not surprisingly, origins were a profound source of anxiety, claims and counter claims. The obsession with origins and causality also reinforced essentialising structures of modernity. The conversation spun endlessly around contested claims to origins as agency, rather than focusing more productively on the variety of contexts and the multivalent constructions of modernity that became possible. Ownership was equated with origins, rather than with creativity, belonging and relevance.

To take one example of the gravitational pull of origins, Wendy Shah notes that Ottoman painters experimenting with European modernist art conceived of their project differently than did European painters, as one without local, indigenous and thus 'authentic' precedent (origins). However participatory, however creative, Ottoman painters' negotiation of European claims to ownership, to genesis, to origins of ideas, forms, techniques and concepts, affected Ottoman painters' own relationship to their work, to their project and to their understanding of the context of their projects.[104] So whether or not ideas were understood or experienced as having developed in local contexts organically created different relationships to it. Did painters understand themselves to be participating in the reconceptualisation of traditions, of customs, of locally owned ideas, forms or techniques with deep roots, or did they perceive themselves to be engaging creatively with foreign traditions? Their answer to this question (as distinct from ours) affected their understanding of themselves and their relationship to their work. The anxiety of authenticity, the attempt to justify change and experimentation as having roots – understood as a claim to the essential capacity of generating modernity – lies at the foundation of this contested claim to origins.

The context of European relationships with the Middle East and South Asia as experienced and perceived by different practitioners complicates any attempt to generalise the mechanics of interaction between the Middle East/ South Asia and 'the West'. It is also the case that these complex interactions did not take place in a political vacuum. As Afsaneh Najmabadi notes in the context of the gender shifts underway in nineteenth-century Iran as a result

---

[103] Flood's persuasive argument for 'routes, not roots' is invaluable for the period he considers, but less so in the deeply interconnected nexus of the circulation of ideas in the nineteenth century. Flood, *Objects of Translation*.

[104] Shaw, *Ottoman Painting*.

of contact with Europe, 'agency would be meaningless outside a matrix of power'.[105] The economic and political power disparity between Europe and other societies effected realms of cultural and intellectual interaction. European countries were aggressive, threatening and dominating, even as their societies offered attractive models and ideas for thought. The conversation thus was effected by these relationships of power. Any discussion of the dynamics of these relationships must take this into consideration and avoid pitfalls of 'Orientalism' or 'nativism' – both of which distort the complexity of these processes.

It is only within this broader context that the nature of the debates, and legitimation of change, becomes clearer. The power disparity between Europe and the Middle East/South Asia shaped arguments to legitimise reform, which themselves often obscured the nature of the reform itself. Justifications for reform reinforced the perception of reform as the adoption or rejection of western models – thus bolstering the construction of modernity as western/foreign and its rejection as indigenous/authentic. In many ways the scholarship on the nineteenth century has fallen into these same worn ruts. On the one hand, the legitimising power of origins is relevant to understanding the discourse on origins. On the other hand, we must not reify their importance, but must instead insist on recognising the legitimising dynamics of this discourse. Some contemporary scholars attempt to establish indigenous origins of modernity by asserting the commensurability of origins, yet this unwittingly reinforces European modernity as normative through its replication. I agree with Sebastian Conrad, who notes that 'the specter of parallels ... that continues to haunt the recent quest for alternative modernities ... [conversely neglects and effaces] the long history of entanglements'.[106] Whether nativist or westernist in content, the language of debate, by centring on claims and counter claims to origins, reinforces the authority of origins, rather than reflecting the complex genealogies of reforms themselves.

Contesting claims of origins and the passionate dance between advocacy and rejection of 'westernisation' are important signals in-and-of themselves, even as the language of argumentation at times obscures the nature of the interaction. Any attempt to try to distinguish intent from argument is also fraught. Did authors mean what they said? In what way could their arguments be read as instrumentalist? To what extent do the arguments suggest a variety of tactics, often simultaneously employed? It is hard to read between the lines, since the lines themselves were shaped both by the need for nativist argumentation, as well as an implicit or explicit comparison to Europe. To take one example, Iranian reformer Mirza Yusuf Khan Mostashir al-Dowleh, in his 1871 treatise, *Yek Kalameh* (One Word), argues for the importance of

---

[105] Najmabadi, *Women with Mustaches*, 5.
[106] Conrad, 'Enlightenment in Global History', 1008.

adopting constitutionalism in Iran.[107] If one ignores the imperatives and constraints of argumentation, one might read him as advocating for the importation of the French constitution to Iran, or for the adaptation of the French constitution in the Iranian context. In my reading, Mirza Yusuf Khan uses France as an example, in classic Montesquieu-esque form, of the empirically demonstrable benefits of rule of law and government accountability. His objective was not to make the French constitution palatable to an Iranian audience or context; his objective was to seek ways in which France's success could be used to convince his audience that rule of law, government accountability and transparency should be similarly embraced in Iran.

The ongoing challenge for scholars of the Tanzimat period broadly conceived is to move away from distortive binaries and the organisational epistemologies of unquestioned definitions and categories. We need to more accurately articulate the ways in which reformists engaged and reshaped both existing traditions and new ideas, in both local and trans-local contexts. Rather than positioning reform along a linear spectrum from imitative to rejectionist, we should turn instead to conceptualising reforms as products of complex, intersecting intellectual networks – networks which operated in local and trans-local contexts, as well as across time. Reformers were engaged not only with ideas from other traditions and contexts, but with ideas from their own. Reforms were as much a product of selection from a local menu of options as they were from other, newly available menus. The choice between one or the other is a false one – the project of reform is more accurately characterised by the profound interaction between them.

I propose that we step back from the quest to ascertain origins and their methodological corollaries: transmission and dissemination. Rather, we should view the nineteenth century as a moment when the various intellectual implications of historicism necessitated the re-evaluation of existing assumptions, about science, about humanity, about religion and about traditions, in a time when multiple and complex networks of intellectual exchange led to global dissemination of these ideas. Such a perspective allows us to conceive of these engagements as universal and to focus on their diversity, as well as the various ways in which they operated in particular contexts.

These stories are lost if approached linearly with the two-dimensionality of European origin and the dissemination to the non-European other. The challenge is to frame the embrace of historicism in Islamic modernist thought, not as the tired story of non-western response to European ideas, nor its reflected inverse, a nativist insistence on the sufficiency of indigenous 'origins' that nevertheless also contributes to subtly reify binaries of derivation and the absence of agency, both imagined and real. Ownership is not origin-dependent; it is about the embeddedness of meaning.

Any methodology implicitly privileges some perspectives over others

---

[107] Gohrab and McGlinn (trans.), *One Word – Yek kalame: 19th-Century Persian Treatise Introducing Western Codified Law*.

as any vantage point permits certain views even as it obscures others. Accepting this, I adopt a methodology that deliberately moves away from attempting to identify itineraries of transmission, to consider instead issues of translation in a complex web of conversations, at times overlapping, at times divergent, but always grappling with similar challenges occasioned by similar paradigmatic shifts and assumptions. European conversations, about science and modernity broadly conceived, were themselves ongoing, as well as participatory in other contemporaneous conversations in other parts of the world. A focus on conversations underlines the simultaneity and multi-directionality of these ideas and allows for Europe to be part of some conversations and not others.

There are myriad ways of conceptualising 'translation'. It is typically used to denote as its object textual and cultural contexts with a particular directionality of moving from one language or context to another, but here the project is to refocus ways in which translation operates multi-directionally, not simply between cultures or languages, but also within them. In particular, this book proposes to examine ways in which Islamic modernists 'translated' ideas across times and traditions, emerging, differently conceived, as new patterns of thought and of knowledge, of new epistemologies and new methodologies, but without the distortion inherent in denying their complex genealogies.

By conceiving of 'translation' in this way, I seek to emphasise the consciousness and agency involved in the myriad of choices made to translate, what to translate, how to translate and, conversely, what not to translate, what cannot be translated, and so forth. This opens up possibilities of exploring ways in which translations move between intellectual contexts, over time and over place, and ways in which translations were fundamentally transformative, even as they could also be preservationist.

Islamic modernists 'translated' Islam within the new epistemological and methodological framework of historicism to generate 'modern' Islam. This was a creative, syncretic and regenerative process, not a superficial, rejectionist, or simply instrumentalist project. Extending the concept of translation, we need to view the Tanzimat and other modernising reform processes more generally, not as hybrid adaptations of western forms to local conditions, but as translations from 'traditional' to 'modern'. The impetus for reform was to address domestic needs; western ideas and forms may have been inspirational, but the process itself was much more than a simple adaptation facilitating importation.

The use of the concept of translation also avoids the pitfall of assuming that the modern is what it claims to be: a rupture, a departure, a denunciation of the past in its framing of its binary, 'traditional'. Translation instead facilitates greater visibility of continuities and recastings within traditions. The concept of translation follows closely the project of Islamic modernism as the modernists themselves viewed it, and privileges an exploration of their terms of engagement, their solutions and their intentions.

Conceiving of the discussion concerning historicism and religion as a three-dimensional set of overlapping conversations foregrounds the dynamics internal to the debates themselves, even as it allows comparisons between debates in different places and the connections between different nexuses of conversations as 'connected histories'. 'Conversation' also highlights European claims to define 'civilisation' and 'modernity,' and locates these claims within local and supra-local contexts. Europe becomes a cluster of locales, with overlapping conversations in the Middle East, South Asia and beyond.

Similarities between reforms, whether in the Middle East, South Asia, Europe or beyond, do not necessarily indicate processes of imitation and adoption with associated causality mapped by routes of transmission. It is not, I believe, a question of finding an Ur text, or a scholarly trail to explain commonalities – there need be no direct route travelled of a particular text – but a diffuse, more powerful impact of the penetration, consciously and unconsciously, of historicism. This is not a story of the seed of modernity planted around the world. I am less interested in attempting to trace linear routes of dissemination of ideas, than with exploring the ways in which these ideas, in their multiple shades, cast new shadows. The appearance of similar ideas in widely divergent areas was because the world was connected, and interconnected, at rapidly growing rates. Similarities were a function of rapidly expanding intellectual networks that created similar intellectual assumptions and explanatory needs. I hope this approach will allow for the multi-dimensionality of these intellectual engagements – over time, over place, in local context and across contexts – to become more visible.

Middle Eastern reform programmes – ranging spatially from Egypt to India and from the Ottoman Empire to Iran, and temporally from the Ottoman and Iranian *Nizam-e Jadid* movements in the early nineteenth century to the Ottoman Tanzimat, Arab *Nahda* and Central Asian *Jadid* movements in the latter half of the nineteenth century – all grappled with the fundamental challenge of growing western expansionist power and the not-unfounded apprehension of loss of sovereignty. Reform was a response to an existential crisis. In seeking to recalibrate political, economic, military, commercial and financial systems to new European military capacities, commercial pressures and diplomatic aggressions, reformers initiated complex processes of substantive change. Some of these changes were inspired by similar solutions to similar problems experienced in Europe; some of these changes grew out of the common conviction that to respond to new needs, administrative and bureaucratic rationalism, centralisation and the concomitant harmonisation, homogenisation and integration into transnational networks were necessary prerequisites. In other words, we should view modernising reform programmes in the nineteenth century as adopting newly available strategies to respond to the internal dynamics of the reforms themselves. Naturally, these were complex and long-term changes, and understanding how to respond to them and how to channel them productively shifted over time, even as they were neither uniform nor static in any given moment or place.

I employ the term 'Islamic modernism' throughout this book for two principal reasons. First, it has entered into scholarly parlance and thus continues to be useful to denote certain broad contours of thought. Second, it is, as Charles Kurzman points out in his compilation *Modernist Islam*, fundamental to the intentionality embedded in the project of religious reform.[108] Muslim intellectuals included in the category of 'Islamic modernist' consciously and deliberately sought to reform religion in ways that they themselves considered in keeping with 'modern' conceptions of scientific method, historicism and rationalism. It thus centres their project on their vision and consequent definition of the modern, on their sketching of the contours of modernity's essential attributes and paradigms, and on their engagement with ways in which these attributes and paradigms both necessitated and allowed for new religious possibilities. Lastly, the term 'Islamic modernist' provides a tentative vocabulary in which to compare 'modernists' from a variety of religious traditions, and to underline ways in which their objectives, challenges and solutions were similar. I use the term 'Islamic modernist' to denote a religious modernist in the Islamic tradition, as distinguished from a 'Muslim modernist' which denoted a Muslim who was committed to modernity, without a concomitant commitment to modernising Islam.

In order to demonstrate the widespread penetration of historicism in the nineteenth century and the fundamentally new intellectual landscape that resulted, I have chosen to explore the contours of Islamic modernism as expressed, both consciously and unconsciously, explicitly and implicitly, in the works of four notable Islamic modernists: Ataullah Bayezidof, Namık Kemal, Syed Ameer Ali and Jamal al-Din al-Afghani. These intellectuals' shared discourse and agendas, together with their enormous geographical breadth and professional diversity, clearly indicate the contours of the conversations they engaged in, as well as some of its varieties.

Ataullah Bayezidof (1841–1911) was a prominent Tatar Muslim scholar, writer and religious figure active in St Petersburg. He variously served as the head of the Muslim Tatar community in St Petersburgh, as Imam of Muslim troops in the Russian army and as a dragoman for the Ministry of Foreign Affairs. Bayezidof is most widely known for having successfully advocated for the construction of the first mosque in the capital city. In response to Renan's 'Islam and Science' lecture, Bayezidof penned a pair of essays on the essence of Islam in history, which he sent to the Ottoman journal *Tercuman-i Hakikat* (The Translation of Truth) in Istanbul, where they were translated from Russian to Ottoman and printed.

Namık Kemal (1840–88), writing from Istanbul and in exile and/or government service in London, Paris, Vienna and the Mediterranean islands of Cyprus, Rhodes and Chios, was a journalist and political activist. A leading

---

[108] Kurzman, *Modernist Islam*.

member of the Young Ottomans, he urged the Ottoman sultan to embrace modernising change, constitutionalism and freedom of the press, while retaining Islam as a foundation for law and morality. Namık Kemal represented the new Ottoman intellectual and public figure, one who was learned in the Islamic tradition and enjoyed a familiarity with European scholarship as well. The majority of his work consisted of articles published in journals, although he also wrote a variety of other works, including his posthumously published *The Complete History of Islam* (*Büyük Islam Tarihi*).

Syed Ameer Ali (1849–1928) was an Indian Muslim of Iranian Shiite descent. He graduated from Calcutta University in 1867, received an MA degree in history with honours a year later, followed shortly thereafter by a law degree. Ali became a leading jurist and professor of law. He spent the years 1869–73 in London where he was influenced by British liberalism and where he became acquainted with many of the leading British administrators of India. Ali wrote extensively on political issues, Islamic history and law and was a founding member of the India Muslim League in 1908. Together with Sir Syed Ahmed Khan (1817–98), Ali is considered the leading Muslim reformer in nineteenth-century India.

Jamal al-din al-Afghani (1838–97) was a peripatetic journalist and pan-Islamist. Afghani claimed to hail from Afghanistan, although Keddie has convincingly demonstrated his Iranian, Shiite, origins.[109] Afghani travelled widely, spending time in the European capitals of Paris, London and St Petersburg, in addition to lengthy stays in Istanbul, Hyderabad, Cairo, Tehran and Afghanistan. In his peregrinations Afghani published and lectured widely and sought to influence modernising elites. As one of the most famous Islamic modernists, he is viewed primarily as an activist promoting a pan-Islamic anti-colonialist agenda, although a close reading of his work demonstrates a genuine and serious engagement with Islamic reform.

This diverse set of intellectuals exemplifies the emergence of new edges and new centres of the intellectual conversations concerning religion and modernity in the nineteenth century. This is apparent in the authorship, audience and language of their works. By profession and training, this group of intellectuals included journalists, a lawyer, a judge, activists, politicians and an imam, not to mention the often-fluid nature of these roles. The authors were members of the new class of public intellectuals that emerged alongside the press, growing literacy and political activism; intellectuals who had broken the monopoly on religious interpretation held by the *ulama*. The burgeoning press was central to the dissemination of their ideas in a new marketplace of exchange and founded on the presumption and formation of a reading public. It was a principle source of their authority, if not livelihood.

These four intellectuals represent a geographically and professionally diverse group, who all engaged in historical writing. They each redefined and relocated Islam by means of a historicist reconstruction of Islamic

---

[109] Keddie, *An Islamic Response*, 5.

history. As modernists, they were committed to fundamental religious reform which they believed was imperative in order to reconcile religious truths with newer, modern, scientific and historical truths. Unlike some of their intellectual contemporaries, however, who did not engage with Islamic tradition and history, these four were as firmly committed to the retention of Islam in the modern, as they were with the adoption of modernity itself.

Additionally, these four intellectuals each penned refutations to Ernest Renan's 'Religion and Science' lecture. This explicit connection with European scholarship and historical claims concerning Islam permitted me to bring these Islamic modernists into conversation not only with their own religious traditions, but also directly with European religious studies scholarship and 'Orientalist' assumptions about the capacity of Islam to modernise. The refutations were all published in journals and were thus written for an explicitly public, international audience that included local and trans-local Muslims and sometimes European Christian readers. The authors avoided technical and specialised terms likely to be unfamiliar to the general public. Although the refutations initially appeared in various languages (Ottoman, Russian, Arabic, French and English), they were quickly translated and shared, thus both confirming and constituting the cosmopolitan network of intellectuals active in the late nineteenth century that linked Istanbul to Paris, Cairo to St Petersburg, Hyderabad to London, Tehran to Berlin, and showcased the profoundly cosmopolitan nature of the intellectual conversation concerning religion and modernity in this expanding Muslim world.

Their differences are no less interesting than their commonalities. As Peter van der Veer, Mohamad Tavakoli-Targhi, Nile Green, Houri Berberian, Afshin Marashi and others have persuasively demonstrated, the contemporaneity and multi-directionality of these transnational conversations suggests that scholarship should focus on their nodes of connectivity and interaction; ways in which they intersect, ways in which they diverge.[110] Indeed, as Holly Shissler and I have argued elsewhere, the Islamic refutations to Renan are arguably more interesting for what they share with Renan, than for the ways in which they disagree.[111]

I do not attempt to provide an intellectual biography of each of these four Islamic modernists. Rather, my focus is on illuminating ways in which the historicist landscape shaped their construction of 'modern' Islam as a way

---

[110] One of the first to make the argument for contemporaneity was van der Veer, *Imperial Encounters*. See also Tavakoli-Targhi, *Refashioning Iran*. For an important discussion of the connectedness of these burgeoning networks facilitated by both print and transportation technologies, see Green, 'Spacetime', and more recently, Green and Gelvin (eds), *Global Muslims in the Age of Steam and Print*. On intellectual (and political) networks of exchange, see Berberian, *Roving Revolutionaries*, and Marashi, *Exile and the Nation*.

[111] Ringer and Shissler, 'The Al-Afghani-Renan Debate, Reconsidered'. See also Ringer, 'Gataullah Baiazitov: An Islamic Modernist in Russia'.

of claiming modernity. As religious modernists, they were principally concerned to demonstrate that Islam had historically served as a motor of progress and civilisation and that, if reformed, could once again do so.

Islamic modernists engaged in a process of identifying Islamic essence as revealed in history, disinterring it from the sediment of ossified tradition, and recontextualising it according to what they believed were the requirements of what Syed Ameer Ali repeatedly referred to as 'the circumstances of the age'. The result was modern Islam – a rationalised, interiorised and fundamentally historicised religion with attendant methodology and hermeneutics of the Quran and Hadith. Islamic modernists believed that modern Islam could generate modernity and enable Islamic countries to reignite what Afghani called the 'torch of civilization'.

The chapters are arranged thematically, around a series of questions and approaches to the issue of historicising and modernising Islam. Some of the authors that I focus on have extensive historical writing that applies to each of these thematic areas; others of them less so. As a result, some chapters draw on some individuals more than others. Throughout the chapters, I emphasise the conversation that modernists engage in with their own traditions, as well as with Ernest Renan, as a quintessential Catholic modernist, and European religious studies and Islamic studies scholarship more broadly. I conceive of Islamic modernism as a project of translation between tradition and modernity, and locate it in the larger field of nineteenth-century religious modernisms.

Chapter 1: Locating Islam

By the nineteenth century, the idea of 'religion' as a universal phenomenon had become firmly entrenched. Religions in the particular were therefore expressions of this universal phenomenon, mapped onto human civilisational evolution. The explanation of difference moved away from a theologically based true/false binary and was relocated onto a universal taxonomy of mankind's religious evolution. In this conception, 'primitive' religions were symptomatic of 'primitive' civilisations, 'advanced' religions likewise belonging to and reflecting 'advanced' civilisations. Historicism, as contextualisation, enabled religions to be located in this taxonomy according to new criteria of civilisational progress.

This chapter explores Islamic modernists' 'location' of Islam in this universal, phenomenological and civilisational taxonomy. The focus is on elucidating their understanding of Islam as part of, and contributing to, universal human history, and ways in which this new set of intellectual paradigms shifted their categorisation and understanding of Islam as a universal religious phenomenon, as opposed to a set of texts, traditions, practices, and so forth. This chapter also elaborates the complex debates that Islamic modernists engaged in with their Christian, religious studies scholarly counterparts, particularly over the position of Islam relative to other monotheistic traditions. The European religious studies taxonomy, not surprisingly, located Islam as inferior to Christianity. Equally unsurprisingly, Islamic modernists argued that Islam was in fact, according to these new phenomenological, civilisational and evolutionary criteria, superior to Christianity. Islamic modernists deployed new intellectual criteria, subtly reshaping older Islamic arguments for superiority based on the Prophet Mohammad's place in the unfolding of Abrahamic revelations, even as they reinforced the ultimate conclusion of Islamic superiority on new 'scientific' grounds.

Chapter 2: Islam in History, Islamic History

The taxonomy of human religions, generated and confirmed as the guiding organisational grammar of European disciplines of religious studies, philology and anthropology, claimed to map civilisational evolution. However, the fixity of the location of particular religions on this map belied its ability to do so. The actual location of the particular in the universal was premised on the essentialisation of religions – on their extraction from historical context. In other words, while scholarship sought to map the history of human evolution via this religious taxonomy, the criteria used to measure and thus locate particular religions on this map was, by nature, ahistorical. Religions were evaluated based on their intrinsic, immutable essences, not as they expressed themselves in history. By representing dehistoricised, essentialised points on an evolutionary continuum, this map was unable to account either for the unfolding of particular religious 'traditions' or for comparative civilisational progress over time and the ways in which 'religion' participated in this.

Islamic modernists, in addition to locating Islam in this universal taxonomy, also explored Islam in history, rewriting Islamic history as the story of transcendent Islamic essence in a sequence of particular historical contexts. They determined the historical laws of progress that dictated the path of the 'torch of civilisation' in order to provide a historical explanation for moments of progress and to understand the reasons for present stagnation. These new Islamic histories chart the interaction of Islam as essence in historical context, beginning with the revelation of the Quran, the Prophet's application of Quranic ideals – God's intent – and the subsequent history of Islamic institutions, from the Rashidun through the Abbasid periods. Modernist reconstruction of Islamic history demonstrated both the enduring relevance of Islam as essence, but also the need to recontextualise it in the present. In making these arguments, modernists were in dialogue not only with European Orientalist scholars, but also with their own Islamic historical tradition.

Chapter 3: The Islamic Origins of Modernity

Modernist Islamic history was deeply prescriptive. Modernists saw in Islamic history the solution to the pressing question of why the Islamic world was 'backward' compared to the dynamic and powerful European great powers. The Abbasid 'Golden Age' was touted by Islamic modernists as empirical proof that Islamic essence, properly manifest in historical context, was a powerful motor of progress and civilisation. In making this argument, modernists claimed not only that Islam had produced superior civilisational levels compared to contemporary Europe, but also that, properly recontextualised, it could do so again. European scholarship accepted the Abbasids as a 'Golden Age', but insisted either that this was the apogee of Islamic potential or, following Renan, that the greatness of the Abbasids occurred despite the Arabs and Islam, not because of them. The prevalent European narrative of the ossification of Islamic institutions and the concomitant rise of dogmatism that prevented intellectual inquiry, creativity and, ultimately, further progress, was by and large accepted by Islamic modernists. However, they insisted that the ossification of tradition was not essential to Islam but rather, historically contingent. Modernists deployed the 'Golden Age' argument to insist on the decontextualisation of Islamic essence and its recontextualisation in the present – the rescue of essence from history. Islamic modernists, by comparing Islam in history to Christianity in European history, asserted the Islamic origins of modernity, thus enabling an indigenous future modern – the reclaiming of the 'torch of civilisation'.

Chapter 4: The Quest for the Historical Prophet

Modernist histories historicised and reimagined the Prophet Mohammad as the embodiment of modern Islam. The Prophet was the 'perfect man' – the prescriptive model of a rationalised, internalised 'modern' Islam. An exploration of the Prophet's character, sensibilities and dispositions illustrates the Islamic modernist's vision of modern Islam.

The historicisation of the Prophet, and the emphasis on his ability to negotiate essence in context, undergirds an entirely new Islamic methodology. The essence of Islam is located uniquely in the Quran and the Prophet becomes an example of accurate understanding of this essence – equivalent to God's intent – and its manifestation in 'laws' and institutions appropriate for his own specific historical context. Prophetic Hadith, therefore, must be historicised, in order to extract their intentionality from their specific manifestation in context. Islamic methodology moves from precedent, as the determination and replication of the Prophet's actions, to precedent reconceived as the Prophet's translation of God's intent into context. The Hadith and Sunna must be gauged for the Prophet's intentionality as it refracted and reflected God's intent. This methodology destabilised the entire premise of the Sunna and effectively unbound 'Islam' from tradition. Tradition as precedent gave way to the continual contextualisation of essence – a 'permanent becoming'. This enabled reformers to go 'back to the Quran' and retrieve God's intent. This innovative hermeneutics of the Quran and Hadith formed the basis for a new methodology for discovering and implementing 'God's intent' in the modern age.

Conclusion: God's Intent – The Re-enchantment of the Sacred in the Age of History

The conclusion outlines the contours of 'modern Islam' and proposes that the 'modern' understanding of the nature of religion resulted from the transformation of the relationship between God and mankind, from one characterised by external recognition of the immanence and 'supernatural' power of God, to one characterised by the internalisation of the Divine in man and the centrality of individual consciousness. Modern religion folded humanism into an enduring eschatological framework, whereby God's intent was consistent with civilisational progress of humankind. I reject the notion that religious modernism is reactionary or anti-modern, or that secularisation and the end of Divine immanence entailed the marginalisation of religion. Rather, I propose that religious modernism's fundamental project was the unification of religion and modernity.

Historicism problematised and revealed tradition to be constructed, yet in its deconstruction lay the possibilities of reconstruction. The truth of the essence of Islam was recovered from the sediment of tradition. Freedom from tradition and dogma enabled freedom to rediscover essence, to recontextualize essence in contemporary context – to reinterpret and reconstruct religion. Modern Islam was cast as a return to truth, the rectification of the distortions of tradition and the reignition of Islam's essential capacity for progress and civilisation. Modern Islam was the fulfilment of the eschatological promise of God's intent, folded into new conceptions of progress and civilisation. Like other religious modernisms, Islamic modernism drew on historicism as disenchantment with tradition, to effect a recontextualisation of religion – the re-enchantment of Islam in the age of history.

CHAPTER

1

LOCATING ISLAM

Religion is 'a yearning after the infinite'.[1]

Syed Ameer Ali (1873)

If we will but listen attentively, we can hear in all religions a groaning of the spirit, a struggle to conceive the inconceivable, to utter the unutterable, a longing after the Infinite, a love of God.[2]

Max Müller (1873)

Introduction

In the nineteenth century, the discipline of religious studies moved away from a centuries-old, purely theological true/false vision, towards one organised along the lines of universal civilisational progress. Scholars of religious studies no longer defined religions as either true or false, but as more true or more false according to new ideas of primitivism and progress. They generated a universal taxonomy that mapped human religious progress from primitive to advanced. Scholars saw religions as particularly valuable sites of scholarship, believing them to reflect the civilisational level of the societies that embraced them. As anthropologist Edward Tylor (1832–1917) explained in his influential book *Primitive Culture*, 'Culture or Civilization, taken in its wide ethnographic sense, is that complex whole which includes knowledge, belief, art, morals, law, custom, and any other capabilities and habits acquired by man as a member of society.'[3] Tylor, in describing cultural difference, also resorted to natural idioms: 'Just as the catalogue of all the

---

[1] Ali, *A Critical Examination of the Life and Teachings of Mohammed*, 310.
[2] Müller, 'Lectures on the Science of Religion', 113.
[3] Tylor, *Primitive Culture*, 1.

species of plants and animals of a district represents its Flora and Fauna, so the list of all the items of the general life of a people represents that whole which we call its culture.'[4] Mapping religious progress was also a means of generating a genealogy of universal civilisational progress. Tylor, an ardent advocate of evolution, argued that 'the general study of the ethnography of religion, through all its immensity of range, seems to countenance the theory of evolution in its highest and widest sense'.[5]

Religion thus emerged as a category of analysis capable of illustrating – and mapping – human civilisational progress writ large. Primitive religions were indicative of primitive societies; advanced religions indicative of advanced societies. In the emerging taxonomy of human civilisational progress, religion played an outsized role in enabling scholars to locate any particular religion, and by extension the particular culture attached to that religion, at a particular point on the spectrum of civilisational progress.

The religious taxonomy defined three broad categories of religions, arranged in sequence from the most primitive to the most advanced. The most primitive category of religion was that of animism. The second, more advanced category consisted of polytheisms and paganisms. The third, most advanced category was that of monotheism. The assignation of a particular religion to one of these categories and its location within that category relative to other religions in the same category depended on its degree of primitiveness. The criterion of primitivism applied both between categories as genus and within categories as species. For example, within the most advanced category, the relative sequence of monotheisms rested not on the chronological order in which these monotheisms emerged, but on an evaluation of which monotheism had more fully rejected residual primitive features.

Imagine this taxonomy represented by a colour spectrum. On the far side we have 'primitivism' – the longest section denoted by red. The red gradually gives way to orange, yellow, green, blue, and eventually, at the other end of the spectrum, purple, representing the most civilised or advanced religions. Polytheisms and paganisms span the middle of the spectrum, denoting their progress away from primitivism but their limitations well short of monotheisms. The colour spectrum thus represented both overall religious progress (from the far end of red to the other extreme of purple), as well as the relationships between different religions represented by the varying shades of colours lying in between. The colour spectrum also represented the concept of boundaries within and between religions, which, while certainly not fluid, were nonetheless blurred. In this way, religions might be located very close to one another within and between the three categories, such that reds might segue to oranges, but also reach definite limits – reds would never bleed into yellows or blues.

---

[4] Tylor, *Primitive Culture*, 8.
[5] Tylor, *Primitive Culture*, 451.

The spectrum of religious difference charted universal religious progress while locating individual religions independently of historical time and place. The relative locations of religions on the spectrum were not historically contingent; they did not depend on when those religions emerged or were practised. Contemporary and ancient religions appeared together on the spectrum, a reflection of their comparability according to the criterion of primitivism, despite their historical/chronological distance. The criterion of primitive versus advanced thus generated a spectrum of religions in a linear sequence, but ranged those religions according to civilisational progress rather than chronology. The spectrum thereby illustrated the torch of civilisation writ large, with the divisions between religious categories representing civilisational ruptures.

The nineteenth-century categorisation of religious difference was thus at once a historical and an ahistorical enterprise. On the one hand, the spectrum charted religious progress as human progress, equating relative degrees of religious development with relative civilisational advancement. On the other hand, the fixity of location for any given religion denied historical change and developments within that religious tradition. While the progressive and static, historical and ahistorical imperatives of this classificatory system appear to be in tension, they were bound up in the same internal logic of religious essence. For nineteenth-century religious scholars, religions had identifiable essences that could be located on the taxonomy as points on a line, or colours on a spectrum. The essence of a religion was thought to derive from the particular time and place of the religion's origin. The origins of religions contained the religious essence, the 'true' inherent nature of religions themselves. European religious studies scholars located the 'essence' of Christianity, the subject of many religious and historical debates within Roman Catholic and Protestant doctrine, in Jesus himself; they similarly located the 'essence' of Islam in the Prophet Mohammad, though, again, not without this location being contested by Islamic modernists who insisted that the location of Islam's essence was the Quran.

Essences, in addition to being located in a religion's origins, defined the inherent extent and limits of possibility for any given religion – much the way that today we might speak of DNA. Religions, over time and space, could and did develop and change. However, these developments and changes were only possible within an extent predetermined by a religion's inherent potential for progress defined by its essence. More primitive religions had inherently narrower limits, while more advanced religions enjoyed inherently greater possibilities.

Nineteenth-century religious scholars also understood that what might appear over time to be the efflorescence of a religion's essence might actually be a departure from this essence in the form of the adoption of 'foreign' elements, corruption of the 'original' and 'pure' religion, and/or digression 'back' to more 'primitive' religious ideas and practices. It was thus a matter of intense disputation whether a particular religion's history represented the 'flowering' of essence, or its disintegration or deformation. As we will explore in the next chapter, Islamic modernists and European Christian scholars disagreed in their analysis of Abbasid era intellectual production. Was it, as Islamic modernists insisted, the expression of Islamic essence? Or was it, as European Christian scholars suggested, the product of non-Islamic influences – and thus not in any way attributable to Islam?

In the nineteenth century, these two projects – (1) the acontextual location of a particular religion's essence on a universal spectrum, and (2) the exploration of the development of a religion in history – were not seen as incompatible, but rather as a matter of focus. The first – the location of essence – represented the bird's eye view. The second – the exploration of context – represented the close-up view of development – a rigorous evaluation of the flowering or corruption of religious essence in history.

Religious Taxonomy

Descriptions of Islam in Islamic modernist histories were inseparable from the larger project of locating Islam in the taxonomy of universal religious cum civilisational progress. Islamic modernists adopted the criteria of religious evolution as they had developed in the European academy of religious studies, and the phenomenological approach to religion as a category of analysis that sustained those criteria.[6] Islamic modernists fully embraced religion as a universal phenomenon and category of classification.

Syed Ameer Ali and Jamal al-Din al-Afghani closely followed European religious studies criteria for primitive versus advanced religions in their location of Islamic essence in the religious taxonomy. For Ali, religion was a shared impulse to respond to and understand the Divine, expressed differently according to the civilisational level of the society that acted on that impulse. Ali echoed Max Müller, the German-educated Oxford doyen of religious studies, when he defined religion as the universal human 'yearning after the infinite'.[7] According to this schematic understanding of religious evolution, primitive religions were expressions of primitive civilisations; advanced religions were expressions of greater degrees of consciousness and understanding of the Divine, possible only in more advanced civilisations. Over time, as the human mind evolved, its capacity for consciousness,

---

[6] On the emergence of the discipline of religious studies, see Masuzawa, *The Invention of World Religions*. On the connection between religious studies, history and theology, see Howard, *Religion and the Rise of Historicism*.

[7] Ali, *A Critical Examination of the Life and Teachings of Mohammed*, 310. Max Müller's famous line: 'If we will but listen attentively, we can hear in all religions a groaning of the spirit, a struggle to conceive the inconceivable, to utter the unutterable, a longing after the Infinite, a love of God', is from Müller, 'Lectures on the Science of Religion', 113.

rationalism and abstraction grew. Consequently, religions moved from the concrete to the abstract, from fetishism to polytheism, and, eventually, to monotheism. Religions, as they mapped onto civilisational levels, thus tracked the developmental stages of the human mind as it moved from infancy to adulthood.[8]

Particular religions were located in this hierarchy of religious evolution according to essential criteria in what was an inherently comparative and classificatory enterprise. Locating Islam in this taxonomy was predicated on the construction of Islamic essence and its comparison with the essences of religious 'others'. Islam, as a monotheism, was juxtaposed with 'primitive' pre/non-monotheistic religions. But even monotheistic religions, while decidedly more evolved than and thus superior to pre/non-monotheisms, were not all equal. Monotheisms, too, were classified and ranked on an evolutionary continuum according to the presence or absence of residual 'primitive' features. Locating Islam in this universal taxonomy thus necessitated comparison to other monotheisms as well as to more primitive religions. To return to the metaphor of genus and species used earlier, one might think of Islam as a species of genus monotheism.

According to phenomenological and evolutionary understandings articulated by Ali, so-called 'primitive' religions were characterised by features thought to stem from incomplete comprehension of the true nature of the Divine. Primitive religions, and the cultures that sustained and reflected them, were incapable of intellectual abstraction or rational comprehension of the Divine. Adherents of these religions, while propelled by the universal urge to know the Divine, were incapable of truly doing so. Their limited (mis)understandings were reflected not only in the nature of their religious beliefs, but in their practices as well. Adherents of primitive religions, ignorant of natural laws, confounded those laws with Divine power in the form of belief in miracles, superstitions and nature worship. Primitive religions, in Ali's view, inclined towards the concrete and anthropomorphic – the worship of trees, stones, fetishes, and, at a more advanced stage, multiple deities erroneously accredited with divine power. Zeus' lightning bolt and Poseidon's storm were thus fundamentally explanatory, based on misattributions of the origin and nature of Divine power.

Most critically, primitive religions were overwhelmingly concerned with obedience, expressed through the mechanistic performance of external rituals. As I have elaborated elsewhere, nineteenth-century religious scholars maintained that rituals were at best prompts for internal reflection – reminders to be 'mindful of God' – and at worst manifestations of an inability to distinguish the rationale that animated and justified these rituals from the performances themselves.[9] Religions that emphasised the perfor-

---

[8] Ali, *Life and Teachings of Mohammed*, 263, 309.
[9] Ringer, *Pious Citizens*.

mance of rituals betrayed a failure to comprehend the intent behind rituals – confounding the intentionality of practice with the performance of practice. According to this view, the performance of ritual was, in and of itself, devoid of value.

In contrast, advanced religions were characterised by greater consciousness of God, expressed in more spiritual, abstract and, ultimately, rational beliefs and practices. Laws of nature were no longer conflated with Divine action. Advanced religions came closer to knowledge of the truth of the Divine, grasped Divine intent, and thus were able to dispense with ritual and embrace the ideals meant to animate individuals as well as individuals' interactions in society. Ali elaborated on the shifting nature of prayer from primitive to advanced religions, noting that while the phenomenon of prayer was common to all 'religious systems', 'savages' believed prayer to be a form of transactional exchange with the Divine and 'castigate[d]' their fetishes 'if supplications [did] not answer their purposes'. In contrast, 'superior' religions recognised that 'prayers are only the utterances of the sentiments which fill the human heart'.[10] Individual spirituality, and internal consciousness of the nature of the Divine, were contrasted with, and held up as superior to, external ritual behaviour. The degree to which religions expressed consciousness of the Divine and comprehension of Divine nature and intent served to locate them on the continuum of religious development.

For Afghani, like Ali, religions were universal human phenomena and could be clearly categorised within a universal religious taxonomy. As Afghani asserted, 'religions, by whatever names they are called, all resemble each other'.[11] However, unlike Ali, who emphasised the direct correlation between religious progress and civilisational progress, Afghani posited criteria of religious superiority on a continuum of rationality and truth, which did not necessarily map onto civilisational progress. All religions, he noted, even the 'false and the basest of religions', maintain a 'belief in a Creator and faith in rewards and punishments'.[12] Religions, however, can be explained by their location along an evolutionary spectrum, which is the 'reason for the special relation of each age to a particular religion and prophet'.[13] Afghani defined religions as sets of beliefs, more or less true, according to the degree to which they were rationally confirmable, or, conversely, irrational and illogical. More primitive religions were less rational and thus less true, and more advanced religions were more rational and thus more true.

---

[10] Ali, *Life and Teachings of Mohammed*, 171.
[11] Afghani, 'Answer of Jamal ad-Din to Renan', 187.
[12] Afghani, 'The Truth about the Neicheri Sect', 168.
[13] Afghani, 'Commentary on the Commentator', 126.

Locating Islam

Syed Ameer Ali

Syed Ameer Ali and Afghani largely concurred with their Christian counterparts, and with the hegemonic grammar of the discipline of religious studies, on the evolutionary classification of religions. They parted ways, however, in their insistence that this grammar clearly demonstrated the superiority of Islam. Islamic modernists embraced the criteria of religious difference as scientific, empirical truths, truths which, according to them, conferred a superior evolutionary position on Islam relative to its nearest taxonomical neighbour, Christianity. They thereby inverted the Christian European religious studies scholars' location of Christianity as the most evolved of world religions.[14]

Ali ranked the various monotheisms according to their relative level of spiritual consciousness and their relative degree of internalisation, or, conversely, externalisation of the moral. In most religions, he maintained, 'the theurgic character predominates over the moral; in some the moral idea is entirely wanting'.[15] Accordingly, Ali emphasised the intensely ritual and performative nature of Zoroastrianism as a way of positioning it as the least evolved of the four monotheisms:

> The Zoroastrian prayed when he sneezed, when he cut his nails or hair, while preparing meals, day and night, at the lighting of lamps, etc. Ormuzd was first invoked, and then not only heaven, earth, the elements and stars, but trees, especially the moon-plant, and beasts. The formulae were often to be repeated, as many as twelve hundred times.[16]

For Ali, the predominance of ritual was a clear measure of absence – absence of understanding of the 'true' nature of God. It was inversely proportional to consciousness of the nature of the Divine. As mankind evolved, 'uncompromising anthropomorphism' declined and 'a more spiritual idea of the Deity' arose, one which recognised that the 'real nature of prayer' was as a 'medium of intercommunication between God and man'.[17] Judaism represented a major evolutionary leap forward from Zoroastrianism, and Christianity another leap forward from Judaism. 'The teachings of Jesus', Ali explained, represented another 'development of the religious faculty of man' since they emphasised spiritual consciousness of God and overtly rejected

---

[14] For a history of the emergence of classificatory systems and the development of 'world religions', see Masuzawa, *The Invention of World Religions*.
[15] Ali, *Life and Teachings of Mohammed*, 170.
[16] Ali, *Life and Teachings of Mohammed*, 172.
[17] Ali, *Life and Teachings of Mohammed*, 173.

'mechanical prayer' that characterised Jewish practice.[18] According to Ali, Jesus recognised the 'true character of prayer' and 'consecrated the practice by his own example'.[19]

Islam, in Ali's systematisation, represented the fourth and final development among monotheisms. Claiming that Islam was the most evolved monotheism involved asserting that Islam most perfectly embodied and expressed the criteria of religious evolutionary superiority: rationalism, spirituality, abstraction, consciousness of the Divine, and so forth. As asserted by Ali, 'it is the distinctive characteristic of Islam that it combines within itself the grandest and the most prominent features in all ethnic and catholic religions, compatible with the Reason and moral Intuition of man'.[20]

In what reads as a rebuttal of European Christian claims that Islam was inimical to rationalism, inherently dogmatic and intellectually moribund, Ali argued that 'in order to understand the primary doctrines of the religion of Mohammed, the first great point to examine is the true significance of the word Islam, for on this hinge some of the most important points involved in the science of religion'.[21] 'Islam', Ali claimed, did not denote 'absolute submission to God's will – as generally assumed'. Rather, Islam, and by extension, Muslim, meant 'one who strives after righteousness with his own strength'.[22] Ali implicitly refuted Christian accusations that Islam by definition denoted passive submission and instead insisted that Islam entailed agency, action and morality. His emphasis on individual consciousness was a rejection of European Christian claims that Islam, along with Judaism, privileged external obedience to dogmatism and laws, in contrast to Christianity's supposed rejection of externalities in favour of an internalised individual spiritual relationship with God.

Afghani

Whereas Syed Ameer Ali ranked religions according to the yardstick of spiritual consciousness and internalisation, Afghani ranked them according to the criterion of truth. Not surprisingly, he located Islam at the far end of the spectrum of truth as the only fully true religion, claiming that the 'Absolute Truth' was located in the Quran.[23] On the primitive end of the spectrum, Afghani located Hindus, Egyptians, Greeks, Chaldeans, Phoenicians and Persians, all of whom he described as 'followers of false beliefs'. He noted, for example, that the Egyptians 'believed in idols, cows, dogs, and cats', the

---

[18] Ali, *Life and Teachings of Mohammed*, 173.
[19] Ali, *Life and Teachings of Mohammed*, 174.
[20] Ali, *Life and Teachings of Mohammed*, 186. Ali uses the word 'catholic' as an adjective meaning 'including a wide variety of things; all-embracing'.
[21] Ali, *Life and Teachings of Mohammed*, 159.
[22] Ali, *Life and Teachings of Mohammed*, 159.
[23] Afghani, 'Commentary on the Commentator', 125.

Greeks 'believed in hundreds of gods and thousands of superstitions', and the Persians 'had hundreds of absurdities engraved in their hearts'.[24]

Christianity fell somewhere in between these extremes. On the one hand, as an Abrahamic monotheism, it constituted an improvement over pagan polytheisms. On the other hand, 'modern' Christians continued to maintain more primitive beliefs that, in Afghani's estimation, were absurd and irrational. Among these he listed belief in 'the Trinity, the cross, resurrection, baptism, purgatory, confession, and transubstantiation'.[25]

In asserting Islam's superiority to Christianity, Afghani was explicitly comparative, contrasting the two in a dichotomous relationship. Afghani measured Islam and Christianity against three metrics, insisting that Islam rested on firmer 'foundations' than did Christianity.[26] The first metric was monotheism. Afghani argued that the Quran articulated a complete, absolute monotheism, unlike Christianity, which was permeated with 'fancies and superstitions' like the Brahman and Zoroastrian religions.[27] Islam, Afghani wrote, 'by the luster of unity [tauhid] ... purifies and cleans off the rust of superstition, the turbidity of fantasies, and the contamination of imaginings'.[28]

The second metric was rationality. The Quran was the repository of the Divine revelation and as such, equivalent to truth itself, in its infinitude. For this reason, Islam was the only religion, according to Afghani, that was entirely consistent with truth. In making this assertion, Afghani argued for the unity of truth – in other words, that Divine truth was in no way inconsistent with other truths – natural, physical or historical. Because Islam was consistent with truth, it was also entirely consonant with reason. With its inherent truth and rationality, Afghani insisted, 'Islam is the only religion that censures belief without proof.'[29] Conversely, Christianity maintained the doctrine of the Trinity, which Afghani asserted was irrational: 'All Christians confess that it is not possible for reason to understand it, which means that one must abandon reason in order to comprehend it.'[30] Accordingly, Christianity could only sustain belief in the absence of rational proof.

Afghani's conception of rationality as a metric of religious difference rested on the distinction he drew between belief and faith. Belief, according to Afghani, was rational and could withstand scrutiny. It was consonant with truth itself. Faith, in contrast, was a requirement of religions that were irrational or incompletely rational. Faith served as a justification in the absence of a religion's ability to withstand rational criticism. Irrational reli-

---

[24] Afghani, 'Commentary on the Commentator', 128.
[25] Afghani, 'Commentary on the Commentator', 128.
[26] Afghani, 'The Truth About the Neicheri Sect', 169.
[27] Afghani, 'The Truth About the Neicheri Sect', 170.
[28] Afghani, 'The Truth About the Neicheri Sect', 169–70.
[29] Afghani, 'The Truth About the Neicheri Sect', 172.
[30] Afghani, 'The Truth About the Neicheri Sect', 172.

gions depended on the ignorance of their followers, or on their suspension of rational thought. For Afghani, faith was indicative of the absence of truth: it constituted blind obedience. Whereas belief stimulated the intellect, Afghani explained, faith inhibited it:

> For superstitious belief is a dirty curtain that intervenes between the holder of such a belief and truth and reality. It prevents the discovery of the reality of a matter. When someone accepts a superstition his reason comes to a stop and he refrains from intellectual movement.[31]

Islam, in Afghani's rendering, was fully consistent with the fundamental unity of truth and with rationality and could therefore support rational belief. Conversely, Christianity, due to the essential irrationality of its doctrines, could not withstand rational scrutiny; adherence to Christianity depended on the maintenance of faith, cast as belief despite inconsistence with truth. Islam's essential compatibility with truth permitted rational belief, whereas Christianity's essential incompatibility with truth could only be sustained by 'blind' faith.

The third metric by which Afghani compared Islam and Christianity was equality. Islam, Afghani maintained, encouraged each individual believer to strive toward the perfection of their soul.[32] This drive to improvement, he explained, depended on the absence of religious hierarchy and/or intermediaries claiming spiritual authority. Other religions, Afghani declared, explicitly naming Christianity, were fundamentally hierarchical and required the 'mediation of priests'.[33] By rejecting the intermediation of priests, Afghani asserted, Luther was 'following the example of Muslims'.[34] Like Ali, Afghani implicitly underscored the importance of the individual's personal and direct relationship to God, free from intermediaries, as a fundamental feature of superior, evolved religions.

Whereas Islam was based on equality and the absence of hierarchy, Christianity was based on hierarchy and inequality. The result was that Islam was fully capable of promoting man's eternal quest for perfection, which in turn generated individual and social morality, order and intellectual progress. Christianity, by contrast, was less able to do so, because some Christian doctrines were implicitly irrational. Christian dogma, such as the Trinity, was unable to withstand rational criticism; since Christianity's institutions could not permit the challenge of rationalism, the Church deliberately inhibited the development of intellectual faculties. A society's civilisational capacity, Afghani believed, depended on its ability to generate intellectual freedom and the scientific advances that this enabled. Islam, therefore, in his

---

[31] Afghani, 'The Truth About the Neicheri Sect', 169.
[32] Afghani, 'The Truth About the Neicheri Sect', 170.
[33] Afghani, 'The Truth About the Neicheri Sect', 171.
[34] Afghani, 'The Truth About the Neicheri Sect', 171.

estimation, enjoyed the essential capacity to serve as a motor of progress and civilisation, whereas less rational and less true religions were endangered by being inherently unable to encourage intellectual growth.

Muslim-Christian Polemics and the Centrality of Law

In addition to the metrics of monotheism, rationality and equality, another salient issue in Islamic modernist arguments for the superiority of Islam over Christianity was the productive function of law. European Christian scholars took the inverse position, arguing that the role of law in Islam was a liability that demonstrated Islam's essential inferiority to Christianity. At stake in the polemics surrounding law was not only the relative position of Christianity vis-à-vis Islam in the taxonomy of world religions, but more importantly, their respective claims to universalism.

European Christian Arguments

European Christian scholars considered religious law to be a manifestation of less advanced religions. Law was symptomatic of more primitive monotheisms and intimately associated with external forms of prescriptive ritual. Accordingly, religions with an emphasis on law were inherently incapable of meeting the spiritual needs of humanity. European Christian scholars constructed a clear binary that associated the presence of law with the absence of a capacity for spirituality, creativity and flexibility. European Christian scholars mapped Christianity and Islam neatly onto this binary, claiming Christianity as non-legal and therefore spiritual/internal, whereas Islam was characterised as legal and therefore external/performative.

For European Christian scholars, Islam's inherent and essential limitations stemmed from its classification, alongside Judaism, as a Semitic religion. Moses and Mohammad, they argued, were first and foremost lawgivers. Abraham Kuenen, a Dutch theologian, wrote in 1882 that the core of Semitic 'essence' was the inclination to monotheism, the 'respect and submission on their knees in the dust to a divine power.'[35] The concept of a divine creator was the 'genius' of Semitic religion, their contribution to universal religious progress.

European Christian scholars cast Islam as a derivative religion, drawing primarily on Judaism for its advance from polytheism to monotheism, but at the same time, inextricably bound to the context of pagan Arabia. Kuenen wrote that 'its entire manner of producing itself was nothing but a copy of the previous revelation of God to the Jews'.[36] Similarly, he asserted that 'it was due to Jewish influence that the moral prescriptions were established that he

---

[35] Kuenen, 'L'Islam', 17.
[36] Kuenen, 'L'Islam', 18.

[Mohammad] imposed in the name of Allah'.[37] Muir, echoing Kuenen, wrote that 'the teaching of Mohammad, taken mainly from the Jews, partly from the Christians, partly also from the Magians, was engrafted on the native worship and tradition of Arabia'.[38]

According to nineteenth-century European historians of Islam, Islam succeeded in forcing pagan Arabians to give up primitive religious and social practices, but shackled Muslims to the inherent formalism of Islamic law. William Muir, a Scottish Islamicist, explained that this deficiency was racial in nature: 'The Arabs, a simple and unsophisticated race, found in the Coran [sic] ample provisions for the regulation of all their affairs, religious, social and political.'[39] European Christian emphasis on the essential, theocratic nature of Islam – the indivisibility of 'religion' and 'politics' – was a trope that emphasised the all-encompassing shackle that was Islamic law. The construction of a binary between law and spirituality, the former associated with Semitic religions and the latter with Christianity, likewise permeated French Hebraicist Ernest Renan's construction of religious difference. He wrote that

> liberty has never been more profoundly damaged than by a form of social organization where religion dominates civil life absolutely . . . Islam is the indistinguishable union of the spiritual and the temporal, it is the reign of dogma, it is the heaviest chain that humanity has ever had to bear.[40]

Islamic and Jewish law were, European scholars argued, by their very nature, dependent on external enforcements and naturally inclined to scholasticism. The ossification of law was thus not contingent on historical developments, it was not the result of the degeneration of an ideal, but rather the fulfilment of Islamic and Jewish religious essence. Judaism and Islam, European Christian scholars argued, were inherently inflexible and organised around the dynamics of imposition and obedience. They lacked the capacity to offer more evolved spiritual or ethical possibilities. In Kuenen's conception, Islam threw a 'thin veil' over other, more primitive religions, which subsequently permeated and transformed Islam, providing new spiritual possibilities and enriching the 'original poverty of Islam'.[41] Sufism and rationalist Mu'tazilite thought were not Islamic in origin, Kuenen argued, but rather the outgrowth of a yearning for rationalism and spiritualism that Islam could not fulfil. Renan concurred, insisting that the brilliant intellectual

---

[37] Kuenen, 'L'Islam', 17, 18.
[38] Muir, *Mahomet and Islam*, 243.
[39] Muir, *The Life of Mahomet and History of Islam*, preface, xxx.
[40] Renan, 'L'Islamisme et la Science',in *Oeuvres Complètes*, vol. 1, 956, as cited in Ringer and Shissler, 'The Al-Afghani-Renan Debate, Reconsidered', 35.
[41] Kuenen, 'L'Islam,' 27, 28–9.

contributions to science in the Abbasid period were made by non-Muslims.[42] The claim that Islam was inescapably legalistic led Kuenen to assert that the rigidly literalist and iconoclastic Wahabi movement represented 'true' Islam – 'Islam itself, nothing more and nothing less'.[43] Muir echoed Kuenen's assertions of the limitations of Islam's essence, arguing:

> There can be no question but that, with its pure monotheism, and a code founded in the main on justice and humanity, Islam succeeds in raising to a higher level races sunk in idolatry and fetishism, like those of Central Africa, and that in some respects, notably in that of temperance, it materially improves the morality of such peoples. But, having raised them to a certain point, it leaves them there. Whether in things secular or things spiritual, there is no advance. The defects of which I have been treating cling to the outer life; and as regards the inner life, there is, in the cold and formal round of Moslem ordinances, altogether wanting the genial and motive power of the Heavenly Father's love.[44]

Islam was characterised as indissolubly tethered to a rigid legalism, which left little room for the possibility of an individual's spiritual or ethical development. European Christian scholars thus constructed a clear binary of law versus spirituality, external versus internal, communal versus individual and intellectually barren versus intellectually fecund. This binary operated within a racialisation of essence, which claimed Semitic religions and peoples as innately intellectually stagnant and moribund and Aryan religions and peoples as inherently intellectually productive and creative. The racial dimensions clearly implied that while Semites had carried forward the torch of universal evolutionary progress from polytheism to monotheism, in so doing they had reached the limits of their evolutionary possibility. Christianity alone had succeeded in transcending Semitic limitations and embracing a superior, more spiritual monotheism. Claiming Protestant Christianity as the most evolved religion on the universal map of world religions was thus a claim not only to evolutionary superiority, but also to futurity – a claim to embody the future religion of mankind.

This Christian claim to the religious future of mankind operated not only in an inter-religious context, but also in the context of intra-Christian polemics. Debates surrounding the location of individual religions in the universal taxonomy ostensibly concerned the location of Christianity vis-à-vis Islam, but equally, if more subtly, concerned the location of Protestantism vis-à-vis Christianity writ large. Protestant Christian scholars, who predominated in the historical and religious studies faculties, were as committed to demon-

---

[42] See Renan, 'L'Islamisme et la Science', in *Oeuvres Complètes*, vol. 1, 956. For a discussion of race and Islam in Renan's argument, see Ringer and Shissler, 'The Al-Afghani-Renan Debate, Reconsidered', 39.
[43] Kuenen, 'L'Islam', 37, 38.
[44] Muir, *Mahomet and Islam*, 246.

strating Protestantism's superiority over other Christian traditions, particularly Roman Catholicism and (Eastern) Orthodox Christianity, as they were to claiming the superiority of Protestantism over Islam and Judaism. Renan, despite hailing from the Roman Catholic tradition, should not be considered the exception to this, influenced as he was by Protestant biblical criticism and given his own reformist religious commitments within Roman Catholicism.[45] In claiming the criteria of religious progress for Protestantism, European Christian scholars explicitly denied those criteria to other religions, including other Christianities. Protestantism, in their definition, was inherently spiritually fulfilling, and served as the motor of intellectual and rational creativity, in direct contradistinction to other religious 'essences'. Rational religion, structured around the internalisation of ethics and predicated on the individual's capacity to develop a consciousness both of Divine nature and of Divine intent, claimed scientific authority in 'othering' all non-Protestant religions and constructing a taxonomy of world religions accordingly.

European Christian discourse on the role and limitations of law and race in religion fitted within the wider conception of universalism. Construction of the universal necessitated construction of the non-universal, or particular. For Protestant scholars, universalism entailed not only spiritual and intellectual capacity, but transcendence – from time and place – from historical context. The non-universal, or particular, conversely entailed boundedness to historical context. Within the overarching classificatory binary of universal versus particular, Christianity, and Protestantism in particular, represented the universal, while Islam represented the particular. Protestant scholars described Protestantism as acontextual and ahistorical, untethered from and transcendent of time and place. In contrast, they described Islam as inextricably bound to the person of the Prophet (and indeed often referred to it as 'Mohammadanism' to emphasise this connection), the place of Arabia, and to the intellectual and creative limitations of Semitic peoples – in other words, to the historical context in which it emerged. We need to read assertions of Islam's fixity and rigidity – whether legal or racial – as assertions of an essential particularism and consequent inability to claim universalism.

Kuenen made these connections explicit in an article entitled 'Does Islam contain the characteristics of religious universalism?' published in 1882.[46]

---

[45] Renan fully acknowledged his intellectual debt to Protestant scholarship, even requesting that if he should die before finishing his *Vie de Jésus*, it should be completed by the liberal Protestant Edmond Henri Adophe Schérer. See Priest, *The Gospel According to Renan*, 38, 58. Renan found Protestantism appealing intellectually, but acknowledged Catholicism's greater emotional and aesthetic appeal. He explained that 'Protestantism appeals to me as a scholar and a thinker, but as an actual religion among the people it is petty: no church-bells, no cathedral, moral coldness.' Renan, *Traveaux et Jours*, 178, as cited in Priest, *The Gospel*, 22.

[46] Kuenen, 'L'Islam', 1–40. Abraham Kuenen (1828–91), a Dutch Protestant theologian, delivered a series of Hibbert lectures in 1882 entitled *National Religions*

Kuenen's opening salvo sought to establish that religions, in their essences, belonged either to the 'particular' or the 'universal' category. He noted:

> Generally we combine in one group universal religions and juxtapose them with religions of particular peoples. There is nothing more natural than this. The difference on which we establish this division jumps immediately to mind and seems to touch on the essence of religion itself.[47]

Kuenen then proceeded to enumerate the characteristics of universal religions. It was not a question of numbers of adherents, he reminded the reader, but of the 'essence and character of the religion'.[48] It was not in dispute that Islam was practised by large numbers of people throughout the world. But this, in and of itself, was not an indication of 'universalism'. Rather, religions had to have the following criteria to be considered universal. First, they had to enable the spiritual development of individuals, which Kuenen described as 'the claim to feel oneself close to God and to feel God close to oneself . . . in short, this is precisely what Islam absolutely does not provide'.[49]

Second, universal religions were inherently 'ethical'. What it meant to be ethical is somewhat elusive in Kuenen's rendition, since his argument insisted on a baseless distinction between law, morality and ethics: 'Islamic law reinforces excellent moral prescriptions, and, what is even better, knows how to introduce them into practice and to energetically push them to be observed. But it is not, for all that, an *ethical* religion.'[50] What Kuenen no doubt meant by the distinction between morality and ethics, was the externality of morality expressed in law, versus the internalisation of individual ethics in the absence of law. The distinction between morality and ethics thus reinforced the distinctions between external/internal, ritual/consciousness that animated claims of Christian superiority.

Third, for a religion to be considered universal, it had to be willingly adopted. As Arietta Papaconstantinou notes, Christian European scholars drew a distinction between 'sincere' and 'insincere' conversion. Islam, 'at least as seen by a scholarly tradition that is overwhelmingly Christian in culture, had little to add theologically to what was already offered by the existing monotheistic traditions, and thus conversion to it [was] largely . . .

---

and Universal Religion. This article was based on his lectures. The Hibbert Lectures were an annual series of non-sectarian lectures on theological issues sponsored by the Hibbert Trust established in 1847 by the Unitarian Robert Hibbert with a goal to uphold 'the unfettered exercise of private judgement in matters of religion'. The inaugural lecture of 1878 was given by the renowned Oxonian religious studies scholar Max Müller.

[47] Kuenen, 'L'Islam', 2.
[48] Kuenen, 'L'Islam', 3.
[49] Kuenen, 'L'Islam', 32.
[50] Kuenen, 'L'Islam', 36.

explained in terms of social or economic benefits, of fear or conformism'.[51] Conversely, 'sincere' conversion to Christianity was typically cast as 'an interiorized, voluntary, individual decision based on faith and dogmatic conviction'.[52]

Willing adoption, in Kuenen's estimation, was indicative of the religion's capacity to provide spiritual and intellectual satisfaction to its adherents. With the exception of the Prophet Mohammad, who, Kuenen conceded, had been a genuinely spiritual individual, and with the further exception of the Prophet's earliest companions, who were moved by the Prophet's own spirituality, religious conversion to Islam, Kuenen held, had never been the result of willing adoption. It would be a mistake to attribute the spread of Islam, Kuenen insisted, to any inherent quality of Islam. Rather, the expansion of a political empire under the banner of Islam created powerful sociopolitical and economic incentives to convert.

After the expansion of the Islamic empire, Kuenen added, Islam became permeated with so many non-Islamic religious and cultural influences that Umayyad and Abbasid era conversions could not be claimed as representing a willing embrace of 'true', which is to say 'original', Islam. In other words, after the immediate disciples of the Prophet, subsequent conversions were purely transactional and could not be considered 'genuine'.[53] Making these claims about the nature of Islamic conversion allowed Kuenen to downplay later Abbasid intellectual and spiritual creativity as inherently un-Islamic.

True Islam, according to Kuenen, was only found in its temporal and spatial origins and therefore intimately bound to the Prophet, to Arabia, and to the Semitic limitations of Arabs. As Kuenen concluded, Islam 'could respond to the needs of the desert inhabitants who witnessed its emergence; it is incapable of satisfying different and more elevated needs'.[54] Islam was quintessentially particularistic and did not meet the criteria of universal religions, which Kuenen reserved for two (Indo-European) religions only: Christianity and Buddhism.[55]

European Christian arguments surrounding whether or not law was an indication of religious inferiority cannot be disengaged from the fact that their starting point was the presumption of Protestant superiority. The taxonomical system of religious progress, together with the criteria used to evaluate and locate religions, derived from these assumptions, even as it claimed scientific authority. European Christian scholars claimed that the criteria they used to locate religions in the universal religious taxonomy emerged as a product of the impartial weighing of empirical historical data and the

---

[51] Papaconstantinou, 'Introduction', in Papaconstantinou, McLynn and Schwartz (eds), *Conversion in Late Antique Christianity, Islam, and Beyond*, 2.
[52] Papaconstantinou, 'Introduction', 1.
[53] Kuenen, 'L'Islam', 2, 24.
[54] Kuenen, 'L'Islam', 38.
[55] Kuenen, 'L'Islam', 3.

construction of scientific categories and definitions, when in fact, their religious commitments were the original cause. Their authority as scholars, and the truth claims they asserted, rested on the edifice of scientific impartiality, but they were clearly animated, consciously or unconsciously, by their own deeply held religious convictions.

The three scholars whose work I drew upon to illustrate the polemics surrounding law – Abraham Kuenen, William Muir and Ernest Renan – were all deeply committed to their faiths.[56] A Dutch Protestant, Scottish Protestant and French Catholic, respectively, they exhibited a remarkable degree of consensus surrounding both the categories of religious superiority and the religious imperatives that sustained them. Despite claims to the contrary, their convictions clearly generated, rather than arose from, these categories of analysis. European historical and religious studies disciplines were permeated with Christian, more precisely Protestant, assumptions and claims masquerading as scientific impartiality and empirically substantiated truth. Yet this in no way precluded the adoption and deployment of these very same scientific theories and methods by Islamic modernists to substantiate radically different conclusions.

Islamic Modernist Arguments

Islamic modernists disagreed with the central premise of Christian scholars that the existence of law signalled an inferior stage of religious development. For Islamic modernists, the relative superiority of a given religion depended in no small part on its capacity to generate and induce civilisational progress. They saw law as a necessary component of a religion's social utility.

Islamic modernist arguments for Islam's superiority to Christianity rested principally on the assertion that, while Islam and Christianity were comparable in essence and shared similar evolutionary and civilisational attributes and ideals, Islam alone enabled the implementation of these ideals – the manifestation of essence in historical context. Syed Ameer Ali suggested that Islam and Christianity were similar in their understanding of truth, when he wrote that 'Mohammed's teachings are in no way opposed to those of Jesus; they are simply complementary to them'.[57] Where Christianity failed, he insisted, was not in Jesus' capacity to perceive truth, nor in its expression of the most evolved and thus civilised ideals (greatly surpassing its forerunner, Judaism), but in its enactment of these truths and ideals. The purpose of religion was to generate civilisational progress. As Ali explained, 'religion ought to mean the rule of life; its chief object ought to be the elevation of Humanity towards that perfection which is the end of our existence'.[58] It was in this project that Christianity miscarried and that Islam, Christianity's successor

---

[56] William Muir (1819–1905), Ernest Renan (1823–92), Abraham Kuenen (1828–91).
[57] Ali, *Life and Teachings of Mohammad*, 185.
[58] Ali, *Life and Teachings of Mohammad*, 185.

in the evolutionary continuum, succeeded through its embrace of the necessity of implementation in the form of law.

Ali, in tracing the evolution of religions, drew a clear distinction between the 'truth' of Jesus's teachings and the ultimate failure of Christianity to adhere to them. In his understanding, over time, Christian practice increasingly diverged from the ideals gifted by Jesus and reverted back to more primitive behaviours, signalled by the preponderance of ritual, the intermediation of priests, and the absence of spirituality. As a result, 'the want of some definite rule for the guidance of the masses in process of time', Ali explained, left Christians 'completely adrift in all that regarded the practice of devotion, and under the subjection of the priests, who monopolized the office of regulating the number, length, and the terminology of prayers'.[59] Consequently, practices degenerated into 'the mechanical worship of droning monks, and the hebdomadal flocking into churches and chapels on one day in the week, to make up for the deficiency of spiritual food during the other six'.[60]

Unlike Christianity, Islam emphasised the centrality of law to the enactment and thus preservation of Divine truth. As Ali explained, 'the work of Jesus was left unfinished ... had a longer career been vouchsafed to him, he would have placed his teachings on a more systematic basis ... It was reserved for another Teacher to systematize the laws of morality.'[61] Ali argued that the manifestation and implementation of truth could not be divorced from truth itself. In other words, social practice was not incidental to the evolutionary location of a religion, but intrinsic to it. He explained that law could be a motor of progress if it was inspired by the ideals of a progressive religion:

> Our relations with our Creator are matters of conscience; our relations with our fellow beings must be matters of positive rules; and what higher sanction – to use a legal expression – can be attached for the enforcement of the relative duties of man to man, than the sanction of religion.[62]

This was both an argument for the social utility of religion, and a staunch defence of the place of law in Islam. It was possible, Ali argued, for intellectual elites to comprehend the Divine in an abstract and rational manner, freeing them from the necessity of law, but such intellectual capacity could not be expected from society at large. Society needed law, just as it needed governance. Laws reflected the civilisational level of the society in which they operated – in other words, their social, intellectual, cultural and religious context. Law was thus the means to an end – the implementation of the essence of Islam.

---

[59] Ali, *Life and Teachings of Mohammad*, 174.
[60] Ali, *Life and Teachings of Mohammad*, 174.
[61] Ali, *Life and Teachings of Mohammad*, 185.
[62] Ali, *Life and Teachings of Mohammad*, 185.

For Ali, Islamic law was not merely consonant with Islamic essence, but the very manifestation of the ideals that comprised that essence. In a lengthy passage, he explained the connection between law and essence:

> The principle bases on which the entire system of the Islamic laws is built, are, firstly (1) a belief in the unity, immateriality, power, mercy and supreme love of the Creator; (2) charity and brotherhood among mankind; (3) subjugation of the passions; (4) the outpouring of a grateful heart to the Giver of all gifts; and (5) accountability for human actions in another existence. The grand and noble conceptions, expressed in the Koran, of the power and love of the Deity surpass everything of their kind. The Unity of God, His immateriality, His majesty, His mercy form the constant and never-ending theme of the most eloquent and soul-stirring passages. The flow of life, light and spirituality never ceases. But throughout, there is no trace of dogmatism. Appeal is made to the inner consciousness of man, to his intuitive reason alone.[63]

For Afghani, like Ali, law performed a necessary social function. He argued in classical Islamic terms that law facilitated the 'promotion of good and avoidance of evil'.[64] Only with the establishment of social order enabled by law, Afghani believed, could individuals be freed to pursue intellectual, moral and spiritual perfection. In an argument evocative of Hobbes, Afghani claimed that intellectual freedom and the development of science were impossible without a stable social order. Moreover, like Ali, Afghani insisted that law must necessarily rest on a divine foundation. It was imperative, Afghani argued, that law be based on religious beliefs and understood as a mechanism for furthering divinely sanctioned justice. If law was not believed to enact Divine intent and further Divine injunctions, its integrity could not be sustained, and social order would disintegrate into chaos. 'Religion is the basic link of the social order', he explained, 'without religion the foundations of civilization could never be firm'.[65]

Ali and Afghani were remarkably similar in their embrace and deployment of the criteria of religious progress. There were, however, minor differences in how they applied the criteria of religious superiority to Islam. One obvious difference is that whereas Ali articulated a direct correlation between religious and civilisational progress, Afghani suggested that the relationship between the form, or expression, of religion, and the generation of progress was crucial to the effectiveness of a given religion. For Afghani, religions were more or less true, more or less false. But their capacity to generate civilisational progress did not map directly onto this hierarchy. As we

---

[63] Ali, *Life and Teachings of Mohammad*, 160.

[64] Afghani's declaration reads as the classic '*al-amr bi 'l-ma 'ruf wa al-nahy an al-munkar*' (enjoining the right and forbidding the wrong), which occurs in the Quran nine times. See the Quran, 3:104, 3:110, 3:114, 7:157, 9:67, 9:71, 9:112, 22:41 and 31:17.

[65] Afghani, 'The Truth About the Neicheri Sect', 131.

will discuss in the next chapter, these differences between Ali and Afghani largely dissolved in their respective historical discussions of the interaction of Islamic essence in history.

In sum, Islamic modernists not surprisingly concurred in locating Islam as the most advanced of all religions. This location was premised on their claim that Islam most perfectly manifested the criteria of religious superiority: rationalism, spirituality, individualism, and so forth – the very same criteria that European Christian scholars claimed as essentially, if not uniquely, Christian. The conflict between Christian and Islamic scholars was thus not about the criteria themselves, so much as ownership of them. The exception to this was the place of law. Was law, as European Christian scholars claimed, symptomatic of primitivism? Or was law, as Islamic modernists argued, a necessary feature that Islam most fully articulated, and Christianity lacked?

The question of law's place as a criterion of religious superiority was central to European Christians' and Islamic modernists' respective locations of Islam and Christianity in the hierarchical taxonomy of progress. It was also pivotal in Islamic modernists' understandings of Islamic history. The crux of the issue revolved around the distinction between the existence of law and its application over time in historical context. As we will explore further in the next chapter, Islamic modernists agreed with European Christian scholars that Islamic law had become ossified but rejected the concomitant assumption that this was an inevitable outcome of the limitations of Islam as a Semitic religion. Islamic modernists insisted, rather, that law had to be historicised as the expression of essence in context and that Islamic reform could restore Islamic law to its function as a motor of progress.

Reforming Islam

Protestant scholars' mapping of their own assumptions of superiority onto the universal religious taxonomy facilitated the accomplishment of their two interrelated objectives. The first and most explicit objective was the harnessing of 'empirical' data culled from the intersection of history and philology to the wagon of Christian superiority. This was visible in the polemics surrounding the place of law in Islam. Christianity was juxtaposed to its religious 'others' – Semitic religions – in order to claim various criteria and characteristics as inherent – essential – to Christianity, namely spirituality, rationalism, and the intimate relationship of the individual to God. The second, less explicit objective, was the authorisation, again on scientific terms, of these specifically Protestant characteristics as the most evolved within the larger contours of Christianity writ large. For European Christian scholars, the location of particular religions on the universal religious taxonomy was a means to provide scientific validity, and truth, to specifically Protestant religious features. This validated their claim to evolutional superiority, but also authorised, particularly in the case of the Roman Catholic scholar

Ernest Renan, religious reform – the absorption of these same criteria both necessitated and enabled a redefinition and reformulation of Catholicism.

Similar objectives animated Islamic modernist scholars. Their explicit battle with European scholars concerning the location of Islam relative to Christianity enabled them to simultaneously advance their argument concerning the imperative of Islamic reform. Islamic modernists' claims that Islam was the most evolved of all religions both necessitated and enabled them to insist that certain inherent features constituted the essence of Islam: rationalism, spirituality, and the intimate relationship of the individual to God. Islamic modernists concurred with their Christian counterparts that the essence of any religion was located in its origins. They also concurred that certain religious characteristics were superior to others. They battled over the ownership of these characteristics – were these characteristics intrinsic to Christianity? Or to Islam? Embedded thus in their claim of Islamic superiority was an implicit imperative to reconcile Islam with these essential characteristics. In other words, Islamic modernists insisted on the necessity of Islamic reform in order to (re)align Islam with these 'modern' criteria of religious superiority.

Epistemology and the Dialogue with Tradition

Islamic modernists' location of Islam in the taxonomy of religions depended on their deployment of the criteria of religious evolution that were developing in the European disciplines of religious studies and history. At the same time, their adoption of these criteria in no way signalled their acquiescence to Protestant superiority. On the contrary, Islamic modernists embraced and implemented these criteria and deployed them to reject the European Christian location of Islam in this taxonomy as inferior to Christianity. They insisted that these very criteria empirically, and thus scientifically, demonstrated the superiority of Islam.

Islamic modernists thus illustrate the fallacy of assuming that engagement with European ideas necessarily entailed a process of uncritical adoption, adaptation or outright rejection. They concurred with their European counterparts on the explanatory capacity of historicism, the interplay between context and essence, and the history of human civilisational evolution as embedded within a hierarchical taxonomy of 'world' religions. Alongside their Christian European counterparts, they participated in locating particular religions on a universal taxonomy, and argued for the superiority of Islam using these new intellectual paradigms. They did not shy away from engaging in Christian–Muslim polemics, and did so using new conceptual and classificatory tools – the same tools that European scholars employed. It is worth underscoring that Islamic modernists did not believe that they had been forced to adopt these intellectual paradigms, or that their adoption of these paradigms would necessarily lead to cultural or religious compromise. On the contrary, Islamic modernists viewed these new paradigms as true

– not culturally conditioned – and thus universally applicable. They were not adopting, adapting or alternatively rejecting European ideas, but were embracing new, universally valid explanatory mechanisms. As historians, we should distance our analysis of Islamic modernist understandings from our own assumptions of the 'cultural' ownership of ideas.

At the same time, we must also avoid insisting that existing 'Islamic' epistemologies were not disrupted. On the contrary, despite Islamic modernists' insistence on Islam's superiority to Christianity and the clear overlap between their arguments and many older Islamic conceptions, the foundations of their claims to superiority were fundamentally different from arguments of truth/falsehood that undergirded conventional claims to Islamic superiority. Previously, following Quranic exegesis, 'Islam' was claimed as the last, final and superior revelation of God to mankind. The Prophet Mohammad, as the vessel and transmitter of this revelation, was the final culmination of Abrahamic prophets.[66] As the 'Seal of the Prophets', Mohammad conveyed God's summons for polytheists to accept monotheism and, equally, for other monotheists to renew their covenant with God by accepting the Quran and the Prophet Mohammad. Jews and Christians, in this traditional explanation, while vouchsafed earlier revelations via Moses and Jesus, respectively, had not safeguarded these prophecies which had, over time, become lost, scattered and forgotten. The communities of Jews and Christians had thus increasingly diverged in belief and practice from the original truth they had been vouchsafed.

Islamic modernists, while undoubtedly influenced by this canonical view of the relationship between Abrahamic religions, advanced very different arguments to claim the superiority of Islam. They described the chronology and sequence of Abrahamic religions in universal as opposed to purely Abrahamic terms, and situated Islam within universal religious evolution, not only within the sequence of Abrahamic prophets. For them, religious difference was evolutionary and grounded in the capacity of religious truth to generate civilisational progress. Despite offering a similar explanation for the abandonment of earlier religious prophecies by the communities that had received them, Islamic modernists' arguments rested on a new epistemological landscape that was profoundly historical, evolutionary and civilisational. The fact that Islamic modernists asserted Islamic superiority over other Abrahamic religions should not obscure the fact that the argumentation deployed to make these claims was fundamentally new.

Locating Islam as the Construction of Essence

The location of Islam in the universal taxonomy of religions as the most evolved monotheism entailed claiming that Islam embodied and expressed the most evolved religious criteria. At the same time, these criteria necessarily

---

[66] See Rubin, 'The Seal of the Prophets', 65–96.

entailed the essentialisation of Islam. Islamic modernists asserted that Islam embodied the criteria of rationalism, spirituality, consciousness of the Divine, and so forth, and in so doing, effectively defined the content and contours of Islamic essence.

The history of religion was permeated with these taxonomical paradigms and animated by these questions and polemics. Religious history found itself at the intersection of two separate yet deeply intertwined projects: the story of universal civilisation, and the story of particular cultures and their location within this universal story. There was a fundamental tension between these two projects. The story of universal civilisational evolution was told by means of the religious taxonomy, generated and confirmed as the guiding organisational grammar of European disciplines of religious studies, philology and history. However, the fixity of the location of particular religions on this map belied its ability to fully convey change over time. The actual location of the particular in the universal was premised on the essentialisation of religions – on their extraction from historical context. In other words, while scholarship sought to map the history of human evolution via this religious taxonomy, the criteria used to measure and thus locate particular religions on this map were, by nature, ahistorical. Religions were evaluated based on their intrinsic, immutable essences, not as they expressed themselves in history. Religious evolution indicated the path of the torch of civilisation, but failed to account for the unfolding of particular religious traditions. By representing de-historicised, essentialised points on an evolutionary continuum, this classificatory map was unable to account either for the unfolding of particular religious 'traditions' or for comparative civilisational progress over time and the ways in which 'religion' participated in this. Syed Ameer Ali and Afghani's views of Islamic history, discussed in the next chapter, were intimately bound up with the historical conditions in which Islam as essence could and did generate progress, as well as with explanations of Islam's failure to do so in the present.

CHAPTER
2

ISLAM IN HISTORY, ISLAMIC HISTORY

A wise man will be saddened when he hears
of how the moving sphere of heaven turns . . .
Both Mars and Venus now oppose our cause
And no man can evade the heaven's laws.
       Ferdowsi, *Shahnameh* (The Book of Kings)

And indeed we have set forth for mankind in this Quran every kind of parable.
       Quran 30:58

Introduction

On 8 November 1882, Jamal al-Din al-Afghani declared that 'sovereignty has never left the abode of science. However, this true ruler, which is science, is continually changing capitals.'[1] In this declaration, Afghani described the history of progress as the repeated taking up and passing of the torch of civilisation. His vision of human civilisational progress, shared by Islamic modernists, was symptomatic of the prevalent nineteenth-century theory of history, one in which history, like nature, adhered to fundamental, rationally discoverable 'self-evident truths' or laws.[2]

The laws of progress writ large determined civilisational progress, and at the more particular level, the interaction between essence and context. Islamic modernists wrote new histories of Islam as the story of the interaction of Islamic essence in historical context governed by the historical laws of progress. As discussed in the previous chapter, locating the essence of Islam on the spectrum of religious progress effectively articulated claims to

---

[1] Afghani, 'Lecture on Teaching and Learning' (given 8 November 1882 in Albert Hall, Calcutta), 103.
[2] Afghani, 'Lecture on Teaching and Learning', 108.

a particular place for Islam within universal religious progress and, to the extent that religion was reflected by civilisation and vice versa, to universal progress writ large. The taxonomy mapped religions in a hierarchy according to how well any particular religious 'essence' met the criteria of religious progress, but was unable to convey the mechanics of progress; it provided no insights into the nature or cause of changes and developments within a religious tradition. Were religions causes of progress, or merely reflections of progress? What were the historical laws, the 'laws of progress', that accounted for periods of civilisational growth as well as periods of stagnation? How did these laws illuminate the path of the torch of civilisation? History was the medium of investigation – the material and methodology that, once understood and deployed, could illuminate a path forward.

Namık Kemal and Syed Ameer Ali in many ways defined the parameters, content and narrative arc of 'Islamic History'. Their works, *The Complete History of Islam* (*Büyük Islam Tarihi*) and *A Short History of the Saracens* (1899),[3] respectively, are remarkably similar in their location of 'Islamic History' in time and space. Both authors began with contextualising the Prophet Mohammad in Arabia, moved to the reception and ultimate success of the Prophet in creating an Islamic community, and then proceeded dynastically through the Rashidun, Umayyad and Abbasid periods. Their books concluded with the ultimate destruction of the Abbasids, who, having endured wave after wave of aggression from the Orthodox Christian Byzantines and Catholic Christian Crusaders, ultimately succumbed to the overwhelming force of the pagan Mongols. Islamic history was constructed as a discreet period of time and place from roughly 500–1258, spanning the lifetime of the Prophet Mohammad in Arabia through the Abbasid period in the Middle East, Andalusia and North Africa, up until the Mongol invasions. Critically, both authors included Islamic Spain in their narratives.

These new Islamic histories must be read as manifestations of Islamic modernists' adoption of the theoretical landscape of historicism and its intendent methodology. Islamic modernists embraced historicism as a scientific method. Above all, they were concerned with claiming impartiality, which they believed constituted a scientific evaluation of evidence.[4] They were careful to substantiate their scholarship with references to primary sources alongside secondary scholarship. They relied on older, canonical Islamic sources as well as more recent European historical works. Ali and Namık Kemal took pains to cite European sources on the civilisational accomplishments of the Abbasids, even if the evidence itself, for Namık Kemal, consisted primarily of lists of Islamic scholarly output. Ali did not hesitate to challenge European scholarship or assumptions of Christian

---

[3] Kemal, *Büyük Islam Tarihi* (*The Complete History of Islam*) was published posthumously in 1975; Ali, *A Short History of the Saracens*.

[4] Bayezidof argued that Ernest Renan, in his 'Islam and Science' article had failed to uphold the standards of modern scholarship. See Chapter 3.

exceptionalism, but whenever he wished to substantiate a point that he believed might be construed as biased, he employed European sources to do so. He did so not because he accorded European scholarship greater authority, but rather to demonstrate his impartiality, accuracy and thus scientific authority. This method reflected his commitment to history as the deployment of the scientific method of historicism: the historicisation of context, the critical evaluation of sources, the weighing of evidence and the empirical examination of the laws of progress.

Uncovering the Historical Laws of Progress

Afghani and Syed Ameer Ali proposed very different models for the relationship of religion to civilisation. Ali maintained that religion and civilisation were partners, and moved along the spectrum of progress simultaneously, hand in hand. The relative level of religion on the spectrum of progress, therefore, was in direct correlation to the level of civilisation; religious progress was lit by the torch of civilisation. Afghani took a more historicist position. The great empires of the past had born the torch of civilisation, he noted, but had not necessarily advanced in terms of religious progress towards greater 'truth'. Afghani therefore proposed a different vision of religion – one that emphasised the form and function of religion, rather than its level of primitivism – as the indicator of civilisational progress.

Afghani: History and the Torch of Civilization

Afghani succinctly described history as the continuous passage of the torch of civilisation when he wrote that

> India was the first origin of the fundamentals of [science], and from there they moved to Babylonia, and from Babylonia to Egypt. From Egypt they moved to the lands of the Greeks and Romans. In every move they acquired a new form, and in each migration they received fresh adornment. They were transferred from one state to another, just as the germs of plants and animals are transformed from a state of imperfection to perfection.[5]

In Afghani's rendering, science 'migrated' through a succession of peoples, each of whom inherited the achievements of others, and added their own contribution. At every stage, science progressed. At the risk of this passage being read simply as an account of the history of science, Afghani emphasised the centrality of science to civilisation. He declared that 'science rules the world. There was, is, and will be no ruler in the world but science.'[6] He then named a succession of conquering peoples, from the Chaldeans, Egyptians,

---

[5] Afghani, 'The Benefits of Philosophy', 116.
[6] Afghani, 'Lecture on Teaching and Learning', 102.

Phoenicians and Alexander (the Great), explaining that their power had been entirely a result of 'science'. This remained true in the present, Afghani insisted, noting that 'the Europeans have now put their hands on every part of the world ... In reality this usurpation, aggression, and conquest has not come from the French or the English. Rather it is science that everywhere manifests its greatness and power.'[7]

By science, Afghani meant two things. First and foremost, he meant scientific method – empiricism, logic, rationalism, and the intellectual freedom to criticize, experiment and create. Scientific method, he believed, sustained the greatest of all sciences – philosophy: 'philosophy is the science that deals with the state of external beings, and their causes, reasons, needs, and requisites'.[8] In a subsequent passage he elaborated that 'the science that has the position of a comprehensive soul and the rank of a preserving force is the science of *falsafa* or philosophy, because its subject is universal. It is philosophy that shows man human prerequisites. It shows the sciences what is necessary.'[9] Second, Afghani used sciences, in the plural, to denote the specific fields of scientific endeavour, ultimately emanating from and governed by philosophy as scientific method – for example, chemistry and botany. Accordingly, 'each of these sciences whose subject is a special matter is like a limb on the body of science'.[10]

In Afghani's reading of the laws of history, societies that encouraged intellectual freedom, and in so doing, enabled philosophy and scientific progress, became dominant, civilising forces; societies that discouraged intellectual freedom faltered and declined. He stated unequivocally that 'the first defect appearing in any nation that is headed toward decline is in the philosophic spirit'.[11] Afghani, unlike Syed Ameer Ali, did not believe that the level of progress of a religion was in and of itself directly related to the capacity of a society to progress. He explained that 'religious beliefs, true or false, are not incompatible with civilization and progress unless they forbid the acquisition of science ... and progress in sound civilization'.[12]

In making this assertion, Afghani was insisting on the evaluation of the function of religion in historical context, not the truth value of its beliefs, or its level of primitivism. Religion, in his view, was an essential foundation of society and law, but this function could be provided even by what

---

[7] Afghani, 'Lecture on Teaching and Learning', 102.
[8] Afghani, 'Lecture on Teaching and Learning', 106.
[9] Afghani, 'Lecture on Teaching and Learning', 104.
[10] Afghani, 'Lecture on Teaching and Learning', 104. One might note that Afghani's conception of the relatedness of all sciences is in stark contrast to classical Islamic admonitions not to 'work on two subjects at once' or to 'mix one subject with another'. See Sheikh Abd al-Latif (c. 1231) on his advice to students, quoted in Makdisi, *The Rise of Colleges*, 88–90.
[11] Afghani, 'Lecture on Teaching and Learning', 105.
[12] Afghani, 'Commentary on the Commentator', 128.

he termed 'false' religions. Afghani cited historical evidence to substantiate this, observing that 'the Greeks, in that century that they were rulers of the world, and at the time that great sages and revered philosophers appeared among them, believed in hundreds of gods and thousands of superstitions'. Likewise, the Persians, 'at the time when they ruled . . . and were considered incomparable in civilization, [nonetheless] had hundreds of absurdities engraved on their hearts'.[13]

Religion, then, was a prerequisite for the promotion of science, but was not in and of itself sufficient. Religion could serve as a motor for progress, but religion could also serve to inhibit progress. One might use the metaphor of an anchor to describe Afghani's view of religion. On the one hand, an anchor provides stability and prevents backward movement. At the same time, an anchor also inhibits forward movement. For Afghani, religion must be evaluated in terms of its function in any particular historical context. When the forms that religion takes (institutions, rituals, laws) are productive of intellectual freedom (and thus philosophy and science), religion is invaluable. However, religion by its very nature tends toward stasis, which inhibits intellectual freedom and prevents progress. One must be vigilant, Afghani believed, in keeping the rust off the anchor chain of religion, so that it could be raised and lowered as needed, both safeguarding progress and enabling forward movement.

Syed Ameer Ali: History as Failed Revelations

Syed Ameer Ali identified the historical law of progress in a lengthy section of *The Life and Teachings of Mohammad* where he explored the universal religious pre-history of Islam. For Ali, Islam appeared at the very end of a long sequence of failed revelations. Ali outlined his views of the historical laws of progress in the history of these failed revolutions, which he constructed as abortive attempts to move from paganism to monotheism.

The dialectic between civilisational progress and inertia animated both Ali's *Life and Teachings of Mohammad* and his later *Short History of the Saracens*. In *Saracens*, Ali presented his reader with what he promised would be a 'survey of the religious and social condition of the nations of the earth about the time of the Islamic dispensation' with an emphasis on 'the causes which had led to the advent of the Great Prophet of Nazareth [Jesus]' and which 'acted with greater force . . . at the period of Mohammed's appearance'.[14] Ali's explication of the causes of Jesus' and Mohammad's appearance reflected his understanding of the laws of progress – laws that governed the possibilities and obstacles for religions to generate progress and civilisation. His treatment of the pre-Islamic context was in effect an explanation of the dynamics of these laws.

[13] Afghani, 'Commentary on the Commentator', 128.
[14] Ali, *Saracens*, 1.

Ali provided four lengthy historical examples of the historical laws of progress as they regulated the interaction between religious 'truths' and civilisational advancement: Aryan religious impact in India, Zoroastrianism in the Middle East, Judaism, and Christianity. He began by noting that humanity moved from 'savageness into barbarism'[15] when 'abstractions and personifications of the powers of Nature [were] subordinated to two comprehensive Principles: Light and Darkness'.[16] He then proceeded to chart the impact of what he termed the Aryan 'conquest' of India and Iran. The Aryans who migrated to India were civilisationally superior to the indigenous peoples and, initially, propelled India from the age of 'savageness' to the relatively superior age of 'barbarism'. Over time, however, the prolonged impact of the conquered 'black aboriginal races'[17] led to the eventual degeneration of the Aryans. Cut off from 'the West', and 'without possessing a system of positive morality embodied in effectual laws',[18] Ali explained that the Aryans degenerated 'back' to a primitive civilisational level, one that he described as resulting in the 'depth of degradation' and 'complete servitude' of women.[19]

The other branch of the Aryans migrated into Persia and expressed their civilizational superiority in the form of Zoroastrianism. Despite the progressive nature of Zoroaster's reforms, they too eventually succumbed to the overwhelming penetration of surrounding inferior civilisations. Ali recounted that Zoroaster's religion, 'at last met with the fate which appears to be the end of every system which does not possess the homogeneity, the practicality, the human sympathy amongst its professors, the absence of all esoteric feelings, which is needful for an universal creed'.[20] As a result, the 'pure', 'symbolical [sic] worship',[21] of Zoroastrianism under the Achaemenids was polluted by contact with the 'influx of all the dregs of Lesser Asia' who accompanied the 'Macedonian conquest'[22] and the subsequent Parthian (Hellenic) rule. Despite the eventual restoration of national unity under the Sassanians, 'social and religious life were lost beyond the power of rulers to restore'.[23] According to Ali, the 'frightful depravation of moral life' led directly to 'the speedy extinction of the nation in its own iniquities' in the form of the Arab conquest, centuries later.[24]

Judaism and Christianity, too, in Ali's conception, were governed by the

---

[15] Ali, *Life and Teachings of Mohammad*, 1.
[16] Ali, *Life and Teachings of Mohammad*, 2.
[17] Ali, *Life and Teachings of Mohammad*, 3.
[18] Ali, *Saracens*, 3.
[19] Ali, *Life and Teachings of Mohammad*, 5.
[20] Ali, *Life and Teachings of Mohammad*, 7–8.
[21] Ali, *Life and Teachings of Mohammad*, 6–7.
[22] Ali, *Life and Teachings of Mohammad*, 8.
[23] Ali, *Life and Teachings of Mohammad*, 9.
[24] Ali, *Life and Teachings of Mohammad*, 10.

same historical laws of progress, whereby their initial revelatory 'truths' were ultimately unable to sustain progress over time. The communities who called themselves Jews and Christians were markedly inferior – civilisationally – to the revelations that they were vouchsafed. Jews, although granted a Divine revelation, varied greatly between different groups. Some Jews found refuge in Arabia, but 'they had brought with their religion the bitter spirit of strife'.[25] Those groups that emigrated into Arabia were unable to maintain the monotheism of Moses' revelation, and instead succumbed to 'the heathenism of their Arab brothers'.[26] Despite having 'an idea of the God of Abraham', they exhibited a materialistic conception of the Deity manifest in 'a statue representing Abraham with the ram beside him, ready "for sacrifice", in the interior of the Kaaba'.[27] According to Ali, most of the Jews had never fully abandoned worship of 'the Teraphim, a sort of household god in a human form', a practice which likely 'strengthened by contact with the heathen Arabs'.[28] On the eve of Islam, Ali described the Jews disdainfully as suffering from 'rigid and uncompromising bigotry on the one hand and a voluptuous epicureanism on the other'.[29]

Christians were equally removed from the initial promise of their revelation. Jesus had been a 'messenger of universal brotherhood and love' who 'trod the paths of humility and mildness'.[30] But, despite his profession of elevated ideals and spirituality, 'Jesus had come and gone, without producing much visible effect.'[31] Christianity had, Ali acknowledged, initially succeeded in extinguishing paganism, only to turn back to its full embrace.[32] Citing Gibbon, he explained that 'after the extinction of paganism, the Christians, in peace and piety, might have enjoyed their solitary triumph. But the principle of discord was alive in their bosom, and they were more solicitous to explore the nature than to practise the laws of their founder.'[33]

As a direct consequence of moral decay, Ali explained, superstition and political factionalism reared their ugly heads. Christians 'sank downward into the common ignorance, and yielded to that worst barbarism – a worn-out civilization'.[34] Christians, he noted scathingly, squandered the possibilities inherent in their revelation: 'Instead of taking an example from the lessons of piety, gentleness and humanity inculcated by their great Master

---

[25] Ali, *Life and Teachings of Mohammad*, 17.
[26] Ali, *Life and Teachings of Mohammad*, 162.
[27] Ali, *Life and Teachings of Mohammad*, 162.
[28] Ali, *Life and Teachings of Mohammad*, 163.
[29] Ali, *Life and Teachings of Mohammad*, 11.
[30] Ali, *Life and Teachings of Mohammad*, 11.
[31] Ali, *Life and Teachings of Mohammad*, 11, 12, 13.
[32] Ali, *Life and Teachings of Mohammad*, 13.
[33] Ali, *Life and Teachings of Mohammad*, 13. Citing Gibbon, *The History of the Decline and Fall of the Roman Empire*, 328.
[34] Ali, *Life and Teachings of Mohammad*, 15.

[Jesus], they [Christians] were animated by the fiercest animosity against each other and against the outside world.'[35] Factionalism and brutality inevitably went hand in hand with moral 'misery' and 'social ruin'.[36] This pathetic condition spread throughout Christian lands, including to Europe, where 'the condition of the people was, if possible, even more miserable'.[37]

These four examples of the failure of Divine revelations to generate lasting civilisational progress illustrate the laws of historical progress as Ali understood them. In his rendering, revelation as an expression of an ideal – a Divine truth – had been provided by God in order to generate progress and civilisation, but, after an initial positive effect, its inherent potential inevitably succumbed to the overwhelming inertia of inferior, primitive civilisations. Societies were unable to qualitatively transform their contexts, and became the victims of their impotence.

Historical laws of progress were thus cast as the conditions of the success or failure of religion to generate progress – progress understood both conceptually as the level of progress of religious beliefs, but also practically, since more advanced religions encouraged and sustained more advanced social practices. God's intent was civilisational progress. Revelations, rays of Divine light, absent fuel to feed them and lamps to protect them, were quickly extinguished by the potency of primitive darkness. According to Ali, civilisational progress necessitated a full rupture with existing social, cultural, political and religious institutions, and the establishment of new ones. Civilisational progress could only be accomplished by the full embrace of the ideal of the 'Supreme Divinity'. The failure of religious communities that had been vouchsafed revelations to remain true to God's intent was thus not only a socio-religious regression, but a failure to embrace Divine intentionality – tantamount in Ali's narrative to faithlessness to God.

The Prophet: Implementing God's Laws

Islamic modernists universally emphasised the barbarity of pre-Islamic Arabia – both religiously and in terms of social practice – as a way of underscoring the radical transformations that Islam wrought on the religious and social landscape of Arabia. Namık Kemal explained that Islam 'showed people the correct path' and that as a result, society abandoned uncivilised practices of 'idol worship, theft, adultery, slander and the burial of infant daughters', and instead 'committed to telling the truth and being trustworthy'.[38] In similar ways, Imam Bayezidof contended that the adoption of Islam as a set of moral and legal precepts imbedded in the Quran enabled social and political progress. He noted that

---

[35] Ali, *Life and Teachings of Mohammad*, 15.
[36] Ali, *Life and Teachings of Mohammad*, 16.
[37] Ali, *Life and Teachings of Mohammad*, 16.
[38] Kemal, *Büyük Islam Tarihi*, 31.

in the *Jahilyya* period there was continuous warfare and conflict. The Prophet changed everything; brought peace and an end of conflict; cleansed the entire Arabian desert of idols and their sites of worship; inaugurated a new era; the Prophet's religious message brought everyone together as fellow countrymen.[39]

Afghani described the intellectual, social and moral transformation enabled by the revelation of the Quran. Prior to the revelation, he noted contemptuously, 'no people were less civilized than the Arabs',[40] whom he described as living 'in the utmost ignorance, like wild animals'.[41] The enactment of the ideals embedded in the Quran into religious laws and prescriptions 'opened the road for man to become man'.[42] Quranic 'ethics' and 'divine policies' were the cause of the superiority and subsequent expansion of the Arabs.[43] Afghani stressed the intellectual possibilities that the Quran enabled – it ushered in the possibility of perfection.[44]

Syed Ameer Ali's evolutionary treatment of civilisational history explicitly located Islam within the purview of these same laws, within a pattern of the repeated unfolding of revelation, but revelations ultimately unable to extricate society from the 'thralldom' of primitivism. The history of monotheistic revelations in the pre-Islamic period was one of aborted civilisational revolution, of humanity trapped in moral dissolution and backwardness. It was also, at a more fundamental level, the story of humanity's faithlessness to God's intent.

Ali described the pre-Islamic context of Arabia as one in which the 'majority of the people were addicted to fetishism of the grossest type'.[45] Providing more details, he noted that

> among the heathen Arabs, the idea of Godhead varied according to the culture of the individual or the clan. With some it rose (comparatively speaking) to the 'divinization' or deification of nature; among others it fell to simple fetishism, the adoration of a piece of dough, a stick, or a stone. Some believed in a future life; others had no idea of it whatever.[46]

Ali concluded that 'neither Christianity nor Judaism had succeeded in raising [Arabs] in the scale of humanity',[47] a failure he attributed partially

---

[39] Bayezidof, 'Islam in Ilimlerle İlişkisi,' (The Relationship of Islam and Science), 46.
[40] Afghani, 'Benefits of Philosophy', 113.
[41] Afghani, 'Commentary on the Commentator', 129.
[42] Afghani, 'Benefits of Philosophy', 114.
[43] Afghani, 'Commentary on the Commentator', 126.
[44] Afghani, 'Benefits of Philosophy', 113–14.
[45] Ali, *Life and Teachings of Mohammad*, 17.
[46] Ali, *Life and Teachings of Mohammad*, 161.
[47] Ali, *Life and Teachings of Mohammad*, 19.

to the challenges of tribalism and idolatry, but partially to the failures of Christianity and Judaism to transform humanity:

> The surface of Arabia had been now and then gently rippled by the feeble efforts of Christianity; the sterner influences of Judaism had been occasionally visible in a deeper and more troubled current; but the tide of indigenous idolatry and of Ishmaelite superstition, setting from every quarter with an unbroken and unebbing [sic] surge towards the Kaaba, gave ample evidence that the faith and worship of Mecca held the Arab mind in a thralldom, rigorous and undisputed.[48]

Even before the revelation of the Quran, the Prophet Mohammad recognised the moral degeneracy of his society. He 'beheld his people sunk in absolute barbarism'[49] and understood that social and political progress alike depended on 'moral regeneration'.[50] Ali repeatedly likened the Prophet's personality to that of Jesus; what distinguished them was not character or essence, but the Prophet's recognition that moral regeneration depended on successful implementation of the revelation, compared to Jesus' failure to do so. The Prophet understood, Ali insisted, that his mandate was not simply belief in the revelation, but its enactment – God 'selected him for the salvation of his people – recalling him to his duty to mankind'.[51]

The Prophet's recognition of the fundamental importance of manifesting essence in context cast him as a conscious actor on the historical stage. If moral and civilisational success depended on implementation, the Prophet was compelled to weigh the ideal – Islamic essence – with its application in context. The Prophet enjoyed a divinely guided, and thus perfect, understanding of the essence of Islam but due to the inescapable boundedness of his own historical context, he was compelled to calibrate ideals within the domain of the possible.

The Prophet's success, measured by the political unification of the peninsula, the embrace of monotheism, and the more 'civilised' social practices that monotheism conveyed, was a means to enable the ultimate, moral triumph of Islam. 'What had once been a moral desert,' Ali concluded, 'was transformed into a garden. Idolatry, with its nameless abominations, was utterly destroyed.'[52] Ali further underscored the connection between morality and cultural progress: 'The reckless freedom of heathenism was abandoned, and manners became decorous, almost austere; gambling and drunkenness were forbidden. Before this time there had been no privacy in

---

[48] Ali, *Life and Teachings of Mohammad*, 19–20, quoting Muir, *The Life of Mahomet and History of Islam*, vol. 1, Introduction, ccxxxix.
[49] Ali, *Life and Teachings of Mohammad*, 33.
[50] Ali, *Life and Teachings of Mohammad*, 33.
[51] Ali, *Life and Teachings of Mohammad*, 36.
[52] Ali, *Life and Teachings of Mohammad*, 149.

houses; from this time, it became customary to have special apartments for women.'⁵³

This was the first genuine monotheistic revolution – the first successful civilisational rupture with paganism. Of all the prophets who had preceded him, Mohammad was the first to successfully elevate degraded, primitive humanity to a 'new moral life' expressed in rule of law, political unity, religious tolerance, increased status for women, rejection of slavery, 'equality and brotherhood of mankind'⁵⁴ and the embrace of a progressive moral code. It was thus the establishment of the 'commonwealth of Islam'⁵⁵ that distinguished Mohammad – his ability to implement the 'laws of God'. Ali described the relationship of the Prophet to his followers thus:

> Mohammed was the source, under Providence, of this new awakening – the bright fountain from which flowed the stream of their hopes of eternity . . . They were all animated with one desire, namely, to serve God in truth and purity, to obey His laws reverently in all the affairs of life. The truths and maxims, the precepts which, from time to time during the past twenty years, Mohammed had delivered to his followers, were embalmed in their hearts, and had become the ruling principles of every action. Law and morality were united.⁵⁶

Ali constructed Mohammad's triumphs as not only Islamic, or Arabian, but as universal advances in human religious progress. Previous prophets, as religious reformers, Ali wrote, had 'departed from this world with their aspirations unfulfilled . . . it was reserved for Mohamed to fulfil his mission and that of his predecessors'.⁵⁷ Mohammad's genius was his understanding of the historical laws of religious progress.

Mohammad succeeded where other prophets had failed, because he understood the importance of implementation. He established prescriptions and laws that furthered Islamic ideals. He was able to implement the ideals of the revelation – the essence of Islam – within the confines of historical context. In so doing, he fundamentally revolutionised his society and ushered in a new civilisational level for mankind. As Ali phrased it, 'success is always one of the greatest criterions of the truth'.⁵⁸ For him, Islam was chronologically the last and yet, in some fundamental way, the first true monotheism. The Prophet was the first to be faithful to God's intent.

---

[53] Ali, *Life and Teachings of Mohammad*, 19.
[54] Ali, *Life and Teachings of Mohammad*, 131.
[55] Ali, *Saracens*, 1–4.
[56] Ali, *Life and Teachings of Mohammad*, 149–50.
[57] Ali, *Life and Teachings of Mohammad*, 150.
[58] Ali, *Life and Teachings of Mohammad*, 89.

'Rashidun' – Syed Ameer Ali's 'Republic of Islam'

The first four Caliphs to assume the mantle of governance of the Islamic community after the death of the Prophet in 632 – Abu Bakr (r. 632–34), Umar (r. 634–44), Uthman (r. 644–56) and Ali b. Abu Taleb (r. 656–61) – constitute a unique era in Islamic historical tradition. This was the first period when the community was governed in the absence of the Prophet, in the absence thus, of Divine guidance via Prophetic mediation. This period was also unique in that these four caliphs were the only leaders in Islamic history who belonged to the early followers of the Prophet – his closest supporters, the age of the 'Companions'. These four caliphs are collectively referred to as the 'Rashidun' – the 'Rightly-guided' – and were distinguished from subsequent rulers as a source of precedent. Syed Ameer Ali adhered to this traditional characterisation of the period, reinforcing the Rashidun as an era of continuity with the Prophetic period – a continuity that hinged on the individual character of the four caliphs.

According to Ali, the Rashidun caliphs were profoundly committed to the ideals of Islam as expressed by the Prophet, and to the continued implementation of these ideals in the form of laws and prescribed religious practices. In Ali's conception, theirs was a period of continuity, marked by their safeguarding of the Prophet's work. For all of these reasons, the Rashidun era, or as Ali called it, 'the Republic of Islam', was a uniquely exemplary period.

At the same time, Ali recognised that this era was also complex and, while discreetly bounded, not uniform. Following classic Islamic historiography, he divided the Rashidun into two periods: the caliphates of Abu Bakr and Umar constituting the first, and the caliphates of Uthman and Ali b. Abu Taleb the second. Ali's divide should not be read as constituting convenient chapter divisions, but as representing significant differences between these two periods.[59] The first period, consisting of the caliphates of Abu Bakr and Umar, was characterized by continuity with the Prophetic period in two senses: intentions of the caliphs and historical context. In Ali's rendering, these first two caliphs were committed to continuing much of what the Prophet Mohammad had initiated, and were largely successful in doing so. The second period, consisting of Uthman and Ali b. Abu Taleb's caliphates, in contrast, witnessed discord as a result of the disruption of outside forces unleashed in the conquests.

The Prophet's 'genius' lay in his ability to appropriately apply Islamic ideals to his own Arabian context – to convey the essence of Islam via 'God's laws'. To a large extent, these ideals were communicated to the Companions by the Prophet himself, and their application was already underway in the Prophet's lifetime. Ali described Abu Bakr and Umar as imbued with the effect of the Prophet, the 'hold' that his 'personality had acquired over

---

[59] Abu Bakr and Umar's caliphates formed the subject of one chapter; Uthman and Ali's caliphates another.

the minds of his followers'.⁶⁰ Accordingly, they envisioned themselves as continuing the Prophet's work. Ali emphasised the continuity of Abu Bakr's caliphate with the time of the Prophet by describing him as resembling the Prophet himself. Abu Bakr 'was extremely simple in his habits: gentle but firm, he devoted all his energies to the administration of the new-born State and to the good of the people'.⁶¹

Ali also emphasised Abu Bakr's commitment to adhering to Prophetic precedent, by quoting in full Abu Bakr's initial public speech to the community upon assuming leadership. Abu Bakr, emphasised the contractual nature of his election, pledging, 'As I obey God and His Prophet, obey me: if I neglect the laws of God and the Prophet, I have no more right to your obedience.'⁶² According to Ali, these 'laws' included efficient and just taxation, good governance, administrative accountability, 'elective government', the promotion of prosperity, equitable and tolerant treatment of non-Muslims, and 'jurisprudence and rules' that 'depended on the Koran'.⁶³

The ideals of Islam and their manifestation were continued in the caliphate of Umar, whom Ali described as a man 'of strong moral fibre and a keen sense of justice, possessed of great energy and force of character'.⁶⁴ Like Abu Bakr before him, Ali portrayed Umar as equally committed to Islamic ideals and to carrying forward Islamic practices and governance.⁶⁵ Yet the caliphate of Umar witnessed a cataclysmic event that threatened the fledgling 'Republic' – one that only Umar's capable guidance succeeded in navigating – the 'Islamic conquests'.

Ali treated the conquests as neither inevitable nor desirable from the Arab standpoint. In his account, the caliphs were forced, however unwillingly, into battle. Ali described the conquest of Persia as stemming from the aggressive actions taken by the Sassanian king 'Yezdjard', who was 'young, energetic' and 'bent not only on driving the Saracens from Hira, but also on conquering their country'.⁶⁶ Forced to defend themselves, the Arab army triumphed over vastly superior Persian forces at Qadisiyyah. Again, reluctantly, the Arab general Sa'd, in order to protect the newly acquired territorial gains, was 'compelled to march upon the royal city' of Mada'in.⁶⁷ This pattern was repeated throughout Ali's narrative of the conquests, with the Arabs forced into combat by Persian forces solely in order to secure or protect

---

⁶⁰ Ali, *Saracens*, 20.
⁶¹ Ali, *Saracens*, 26–7.
⁶² Ali, *Saracens*, 21–2. Ali follows Tabari closely on this quotation, but omits any reference to the other conflicts surrounding Abu Bakr's 'election' as discussed at great length in Tabari and other classical historical sources.
⁶³ Ali, *Saracens*, esp. 62–3.
⁶⁴ Ali, *Saracens*, 27.
⁶⁵ Ali, *Saracens*, 43–4.
⁶⁶ Ali, *Saracens*, 28
⁶⁷ Ali, *Saracens*, 27–43.

their territories. Reluctantly, the Arabs expanded their realm. Equating Arab 'defensive' conquests to relatively recent British actions in India, Ali noted that 'like the British government in India, when threatened by the Sikhs in 1848, the Caliph had no choice but to repel the Romans, and reduce the tribes to subjection'.[68]

Ali described the lead up to the battle of Nihavand that destroyed the Persian empire as forced on the Arabs by an aggressive Persian ruler: 'It now became clear to Omar that the ban against an advance towards the east must be withdrawn. In self-defense, nothing was left but to crush the Chosroes, [the Persian emperor] and take entire possession of his realm.'[69] With a matter-of-factness that stands in stark contrast to the enduring pathos of Ferdowsi's lament for the fall of Persia in the *Shahnameh*, Ali described the events briefly with sparing use of adjectives: 'The Persians, who outnumbered the Saracens six to one, were defeated with terrible loss ... Persia thus passed under Moslem domination.'[70] Ali's account emphasised the inevitability of Arab conquest as the consequence of their newly acquired civilisational superiority. For this reason, he de-emphasised the importance of battles or strategy as reasons for Arab military success, instead suggesting a civilisational inevitability of the conquests with his passing mention of the overwhelming military odds that the Arabs, time and time again, effortlessly triumphed over.

The conquests, as a 'clash of civilizations', juxtaposed Islamic governance with the 'galling oppression' and injustice of Persian Sassanian and Byzantine rule. Their difference was the inescapable outcome of civilisational superiority. Islamic governance was first and foremost a civilising mission, designed for the betterment of all. Ali listed the various administrative reforms undertaken in lands conquered from Persia and Byzantium. These included establishing land rights for peasants and land-holders, restoring aqueducts, establishing progressive taxation, fostering trade, protecting Christians and other minorities, and generally, 'organizing the administration of the new Empire'.[71] Moreover, Ali emphasised religious tolerance as a fundamental principle of Islamic governance. He insisted that 'liberty of conscience was allowed to every one [sic], and the Moslems were ordered not to interfere with the religion of the people'. Ali described how over time, implicitly as a result of good governance and the superior civilisation that produced it, 'the bulk of the people, without any such compulsion as is used by some modern nations for the conversion of unorthodox communities, adopted Islam'.[72]

Ali's narrative of the conquests as thrust unwillingly upon the Rashidun was a deliberate strategy designed to counter Christian representations of

[68] Ali, *Saracens*, 34.
[69] Ali, *Saracens*, 32.
[70] Ali, *Saracens*, 33. For Ferdowsi's treatment, see Ferdowsi, *Shahnameh: The Persian Book of Kings*, 832–54.
[71] Ali, *Saracens*, 33, 42–3.
[72] Ali, *Saracens*, 33–4.

the Prophet as instrumentalising Islam in the name of political conquest, epitomised by the famous line in Gibbon's *The Decline and Fall of the Roman Empire*: 'Mahomet, with the sword in one hand and the Koran in the other, erected his throne on the ruins of Christianity and of Rome.'[73] Ali's emphasis on the Prophet's character, his sacrifices and sufferings in the cause of moral progress, deliberately countered the enduring Christian trope of the Prophet as an immoral charlatan.[74] The Arab conquests overthrew decadent empires of Byzantium and Persia and ushered in a new level of civilisation in Islamic lands.

Unlike Abu Bakr, whose brief rule followed on the heels of the Prophet's own, Umar's rule was significantly longer and witnessed the zenith of the conquests. Umar was forced to innovate as exigencies demanded. Ali credited Umar with articulating new Islamic practices that exemplified Islamic ideals, such as the famous 'Divan' or, as he termed it, the 'department of finance'.[75] This illustrates his crucial distinction between precedents in application and precedents in intent; precedents as commitments to the ideal and precedents as expressions of the ideal in particular historical circumstances.

The premature death of Umar and the weak character and leadership of Uthman,[76] despite his 'virtue and honesty',[77] meant that the primitive forces that Umar had successfully held at bay re-emerged. Umar 'had held the helm with a strong hand, and severely repressed the natural tendency to demoralisation among nomadic tribes and semi-civilised people when coming into contact with the luxury and vices of cities'[78] that was an inevitable consequence of the conquests. The conquests, and the enormous wealth and power that accompanied them, led to the 'loss of those qualities of frugality, austerity, and self-sacrifice'[79] and ultimately, when Umar was no longer 'at the helm', encouraged the worst excesses of primitive behaviour in the Islamic community.[80] After Umar's death, 'the unruly spirit of the Arab

---

[73] Gibbon, *Decline and Fall*, vol. III, ch. L, 1718.
[74] Mohammad's insincerity and deployment of Islam to trick his followers is a common theme that dates to the earliest Byzantine accounts of Mohammad, and is reinforced in the popular medieval *Golden Legend*, which was written by Jacobus de Voragine in 1275 and first translated into English in 1483. Not coincidentally, it was frequently printed in English and French in the early nineteenth century. On Byzantine accounts, see Mango and Scott (trans.), *The Chronicle of Theophanes Confessor*, especially 464–5.
[75] Ali, *Saracens*, 43–4.
[76] Ali, *Saracens*, 46, 48,
[77] Ali, *Saracens*, 46.
[78] Ali, *Saracens*, 43.
[79] Ali, *Saracens*, 30.
[80] Interestingly, Tabari records Uthman as concerned with the perils of wealth, not Umar. See 'Uthman's letters to his officials and governors and to the common people', Tabari, *History*, vol. XV, 5–8.

broke forth'[81] and tribalism, factionalism, and other expressions of primitive pre-Islamic civilisation that had not been fully tamed by Islamic governance, reasserted themselves, severely testing Islamic institutions.

Uthman's election as caliph marked a fundamental watershed in what Ali termed 'the Republic', a divide between the firm guidance of Abu Bakr and Umar on the one hand, and the inability of Uthman and Ali b. Abu Taleb to control the forces unleashed by the conquests on the other. Described by Ali, Uthman's election 'proved in the end the ruin of Islam ... Uthman was quite unequal to the task of government. He fell at once ... under the influence of his family'[82] – the Umayyads – the Prophet's fiercest opponents who had only 'adopted Islam from motives of self-interest'.[83] Uthman, under the sway of his relative Marwan, 'an evil genius',[84] reversed many of Umar's policies, replaced capable provincial governors with his close relatives, granted state lands to his kinsmen 'to gratify their grasping demands,'[85] and withdrew 'privileges which had been granted to non-Muslims'.[86]

As recounted by Ali, the fourth Rashidun caliph, Ali b. Abu Taleb, despite his admirable characteristics, was unable to turn the tide. He was too preoccupied with the 'civil war' to 'remedy the evils of the previous administration'.[87] With his death, the Rashidun period came to a close. In the words of Ali, 'with Ali [b. Abu Taleb] ended the Republic of Islam'.[88] The shift from Ali b. Abu Taleb's caliphate to the subsequent caliphate of Muʾawiya ibn Abu Sufyan signalled a fundamental rupture in Islamic history. It was the end of governance by the Prophet's Companions, those who were directly inspired by Mohammad and the ideals of Islam, who had proven themselves to be the Prophet's staunch defenders in the long years of opposition and persecution they endured together, partners in the enterprise of implementing the 'laws of God'.[89]

In his construction of the Rashidun period, Ali emphasised cohesion and continuity. Political unity, for him, was a *sine qua non* for cultural and moral progress, as well as just, rational and accountable Islamic administration. Political unity and progress went hand in hand, as did the inverse: factionalism and civilisational slippage. He described Islamic administration as facilitating unity, but also depending on it. Unity was fragile in the Rashidun

[81] Ali, *Saracens*, 22.
[82] Ali, *Saracens*, 46.
[83] Ali, *Saracens*, 45.
[84] Ali describes Merwan (Marwan) as an 'evil genius' twice in the space of one page – virtually the entirely of his treatment of Uthman. Ali, *Saracens*, 48.
[85] Ali, *Saracens*, 59.
[86] Ali, *Saracens*, 60.
[87] Ali, *Saracens*, 60.
[88] Ali, *Saracens*, 54.
[89] The end of Ali's caliphate as the end of 'the Republic' of the Rashidun is emphasised by the beginning of a new section of chapters in Ali, *Saracens*, entitled 'The Umayyads'.

period and when broken, ushered in violence, oppression and suffering. Ali's understanding of the powerful link between political unity and civilisational progress led him to emphasise unity and understate factionalism and dissent in the Rashidun period. He only admitted political factionalism in Uthman's caliphate, with Ali b. Abu Taleb as its ultimate sacrificial victim. Moreover, he blamed the shortcomings of the second two caliphs primarily on external challenges, not on internal character flaws or divisions within the Islamic community. Ali's treatment of the conquests reinforced the Rashidun as a period of cohesion and continuity, only divided by the intrusion of outside forces.

Ali was particularly concerned with emphasising unity among the Rashidun caliphs. He underplayed and even erased divisions and discord amongst the Prophet's Companions, particularly amongst the four Rashidun caliphs themselves. He omitted elements of the traditional narrative that described factionalism that emerged immediately upon the Prophet's death. He was particularly careful to omit references to the tensions between the Ansar and the Qurayshi triumvirate of Abu Bakr, Umar and Abu Ubayda, or to Abu Bakr's conflicts with Ali b. Abu Taleb and Fatima.[90] He completely glossed over the six-month period during which Ali b. Abu Taleb refused to give Abu Bakr allegiance, instead noting that '[Abu Bakr's] election was accepted with their usual devotion to the Faith by Ali [b. Abu Taleb] and the chief members of Mohammed's family'.[91] In *Saracens*, Ali again passed quickly over the divisions that arose within the community following the Prophet's death, making no reference to the seminal meeting of the Ansar in Medina, or to Ali b. Abu Taleb's opposition to what Ali, in passing, acknowledged was the 'hasty' election of Abu Bakr.

These erasures are central to Ali's reconceptualisation of the meaning of the Rashidun period. For him, it was important to stress the Rashidun caliphs' understanding of the Prophet's mission and their dedication to its ideals. The portrayal of each of the Rashidun caliphs as directly inspired by the Prophet and committed to his vision of Islam, enabled Ali to emphasise Rashidun continuity with the Prophetic period, but a continuity not in replication so much as in intent. For Ali, Rashidun's – 'Rightly-Guided' – took on new meaning.

Ali's emphasis on all of the Rashidun caliphs being directly inspired by the Prophet suggests to the readers that, for him, the continuity of the Rashidun, the period's relevance and, ultimately, its capacity to serve as precedent, derived from the caliphs' understanding of and commitment to the ideals of Islam as outlined by the Prophet. It was less important for them to replicate the specific laws, than for them to understand the Prophet's intent. Precedent, thus, for Ali, should not be understood literally.

---

[90] On the key events surrounding the death of the Prophet and the Ansar's meeting at the Saqifa, see Tabari, *History*, vol. XX, and Madelung, *The Succession to Muhammad*.
[91] Ali, *Saracens*, 20–1.

Precedent should not consist of the replication or adherence to specific laws and practices; it should instead consist of faithfulness to the intent behind the laws. For this period to function as precedent, Ali emphasised the personal connection that each of these four individuals had with the Prophet; each understood the Prophet's intentions, and each was committed to fulfilling them.

In many ways, Umar was the central character in understanding Ali's concept of precedent. Umar was caliph at the pivotal moment between the two sub-periods of the Rashidun – the moment when the community was faced with new challenges requiring new solutions. Umar's success was partly due to his fidelity to the Prophet's intent and partly a result of his capacity to articulate new laws to address new challenges. Umar, like the Prophet himself, successfully navigated the ship of the community through new, uncharted, waters.

The Rashidun were thus portrayed as individuals able to channel the Prophet's intent. God's intent was thus manifest in the Prophet and the Prophet's intent communicated and committed to by the Rashidun. In this way, the Prophet was divinely guided, and the Rashidun were 'rightly guided' – God's intent was channelled to them via the Prophet. Because of the Rashidun's commitment to the ideals of Islam as communicated by the Prophet, despite varying abilities to articulate those ideas into practice, Ali termed this period the 'Republic of Islam'. The four caliphs were animated by the true ideals of Islam. Ali emphasised the uniqueness of this period through the stark contrast he painted between the fourth and last of the Rashidun, Ali b. Abu Taleb, and Mu'awiya, the first of the Umayyad caliphs.

Ali was also attentive to ways in which the historical laws of progress defined the Rashidun period. The push and pull of new and old civilisational forces proved the enduring power of the laws of progress that he identified in the pre-Islamic period. Yet, unlike the pre-Islamic period, the Rashidun did not witness a reversion to the pre-existing level of civilisation. The Islamic revelation did not succumb to primitivism as had, historically, the earlier revelations of Zoroaster, Moses and Jesus. Ali suggested that the institutions of Islam, while weakened, did not crumble, and thus successfully prevented a full backslide into pre-Islamic primitivism. The Rashidun period witnessed a Manichean tug of war, between Islamic institutions animated by progressive ideals, and primitive forces holding them back from their potential fruition, but one in which Islamic institutions ultimately triumphed.

The two competing forces of progress and backwardness were exemplified by the dichotomy between Mecca and Medina, which Ali likened to the equally antagonistic relationship between Athens and Sparta. Medina, the equivalent of Sparta, maintained a commitment to the ideals of Islam and the 'laws of God'. Residents of Medina were committed to political unity and republican ideals of liberty, equality and fraternity, alongside freedom for women and tolerance of non-Muslims. They were described as 'sincerely devout',[92] altruistic, 'austere in their manners',[93] intellectual, rational and civilised. These superior character traits expressed themselves in their refined table manners – their 'manners and customs' – the washing of hands 'both before and after dinner, just as among the ancients and in the Middle Ages in Europe',[94] monogamy,[95] and modest dress for women.

Mecca, corresponding to Athens, represented the inverse. Mecca and its inhabitants were depicted as consisting primarily of Qurayshi tribes who only adopted Islam out of necessity, and quickly fractured along old tribal divisions upon the death of the Prophet. Residents of Mecca were described as 'self-interested',[96] impious, licentious, 'frivolous', 'reckless',[97] irrational and uncivilised. Their depravity manifested itself as adherence to pre-Islamic (read non-Islamic) 'primitive' customs and mores, including warfare, bloodlibel and polygamy. This 'old story of Athens and Sparta',[98] here replicated in the conflict between Mecca and Medina, was a story of the conflict between old and new civilisational levels, between the pre-Islamic 'backward' and the Islamic 'progressive'.

Umayyad Dissonance

In Syed Ameer Ali's rendition, the Umayyads were in many ways a significant departure from the 'Republic'. They embodied the end of an era, the end of the caliphate of the Prophet's Companions who could rightfully claim to have been directly inspired by the Prophet and to have been amongst his closest supporters. The Umayyads also signified the end of the centrality of Medina, even of Arabia, as the conquests extended the borders of the empire to encompass most of the Persian empire and much of the Byzantine empire as well. These conquered areas were both the most populous and the wealthiest. The broadening theatre of rule accompanied the change in the centre of political gravity, from Medina to Damascus, the site of Caliph Mu'awiya's new capital. Most importantly for the modernists' rendition of Islamic history, the Umayyads signified the end of the application of republican ideals of equality, justice and 'democracy,' the end of the harmony of Islamic ideals expressed in institutions – of Islamic essence appropriately manifest in context. Not surprisingly, Ali described Mu'awiya as the antithesis of his arch opponent, Ali b. Abu Taleb. Mu'awiya was an 'Atheist', and only concerned for his own political well-being. 'Like the Borgias and the Medicis in later times', Mu'awiya was unscrupulous, 'frequently resort[ing]

---

[92] Ali, *Saracens*, 56.
[93] Ali, *Saracens*, 56.
[94] Ali, *Saracens*, 67.
[95] Ali, *Saracens*, 69.
[96] Ali, *Saracens*, 45.
[97] Ali, *Saracens*, 56.
[98] Ali, *Saracens*, 56.

to poison and the dagger to remove an inconvenient enemy or an impossible friend'.[99]

Mu'awiya's triumph represented the triumph of the 'Meccans' over the 'Medinans', of Athens over Sparta, of backwardness over progress – the reassertion of primitive forces of tribalism, discord and inequality. Yet the Umayyad period did not usher in the complete degradation of Islamic ideals. It did not spell the failure of Islam. Unlike Christianity or Judaism, whose truths eventually surrendered to the forces of primitivism, the essence of Islam, and the civilisational advances that Islam had enabled, were shaken, but not destroyed. The 'genius' of the Prophet in expressing the 'laws of God' in institutions meant that the Islamic ideals which animated these institutions, rather than being lost, were carried into new lands and formed the basis of Umayyad governance. The Umayyads, insofar as they remained 'Islamic', continued to spread Islamic ideals. They were the unworthy vessels of civilisational progress.

The Umayyad period was characterised by the ongoing clash of civilisations – the perpetual dialectic of the laws of progress. On the one hand, Islamic institutions brought progress and ushered in a new level of civilisation. On the other hand, these institutions were unable to fully triumph over residual cultures and institutions of backwardness. Islamic governance in the Umayyad period, despite the abandonment of many key ideals, remained a vehicle for the spread of Islam and a foundation of governance. The conquests, according to Ali, were indicative of Islamic civilisational superiority. Islamic governance under the Rashidun and, to a lesser extent, under the Umayyads, was significantly more progressive than the Byzantine and Persian systems that it replaced.

The lackluster commitment, if not outright denunciation, of the ideals of Islam by the majority of the Umayyad caliphs released the tribalism, discord and inequalities that the Rashidun 'Republic' had not succeeded in eradicating. These latent forces of primitivism were aggravated by the penetration of inferior Persian and Byzantine mores and practices into Umayyad customs and practices. In contrast with the austerity and simplicity of the Prophetic and early Rashidun periods, the Umayyads eagerly adopted the 'pomp and pageantry of the Persian and Byzantine monarchs'.[100] The impact of inferior Persian and Byzantine civilisational customs was not limited to 'various customs and rules of etiquette in vogue among the old Persian kings', but also included the use of eunuchs, the harem, and with it, increased female seclusion.[101] According to Ali, these backward cultural institutions were clear signs of the vigour of older customs, and were neither Arab nor Islamic. He stressed that these older, more primitive customs 'took root in the Ommeyade [sic] court' despite

[99] Ali, *Saracens*, 71.
[100] Ali, *Saracens*, 71.
[101] Ali, *Saracens*, 198, citing Von Kremer, *The Orient Under the Caliphs* (1875).

the fact that they were 'reprehended and denounced by Moslem doctors and divines'.¹⁰²

Despite the adoption of these primitive practices, the Arab Umayyads did not fully succumb to the level of civilisation of the conquered peoples: 'Byzantine license and Persian luxury had not destroyed the simplicity and freedom of the desert.'¹⁰³ In particular, Ali insisted that elite women in the Umayyad period continued to be respected for their intellectual pursuits, and were not secluded from social interactions in mixed gender company: 'the high-bred Arab maiden could still hold converse with men without embarrassment and in absolute unconsciousness of evil'.¹⁰⁴ Ali's insistence that inferior cultural practices adopted in the Umayyad period were residues of primitive pre-Islamic civilisations, and neither originally Arab nor originally Islamic, meant that they constituted historical detritus, neither essential nor intrinsic to Islam – a digression from the ideals of Islam, not their inevitable consequence.

Muslim Spain fully illustrated this ongoing civilisational dialectic between the implementation of progressive Islamic ideals and the drag of backward cultural forces. It proved Ali's contention that the key to the generation of progress and civilisation was the correct application of Islamic essence in context. The juxtaposition of Umayyad Spain with the Damascene Umayyads provided empirical historical proof that, when embraced and appropriately implemented, Islamic ideals were innately generative of progress and civilisation. According to Ali, Spain prior to Muslim rule was the epitome of a primitive civilisation. Unlike North Africa, which had fallen under Muslim rule and was consequently 'enjoying the blessings of toleration and justice, and was advancing with rapid strides in the path of material prosperity', Spain 'groaned under the iron heel of the Goth. Never was the condition of the country or of the people so bad or so miserable as under the grinding yoke of the Gothic kings.'¹⁰⁵ Ali described Spain as a country devastated by inequality, oppression and licentiousness: 'The country was split up into immense domains whose owners, lay and cleric, lived in palatial mansions where they spent their days in riotous and wicked indulgence.'¹⁰⁶ Whereas the rich were 'exempt from taxation', the middle classes were 'reduced to ruin and misery' and industry and commerce were stifled.¹⁰⁷

The situation was even more dire for those who cultivated the land, whom Ali described as 'serfs' and 'miserable herds of slaves'. The majority of the population was 'sunk in the grossest superstitions, their moral state was

---

¹⁰² Ali, *Saracens*, 198, 199, 204.
¹⁰³ Ali, *Saracens*, 200.
¹⁰⁴ Ali, *Saracens*, 200.
¹⁰⁵ Ali, *Saracens*, 106.
¹⁰⁶ Ali, *Saracens*, 107.
¹⁰⁷ Ali, *Saracens*, 106.

as depraved and degraded as their material condition was wretched'.[108] Oppression was not reserved for the peasants, but also for non-Christians, namely the Jews, who 'suffered terribly from the persecutions of the kings, the clergy and the nobles'.[109] In short, 'the impoverished and ruined citizen, the wretched slave, the miserable serf, the persecuted and hunted Jew, all waited for the relief which was so long in coming'.[110]

This 'relief' took the form of Islamic rule, which ushered in a period of justice, equality, prosperity, and intellectual and cultural achievements. Ali described Islamic rule as producing 'a social revolution', one that he likened to 'the great upheaval in France in the eighteenth century, without its evil or appalling consequences'.[111] The 1789 ideals of *Liberté, Égalité, Fraternité* were exactly those that animated Islamic rule: 'the democratic teachings of Islam had levelled all distinction of race and colour'. Even the Christians themselves, according to Ali, 'preferred the mild, generous, and beneficent rule of the Saracen to the grinding tyranny of the Goth or Frank'.[112] Under the Gothic kings, Spain had been a wasteland; 'the Arabs turned Spain into a garden; they organized a model administration, and gave impetus to the arts and sciences'.[113] 'Never,' he wrote, 'was Andalusia so mildly, justly, and wisely governed as by her Arab conquerors.'[114]

Spain reached the apogee of civilisation – a level as yet unattained in either the lands under Damascene Umayyad rule or, significantly, in Europe. Under Islamic rule, Ali wrote, Spain was 'the marvel of the Middle ages ... when all Europe was plunged in barbaric ignorance and strife, [it] alone held the torch of learning and civilization bright and shining before the Western world'.[115] For Ali, Spain provided irrefutable proof of the civilisational potential of Islam. The harmony of essence correctly applied in context enabled this civilisational leap; institutions animated by Islamic essence were motors of progress and civilisation. Ali made this view apparent in a passage explaining: 'the Saracen settlers ... were led towards industry by the teachings of the Prophet, which made labour a religious duty. They accordingly took in hand with unequalled energy the material

[108] Ali, *Saracens*, 107.
[109] Ali, *Saracens*, 107.
[110] Ali, *Saracens*, 107.
[111] Ali, *Saracens*, 112.
[112] Ali, *Saracens*, 114.
[113] Ali, *Saracens*, 117. This is the second instance when Ali describes the transformation of desert or wasteland into a 'garden'. The first instance was accomplished by the Prophet Mohammad. See *Life and Teachings of Mohammad*, 52.
[114] Ali, *Saracens*, 115. Here Ali is quoting 'another well-known writer', presumably European, but unnamed.
[115] Ali, *Saracens*, 115. It is noteworthy that Ali describes the beneficial results of Muslim rule in his own words, but when asserting comparative civilisational superiority with Europe, typically opts to cite Western authors, here Dozy (1820–83), *The History of the Almodhades* (1847).

development of Spain, which had hitherto lain sterile under the Christian government.'[116]

The garden that was Spain was eventually demolished by invading Christian armies, never again to achieve the level of civilisation it had enjoyed under Islamic rule. Some decades later, the Damascene Umayyads too were overthrown by the Abbasid dynasty, in the name of a 'return' of rule to the Prophet's family. At first glance, the Spanish and Damascene Umayyad empires read as two very different stories, one of decline, the other of advancement, yet despite their very different trajectories, Ali ultimately attributed the downfall of both empires to the dissonance that existed between Islamic ideals and practice.

The Arabs in Spain, despite their embrace of the 'republican' ideals of *Liberté, Égalité, Fraternité*, never succeeded in fully implementing these ideals. However beneficent, however 'wisely governed', tolerant and liberal, the Arabs could not escape their origins, their racial predilections, 'the old tribal jealousies of the desert'.[117] Likening Islamic Spain to the British Empire, Ali explained the discrepancy between the ideals of Islam and their implementation:

> The democratic teachings of Islam had levelled all distinctions of race and colour; but in distant lands, which he had entered with the help of his sword, the Arab could never rise superior to the intense pride of race which has always formed an essential characteristic of his nature. Like the Anglo-Saxon, he considers himself the noblest of God's creation.[118]

The indigenous peoples who had converted to Islam resented the hypocrisy of Arab superiority, which ran counter to the teachings of Islam, and 'insisted upon home rule [!] in a modified shape: to be governed, in fact, by members of their own race'.[119] The discord between ideal and practice led to increased revolt and 'discord' and contributed significantly to the weakness of the Spanish Umayyads. This weakness was seized upon by the natural religious fanaticism of Spaniards, who ultimately drove the Muslims out of Spain.[120] Yet the Christian triumph was short-lived; Christian fanaticism could not sustain the superior level of civilisation that Islam had generated. The Spaniards 'did not understand that they had killed their golden goose ... the Moors were banished; for a while Christian Spain shone, like the moon, with a borrowed light; then came the eclipse, and in that darkness Spain has

---

[116] Ali, *Saracens*, 117.
[117] Ali, *Saracens*, 117.
[118] Ali, *Saracens*, 118. This is a thinly veiled condemnation of British liberalism in the service of Empire. For a discussion of liberalism's inherent inequalities, see Mehta, *Liberalism and Empire*.
[119] Ali, *Saracens*, 118.
[120] Ali, *Saracens*, 117, on the Spanish tendency to fanaticism.

groveled ever since'. Ali portrayed Spain as languishing 'in the general stagnation and degradation of a people which has hopelessly fallen in the scale of the nations, and has deserved its humiliation'.[121]

The Damascene Umayyads were not nearly as progressive as their Andalusian counterparts. The discrepancy between ideal and practice was much more pronounced, and as a consequence, their achievements far less substantive. Like the Spanish Umayyads, the Damascene Umayyads suffered from delusions of racial superiority, which prevented them from adhering firmly to Islamic ideals of equality:

> This selfish policy ... was successful so long as the subject nationalities had not learnt their strength. The revolution which wrested the supreme power from the Ommeyades [sic] and transferred it to their rivals broke their monopoly. Henceforth the non-Arabs, as common subjects of a great and civilized empire, assumed their proper place as citizens of Islam ... and enjoyed equal consideration with the Arabs.[122]

With some notable exceptions, Ali articulated this dissonance between Islamic ideals and the rule of the Umayyad caliphs in civilisational terms. Recalling the Mecca–Medina divide that had existed in the Prophetic and Rashidun periods, a similar divide pervaded the Umayyad period. Ali described the split occurring on the accession of the first Umayyad, Mu'awiya, to the throne. When the Umayyads, longstanding enemies of the ideals of the Prophet, assumed power, 'pious' men withdrew from affairs of state, concentrating instead on intellectual pursuits.

The resentment that pious adherents of 'true' Islam felt for the inequalities embedded in Umayyad rule intensified with the conversion of subject peoples to Islam. The ideas embedded in the Quran, described by Ali as 'proclaiming the equality and brotherhood of man', were not articulated in Umayyad policies. As a consequence, 'political disabilities and invidious social distinctions gave rise among the Persians to a strong and natural sense of injustice'.[123] Dissent was articulated as a call to 'return' to the Islam of the Prophet, under the leadership of the family of the Prophet, the *ahl al-bayt* (the people of the house). Over time, however, as it became clear that the Shiite Imams, or, to use Ali's terminology, the 'apostolic Imams', could not mount a political movement, the Abbasids capitalised on their clan ties with the Prophet to champion their cause. Ali cast the Abbasid overthrow of the Umayyads as a popular, grass-roots revolution in the name of a 'return' to the ideals of the Prophet.

---

[121] Ali, *Saracens*, 564, quoting Lane-Poole (1854–1931), *The Story of the Moors in Spain* (1886).
[122] Ali, *Saracens*, 402.
[123] Ali, *Saracens*, 173.

Abbasid Harmony – The Golden Age

The replacement of the Umayyads with the Abbasids signified more than a dynastic turnover. For Syed Ameer Ali, this was a 'revolution' – a watershed moment that constituted a 'return' to the ideals of the Prophet, championed by the Prophet's own clan, the Banu Hashem. Despite not being direct linear descendants of the Prophet, as were the Shiite Imams, the Abbasids owed their success to their ability to symbolise an alternative to the Umayyads, whose defects were articulated in terms of impiety and 'deviation' from the Prophet's vision of Islam.[124] Ali, a Shiite Muslim himself of Iranian descent, replicated this Abbasid-era Shiite historical narrative.

Ali took the idea of the 'revolution' even further than the Abbasid-era historical narratives that he used as sources.[125] For him, the revolution lay less in the Abbasid's ability to effectively harness dissatisfaction with the Umayyads than in the civilisational progress that the Abbasids enabled. Contrary to the dissonance between Islamic ideals and practice that characterised the Umayyads, the Abbasids facilitated their harmonisation. 'A greater revolution than this,' Ali wrote, 'has scarcely been witnessed either in ancient or modern times; it gave practical effect to the democratic enunciation of the equality and brotherhood of man.'[126] The harmonisation of ideas and practice unleashed the agency embedded in the essence of Islam, and successfully generated the greatest Islamic civilisation of all times. The revolution was thus explicitly civilisational. The ideals of Islam, firmly embraced and expressed in the institutions of the caliphate, were the cause of civilisational progress. The 'Golden Age' that resulted served as empirical proof of the civilisational capacity of Islamic ideals, when properly manifest in context.

Islamic modernists described Abbasid civilisation as the fruit of the union of ideals and their implementation. These ideals were those first communicated by the Prophet, and subsequently embraced by the Rashidun: *Liberté, Égalité, Fraternité*. The superiority of the Abbasids lay not in their familial ties to the Prophet, but in the harmony they created, for the first time since the Rashidun period, between Islamic ideals and practices. Abbasid caliphs

> endeavored by an active and liberal administration, and by grand and useful enterprises, to merit the veneration and love of their subjects. They devoted themselves to the building of new cities, to the construction of roads, caravanserais, canals, fountains, the formation of charitable and educational institutions,

---

[124] On the complex relationship of the Abbasids to their Umayyad predecessors, see El-Hibri, 'The Redemption of Umayyad Memory by the Abbasids', 241–65.

[125] This is the case for Namık Kemal, Bayezidof and Ali. In addition, Ali referenced Shiite histories, which may have emphasised the impiety of the Umayyads.

[126] Ali, *Saracens*, 402.

the stimulation and protection of letters, and the promotion of commerce and all arts of peace.[127]

It was a period that saw the enactment of the 'principle[s] of racial equality', 'legitimate government', 'constitutionalism', 'justice' and 'civil rights among non-Moslems'.[128] Under the most progressive of Abbasid caliphs, Ali noted the high position occupied by women, who 'held their own against men in culture and wit, took part in poetical recitations, and enlivened society by their grace and accomplishments', thereby demonstrating their civilised 'manners and customs'.[129]

The fall of the Abbasid dynasty in no way tarnished their achievements. Unlike the demise of the Damascene and Spanish Umayyads, the dissolution of the Abbasids did not stem from internal dissonance or inherent deficiencies. The Abbasids were overthrown by the relentless belligerence of backward cultures – symptomatic of the perpetual combat between the forces of primitivism and progress. The Islamic realm under the Umayyads and Abbasid dynasties was continually plagued by Byzantine incursions. It was not until the appearance of the Crusaders, however, that the foundations of empire were seriously shaken. Ali, citing an unnamed 'clever writer', explained the civilisational clash between the enlightened rule of the Abbasids and the 'religious fanaticism' of the Crusaders: 'The Crusades form one of the maddest episodes in history. Christianity hurled itself at Mohammedanism in expedition after expedition for nearly three centuries ... every atrocity the imagination can conceive [of] disgraced the warriors of the Cross.'[130]

Although the Abbasids were 'rescued from the dangers of the Frankish onslaught' by Saladin and others, the empire had been sufficiently weakened from years of assault by 'herds of wild and desperate savages'[131] to be unable to resist 'the Tartaric wave which swept away all the civilization and culture of the East'.[132] The 'destroying hordes of Chengiz, sweeping over Western Asia, had engulfed in ruin every vestige of Saracenic civilization'.[133] The Abbasid empire never recovered from the Mongol invasion. As Ali recounted, 'The civilization of centuries was completely destroyed, and the people were plunged into a depth of barbarism in which the remembrance

---

[127] Ali, *Saracens*, 212–13.
[128] See Ali, *Saracens*, for an extensive description of Abbasid administration, especially 403, 404, 406, 422.
[129] Ali, *Saracens*, 455.
[130] Ali, *Saracens*, 321.
[131] Ali, *Saracens*, citing Mills, *The History of the Crusades For the Recovery and Possession of the Holy Land* (1820).
[132] Ali, *Saracens*, 472–3.
[133] Ali, *Saracens*, 216.

of their former greatness and their whole future were alike engulfed.'[134] The level of civilisation that the Abbasids achieved was never regained, and 'the gloom of night settled on Western Asia'.[135]

The Abbasid 'Golden Age' constituted the civilisational pinnacle of Islamic history. It was the full flowering of Islamic potential, unfolding since the time of the Prophet – a realisation of latent possibility enabled through the harmonisation of essence and context. For Islamic modernists, the Abbasid period was civilisationally superior to earlier historical moments – even the time of the Prophet and the Rashidun 'Republic'. The 'return' to the ideals of the Prophet as claimed in Abbasid historiography, gave way to a 'return' to the harmony of ideals and practice first witnessed in the Prophetic period. It was not about returning to past precedent as specific practices, but to past precedent as harmony between essence and context.

Rewriting Islamic History – Islamic Modernists' Dialogue with Islamic Historical Tradition

Modernists were formed in and informed by the classical Islamic historical tradition. They relied for the entirety of their information on Islamic historians, whether directly as primary sources, or indirectly via European histories that were based on a few 'canonical' Abbasid sources.[136] European scholars by and large accepted the Abbasid historical tradition as accurate, reproducing it uncritically in their own histories, as did Syed Ameer Ali and Namık Kemal.[137] Islamic modernists and European scholars replicated classical periodisation and dynastic organisation; even their renditions of particular character traits of individual caliphs adhered to common Abbasid historiographical tropes.

Despite the unmistakable imprint of Islamic historical tradition on Islamic modernist histories of Islam, Islamic modernist histories constituted fundamental rewritings of Islamic history. Indeed, this could not be otherwise,

---

[134] Ali, *Saracens*, 394.
[135] Ali, *Saracens*, 398–9.
[136] Namık Kemal drew on 'Ibn al-Athir, Ibn Khaldun, Abu al-Feda, Masudi, Biladeri, al-Siyuti, Tabari, al-Makari, Ibn Hisham, Wakidi, Mahmud b. Ishaq, Bukhari (and "such")'. See Kemal, *Büyük Islam Tarihi*, 20. Syed Ameer Ali primarily drew on al-Shahrestani (d. 1153), Ibn Sa'd (d. 845), Tabari (d. 923), Ali Ibn al-Athir (d. 1233) and Ibn Ishaq (d. 761). He thus displayed a familiarity with a variety of Sunni and Shiite authors, from a range of time periods. He drew most heavily upon the works of Tabari, Ibn Ishaq, ibn-Athir and Ibn Sa'd, along with Hadith and the Quran. European histories, like Muir, had relied heavily on Tabari. As Muir explained, 'The great treasury of tradition in which the historian must draw is the Annals of TABARI, happily styled by Gibbon the Livy of the Arabians.' Sir William Muir (1819–1905), *Annals of the Early Caliphate from Original Sources*, vi.
[137] For a history of Western historical scholarship on Abbasid historiography, see Donner, *Narratives of Islamic Origins*, esp. 5, 8.

since the interpretation of the meaning of historical events is necessarily a product of a particular understanding of the nature and patterns of history itself. Abbasid historians had very different conceptions of history than did Islamic modernist historians. Abbasid historians served as the principle source of historical data for Islamic modernists, but modernists applied a distinctly historicist epistemology and methodology to their own interpretations of this data. Islamic modernists fundamentally restructured the historical contours of history, and with it the meanings attendant in Islamic history.

It is difficult to speak of a coherent Islamic historical tradition, or 'canon,' given the enormous diversity of historical writing, not to mention the range of sectarian and intellectual positions represented in any given genre. In what follows, I do not attempt to capture the breadth of Islamic historiography, but rather, to make some general characterisations about the methods and historical epistemology implicit in the classical Islamic historical tradition in order to contrast it with that of the Islamic modernists.

The Abbasid period witnessed a rewriting of history that was preponderant in shaping subsequent historiography up to the present day.[138] The canon of 'classical' Islamic historical tradition is represented as beginning in the eighth and reaching its culmination in the ninth century in the form of Sunni Hadith-centred historical chronicles. Muhammad ibn Jarir al-Tabari, Quranic exegete and 'the *imam* of *Hadith* historiography',[139] is generally hailed as the 'the representative product of the early Islamic historiographical tradition, if not, indeed, as the culmination and crowning glory of that tradition'.[140] He enjoyed a 'massive reputation even in his own lifetime' and 'composed what was by far the most explicit defence of the *Hadith* method in historical writing, while his annalistic arrangement enshrined a style that lasted until the modern times'.[141] Tabari's universal history, *The History of Prophets and Kings* (*Tarikh al-rusul wa'l-moluk*) is ubiquitously hailed as 'the preeminent example of the annalistic tradition'.[142]

From Pastiche to Narrative

Western scholarship on Islamic historiography since the nineteenth century has been principally concerned with determining 'what really happened' in Islamic history, with particular attention to uncovering the 'origins' of Islam. Not surprisingly, Islamic modernist historians, like their nineteenth-century European counterparts, were concerned to determine Islamic origins, to decipher 'what really happened' in the Prophetic period. The obsession with

---

[138] On the process of constructing a pre-Islamic past in the Abbasid period, see Drory, 'The Abbasid Construction of the Jahiliyya'.
[139] Khalidi, *Arabic Historical Thought*, 73.
[140] Donner, *Narratives of Islamic Origins*, 128.
[141] Khalidi, *Arabic Historical Thought*, 73.
[142] Robinson, *Islamic Historiography*, 32.

origins derived from the conviction that essence was generally located in origins. Essence, in turn, explained the unalterable characteristics of a religion and located a religion on the taxonomy of world religions. The determination of essence went hand in hand with the ability to distinguish essence from context. It was imperative to understand the contours of context, in order to isolate and extract essence. Historicism as method depended on the reconstruction of past context – the piecing together and weighing of 'empirical' evidence. History as science was true and impartial. Unlike Abbasid historians, for whom narrative only gestured at the divine preserve of truth, Islamic modernists and their European counterparts believed that history was akin to an archaeological sifting of data in the quest to recover a primordial essence. They approached texts as repositories of truth, as collections of evidence, not as narrative constructions of meaning. 'What really happened' was thus not an innocuous question, but one deeply embedded in classifications of religions based on claims of essence – the victor in the heady contest over origins claimed the spoils of civilisation.

Scholars typically characterise Abbasid historiography in the ninth century as the final phase in a long process of the accumulation of sources. Abbasid chronologies were understood as largely devoid of authorial intentionality – as un-authored pastiches of inherited sources – products of a 'compiling rather than a composing' to borrow Chase Robinson's terminology.[143] The recognition of Abbasid fingerprints on the sources, however, gave rise to what one might call the forensic analysis of the texts – an attempt to 'read out' distortions resulting from Abbasid ideological and sectarian perspectives, with the aim of distinguishing 'factual' from 'fabricated' sources, in the ongoing quest to determine 'what really happened'.[144]

Jacob Lassner was one of the first historians to suggest that scholars be more attentive to the relationship between Abbasid authors and their audiences. For Abbasid historians, he notes, history was not either 'true or false', but was rather a 'metatruth' dependent on the recognition of Abbasid references.[145] In order to understand this 'metatruth', the modern reader must appreciate the particular relationship between author and audience in the Abbasid period:

> The link between the author's message and the remembrance of things past can be extremely elusive, however, for both the author and medieval reader ... were originally partners in the act of transmission. Informed contemporaries would have recognized the historical allusions ... The partnership has not survived ...

---

[143] Robinson, *Islamic Historiography*, 94.

[144] On the long and storied Western scholarship on Abbasid historiography, see Donner, *Narratives of Islamic Origins*, and Robinson, *Islamic Historiography*. For an exploration of the variety of historical writings, see Khalidi, *Arabic Historical Thought*.

[145] Lassner, *Islamic Revolution*, 12–13.

the reader of Abbasid times has been replaced by a modern counterpart who is, quite naturally, less informed as to the particulars of the discourse.[146]

More recently, Tarif Khalidi and Tayeb El-Hibri have taken up this charge and articulated a fresh hermeneutic approach. El-Hibri argues against conceiving of Abbasid historical texts as the products of a gently curated accumulation of materials, instead suggesting that their unmistakable continuity of voice demonstrates convincingly that they were products of a fundamental redaction and rewriting of history.[147] Rejecting the 'pastiche' view of Abbasid historical method, el-Hibri and Khalidi propose that we conceive of Abbasid historiography as narrative. Abbasid historians were less concerned with recording 'what really happened' than with attempting to derive meaning from history. Abbasid histories should be understood as 'texts of representation', El-Hibri argues, not 'factual testimonies preserved in time'.[148]

The imprint of the Abbasid period on Islamic historiography was so profound, El-Hibri explains, that we must begin with a more substantive exploration of Abbasid context. It is not enough, he argues, to recognise the ways in which Abbasid intellectual and political sectarian positions may have shaped the historical tradition. Offering a more capacious understanding of context, El-Hibri suggests that we need to recognise the assumptions and techniques employed by Abbasid historians. In particular, we must appreciate that Abbasid historians were the heirs to a long-standing biblical tradition of parable. El-Hibri explains that 'the medieval reader did not read the chronicle for its factual value. Rather, he was reading through the fabric of the text in pursuit of a historical process that was predicated on a multiplicity of received dramas.'[149] Abbasid history, El-Hibri suggests, was written, and read, as 'a largely parabolic cycle of literary narrative'.[150]

As opposed to a forensic approach that tries to read between the lines – to distinguish ways in which ideological and political commitments obscure historical 'facts' – a parabolic approach shifts our focus towards decoding the meanings both drawn from and assigned to events by Abbasid authors. Like the prevalence of symbolism in Venetian Renaissance painting, parables were only meaningful if author and audience both spoke the same symbolic language. As El-Hibri explains, 'to a medieval reader, the issue was not how to separate the true (historical) parts of the story from the fictional. Such a dichotomy was a non-issue because historical interpretation ... formed an integrated part of an interconnected worldview.'[151] Only by reflecting on the ways in which parable informed the construction of the Abbasid historical

---

[146] Lassner, *Islamic Revolution*, 14.
[147] Khalidi, *Arabic Historical Thought*, 8; El-Hibri, *Parable and Politics*, 17–25.
[148] El-Hibri, *Parable and Politics*, xi.
[149] El-Hibri, *Reinterpreting Islamic Historiography*, 52–3.
[150] El-Hibri, *Parable and Politics*, ix.
[151] El-Hibri, *Reinterpreting Islamic Historiography*, 54.

narrative, El-Hibri insists, can we begin to understand the Abbasid 'projection of a certain type of historical representation on the earlier period of Islamic history'.[152]

That Abbasid historians would have made use of parable is not surprising, given that the Quran, as the self-acclaimed continuation and ultimate fulfilment of a long line of earlier Abrahamic prophecies, contains many stories of prophets and messengers. Khalidi notes that there was great interest in deciphering parable in the Quran and the older biblical tradition 'in the early-Islamic milieu, a milieu much more porous than it was to become later on when the full weight of legalism began to be exerted'.[153]

The development of parabolic interpretation based on the Quran and applied to the early Prophetic period followed the established contours of biblical parabolic interpretation, in no small part due to Jewish and Christian converts to Islam in the Umayyad and Abbasid periods. According to El-Hibri, 'these converted masters of storytelling not only revived the memory of biblical accounts in exegetical literature but crafted a whole new saga for the life of Muhammad, his companions, his Hashemite relations, and his successors in a trajectory that continued the biblical style of novelistic and parabolic accounts'.[154]

This parabolic method was absorbed into an emerging Islamic historiography, as evidenced by the history of Ibn Ishaq (704–68), a prominent Islamic historian, who 'lived at a time when extensive traffic in Jewish stories (*akhbar*) was still permissible'.[155] According to Khalidi, Ibn Ishaq was one of the first to 'integrate Muhmmad's life into the history and hagiography of Near-Eastern prophecy and to arrange that life sequentially by subordinating *Hadith* to interpretation and chronology'.[156] Ibn Ishaq made explicit use of Abrahamic parable to give meaning to the Prophet's biography.[157]

Despite a later, post-Mihna generation of historians that placed less emphasis on parable and more on the literal adherence to Hadith, 'fragments of biblical resemblance are woven throughout the fabric of Abbasid representation' and continued to animate historical interpretation.[158] Tabari

---

[152] El-Hibri, *Parable and Politics*, xi.
[153] Khalidi, *Arabic Historical Thought*, 69.
[154] El-Hibri, *Parable and Politics*, 3.
[155] El-Hibri, 'A Note on Biblical Narrative and Abbasid History', 64. Khalidi notes that 'the inclusion of non-Muslim informants, mainly Christians and Jews, is of course tacit acknowledgment of the expertise of these communities in pre-Islamic history in general and in biblical history in particular'. Ibn Ishaq would later be criticised for having accepted Jewish and Christian sources and informants. See Khalidi, *Arabic Historical Thought*, 38, 39.
[156] Khalidi, *Arabic Historical Thought*, 39.
[157] For an example likening the Prophets Mohammad and Johan, see Khalidi, *Arabic Historical Thought*, 36.
[158] El-Hibri, 'Biblical Narrative and Abbasid History', 64. The Mihna was imposed by Abbasid Caliph al-Ma'mun in 833 and lifted by his successor, Caliph al-Mu'tasim

exemplifies this latter period. According to Khalidi, Tabari 'composed what was by far the most explicit defence of the *Hadith* method in historical writing', but at the same time, continued to deploy parable as both content and method. Tabari 'project[ed] a vision of history inspired by the regular rhythms of Qur'anic narrative'.[159] As El-Hibri explains, Abbasid historians sought meaning as revealed through history. 'Stories about the caliphs and their viziers', he notes, 'ring much like the sections of "*qisas al-anbiya*" (Stories of the Prophets) preserved in Tabari's work and others sources'.[160] 'Abbasid history', according to El-Hibri, 'was intended by narrators to be read in relation to the history of the Rashidun and other previous rulerships ... as a language of resolution for cycles of political and moral tribulation that spanned the history of peoples who dwelt in the shadow of kingship and prophecy.'[161]

The use of parable in Abbasid historiography is not only important for recovering the relationship between Abbasid author and audience, for illuminating authorial intentionality and meaning; the predominance of parable as content and method is also suggestive of the Islamic historical epistemology – what Khalidi terms the 'epistemic canopy' – that informed Abbasid historiography.

God's Sunna: Islamic Historical Epistemology

The term God's *Sunna* – *Sunnat Allah* – is infrequently used. According to the *Encyclopedia of the Qur'an*, God's *Sunna* 'either denotes God's way (*Sunna*) of dealing with the as-yet unbelieving people of the world, or it is a word for the behavior of those rebellious unbelievers who refuse to comply with divine institutions by declining to submit to divine messengers'.[162] Along the same lines, the *Encyclopedia of Islam* notes that *Sunnat Allah* appears in the Quran to connote the 'norms of God' – but, again, emphasises that this typically refers to God's actions towards pre-Islamic peoples.[163]

I would like to extend the meaning of God's *Sunna* to include the historical epistemology attendant in Abbasid historical conceptions of God's interventions in the world. If we understand history as conceived by Abbasid historians to be the story of God's relationship to mankind, from the Creation of the world through to the end of time, then God's *Sunna* is the theory of history itself as revealed in the Quran that animated Abbasid historiography and became firmly established in Islamic historical tradi-

---

in 848. On the effect of Hadith-focused jurisprudence on historical writing, see Khalidi, *Arabic Historical Thought*, 70–8.
[159] Khalidi, *Arabic Historical Thought*, 78.
[160] El-Hibri, 'Biblical Narrative and Abbasid History', 67.
[161] El-Hibri, *Parable and Politics*, 306.
[162] McAuliffe (ed.), *Encyclopedia of the Qur'an*, 164.
[163] Martin (ed.), *Encyclopedia of Islam*, 667.

tion. History becomes, as Khalidi notes, 'a universe full of God's signs (*ayat*)'.[164]

The Quran, in explicit continuity with the Bible, recounts God's interventions both in nature and, more importantly, in the affairs of mankind. History is punctuated by God's repeated sending down, or deputising, of prophets and messengers. According to Uri Rubin, al-Baydawi counted as many as 124,000 prophets and messengers referenced in the Quran.[165] One after the other, messengers brought 'clear arguments, scriptures, and the illuminating book'[166] from God to their respective peoples.[167] The Quran represents all revelations as part of 'the same divine revelation',[168] all part of the same Divine objective: the embrace of God's covenant. Specifically, the covenant prescribed particular belief (monotheism, recognition of God as the bearer of the Quran, and acceptance of the Prophet Mohammad as God's messenger) and ritual behaviour (law and prescriptions of piety). In the Quran, God exhorts people to 'follow what has been revealed'[169] and to 'serve nothing but God'.[170] More generally, the covenant enjoined pious and just behaviour.

In the historical pattern of prophecy apparent in the Quran, prophets are repeatedly invited to accept Gods' covenant and repeatedly prove unfaithful, until the coming of the Prophet Mohammad.[171] As Khalidi explains, 'prophecy in the Qur'an is thus a cyclical phenomenon, doomed to a failure from which it can only be rescued by a final revelation. The Muhammadan experience is at once the exemplar and the triumphant completion of that futile cycle.'[172]

The sum total of God's interventions thus indicates God's *Sunna* – the 'way' of God – in other words, God's intent as manifest in historical patterns of behaviour. The covenant, as the embodiment of the 'straight path' of righteous belief and behaviour, the *sirat al-mustaqim*, structured God's actions. God rewarded and/or punished individuals and entire peoples according to their faithfulness to the terms of the covenant, depending on their adherence to 'the straight path'. God's immanent interventions had

---

[164] Khalidi, *Arab Historical Thought*, 9.
[165] Rubin, 'Prophets and Prophethood', 249. Rubin is referencing Nasir al-Din Abu al-Khair Abdullah Ibn Umar al-Baydawi's (d. c. 1286) *tafsir*, entitled *The Lights of Revelation and the Secrets of Interpretation* as edited by H. L. Fleischer in 1846–8.
[166] Rubin, 'Prophets', 254, referring to Quran 35:25, 3:184, 57:25.
[167] Messengers (*rasul/rusul*), unlike prophets (*nabi/anbiya*), typically deliver messages/law. See Rubin, 'Prophets', 255.
[168] Rubin 'Prophets', 252.
[169] Rubin 'Prophets', 253.
[170] Rubin 'Prophets', 256, referring to Quran 41:14.
[171] Donner, *Narratives of Islamic Origins*, 130.
[172] Khalidi, *Arabic Historical Thought*, 68–9.

an eschatological purpose: to guide mankind on the path to salvation.[173] Reward and punishment thus had rationales – they were not random or meaningless.[174] At the same time, God, while not irrational, was not fully comprehensible by means of human reason. The impossibility of circumscribing God's *Sunna* is evident in Quran 3:26, where listeners are enjoined to acknowledge God as all-powerful, unbounded by any constraints:

> Say, 'O God, Master of Sovereignty. Thou givest sovereignty to whomsoever Thou wilt, and wrestest sovereignty from whomsoever Thou wilt. Thou exaltest whomsoever Thou wilt, and abasest whomsoever Thou wilt. In Thy hand is the good. Truly Thou art powerful over everything. Thou makest the night pass into the day, and Thou makest the day pass into the night. Thou bringest forth the living from the dead, and Thou bringest forth the dead from the living.'[175]

The centrality of parable in the Islamic historical tradition indicates a particular conception of the nature of history. History was a product of God's immanence – of God's interaction with mankind and the natural world. As Khalidi explains: 'The whole of history is present at once to God. Within this design, events are arranged in clusters, repetitive in form. This means that a Qur'anic *qissa*, or tale, is closer in function and meaning to a ... "parable" than it is to a story or narrative.'[176] Abbasid historians not only explored the meaning of parable, but deployed parable to construct meaning. Abbasid historians thus linked events across time and space, reshaping them to adhere to the parameters of parabolic meaning. Historians believed that they could determine patterns of God's interventions in history and that these patterns recurred across time and space as God's *Sunna*. 'Narrators may have invented an account,' El-Hibri writes, 'that bore little resemblance to reality and much to biblical legend.'[177] History, as the sum total of God's interactions, was possible to learn from but impossible to reduce to a simple set of laws. God was not irrational, but nor was God fully comprehensible within the limits of human reason. God was just, merciful and all-knowing, but ultimately, unknowable.

Abbasid historical method of interpretation via parable was thus built on the foundation of the perceptibility of God's *Sunna*. God's interactions with earlier prophets were understood to be relevant, and thus applicable across all time/space. Historians sought to understand the causal relation-

---

[173] 'The straight path' (*sirat al-mustaqim*) appears thirty-three times in the Quran. As an indication of its significance, it appears first in the *Fatiha*, the 'opening' verse of the Quran, the verse most often used in prayer.
[174] As Rubin notes in 'Prophets', 259, 'destruction is never arbitrary or unjust'.
[175] Nasr, *The Study Quran* 3:26. I owe this reference to El-Hibri, *Parable and Politics*, 291–2.
[176] Khalidi, *Arabic Historical Thought*, 8.
[177] El-Hibri, 'Biblical Narrative and Abbasid History', 67.

ships between God and man, even as they appreciated the limitations of doing so. Parables were tools of comparison, of analogy – the attempt to assign meaning to events within the purview of past parables and precedents. Abbasid historians were following Quranic methodology in adopting parable as an explanatory mechanism. Parables appear repeatedly in the Quran.[178] God speaks in parables (Quran 16:75–6), as does the Prophet Mohammad, on occasion. For example, we read in Quran 17:89: 'And indeed We have employed every kind of parable for mankind in this Quran. Yet most of mankind refuse aught but disbelief.' God's reminder of His use of parable is repeated, nearly exactly in Quran 18:54: 'And indeed We have employed every kind of parable for mankind in this Quran. And man is the most contentious of beings.' Quran 30:58 again emphasises the Quran as a parable itself: 'And indeed we have set forth for mankind in this Quran every kind of parable.' Perhaps the most famous mention of parable appears in Quran 24:35:

> God is the Light of the heavens and the earth. The parable of His Light is a niche, wherein is a lamp. The lamp is in a glass. The glass is as a shining star kindled from a blessed olive tree, neither of the East nor of the West. Its oil would well-nigh shine forth, even if no fire had touched it. Light upon light. God guides unto His Light whomsoever He will, and God sets forth parables for mankind, and God is Knower of all things.[179]

Parable elucidated the meaning of history and consequently was central to Abbasid historical methodology and epistemology. The implication of parable is that history is repeatable – not in the discrete sense of particular events, but in the holistic sense of God's *Sunna* being eternally applicable. As suggested in Quran 17:39, 'That is from the wisdom thy Lord has revealed unto thee', there are 'moral lessons which must be derived from the history of past generations'.[180] History is flat – there are no fundamental contextual ruptures; parable, as God's *Sunna*, is permanently relevant.

This notion of the repeatability, and thus the perpetual relevance of the past, is manifest in the predominantly cyclical nature of pre-modern history. Historical unpredictability was not a matter of the obscurity of content – the 'wheel of fortune' turned endlessly on the same worn axis – but of speed and/or distance. History followed the same patterns, making parable an explanatory mechanism, but it was never clear how fast the wheel was turning, or how large its circumference was. As El-Hibri explains, 'The mill as a motif of the tragic turns of life on earth was connected to a wiser cosmological perception among medieval authors, who compared the astrological turn of the

---

[178] The word 'parable' (*mathal*) appears thirty times in the Quran but, surprisingly, is not included in the index of *The Study Quran* (Nasr).
[179] Nasr, *The Study Quran* 24:35.
[180] Rubin, 'Prophets', 253.

zodiac to the image of a mill.'[181] As an illustration, recall Ferdowsi's deployment of an astrological 'revolving' of heaven's fortune to foreshadow the fall of the Sasanian empire, a prediction that is ultimately fulfilled by the murder of Yazdegird III, the last Sasanian Emperor, at the hands of a miller:

> A wise man will be saddened when he hears
> of how the moving sphere of heaven turns . . .
> Both Mars and Venus now oppose our cause
> And no man can evade the heaven's laws.[182]

In the Shadow of Kingship and Prophecy[183]

Abbasid historiography divided history into three principle eras: the era of prophets, the era of kings, and the era of the Prophet Mohammad that served as the pivot between them.[184] It is no coincidence that Tabari's famous history was entitled *The History of Prophets and Kings* (*Tarikh al-rusul wa'l-moluk*). He was not the exception. Ibn Ishaq's *Life of the Prophet* (*Sirat rasul Allah*) was originally structured as two or even three divisions. The first, a since-lost preface, concerned itself with the sequence of biblical prophets prior to and leading up to the Prophet Mohammad.[185] While not all Abbasid historical works attempted to be as inclusive, these self-styled 'universal' histories, like those of Ya'qubi, Mas'udi and Ferdowsi, all began with Creation.[186]

---

[181] El-Hibri, *Parable and Politics*, 121.
[182] Ferdowsi, *Shahnameh*, 'The causes of Yazdagird's Murder', XV, 78–90.
[183] I take this subtitle from El-Hibri, *Parable and Politics*, 36.
[184] In addition to many universal histories, Abbasid historical literature was often subdivided by genre, depending on which time period it covered. Works that dealt with the pre-Islamic period were termed *al-Mabda'* or *al-Mubtada'* (A Book on the Beginnings); literature about Mohammad was termed *Sira* (Biography of the Prophet), and the genres of *Tarikh al-khulafa* (History of the caliphs) dealt with the post-Prophetic period. See Robinson, *Islamic Historiography*, 135. There were also other literary forms such as *siyasa* (political theory, or 'mirrors for princes'), *adab* (belles-lettres) and *hikma* (philosophy), which also dealt with the post-Prophetic period and were often historical in nature; see Khalidi, *Arabic Historical Thought*.
[185] On the reconstruction of Ibn Ishaq's preface to this *sira* of the prophet, the '*Kitab al Mubtada*', see El-Hibri, 'Biblical Narrative and Abbasid History', 64, citing Newby, *The Making of the Last Prophet*, 10–12. According to El-Hibri, there was a 'close tie between this work by Ibn Ishaq and the Abbasid narratives'. On Ibn Ishaq's historical periodisation, see also Khalidi, *Arabic Historical Thought*, 35.
[186] Shiite historian Ahmad b. Abu Ya'qub al-Ya'qubi (d. c. 900) wrote a universal history beginning with Creation and ending in 872. Al-Mas'udi's famous history also began with Creation. As Robinson observes, 'the underlying historical vision is both God-centered and teleological: history has a purpose, and the purpose of pre-Islamic history is to provide a sort of *praeparatio evangelica* for the events of the early seventh century and what followed'. See Robinson, *Islamic Historiography*, 136 and 137. Another example is Abu Rifa'a Umara ibn Wathima al-Farisi's (d.

This conception of history also informed Tabari's attempt to determine the correspondence between Iranian and Islamic genealogies of prophets and kings.[187]

The era of prophets began with the Creation of the world by God, with the beginning of time itself, and proceeded through a long series of messengers and prophets – the intermediaries between God and mankind – starting with Adam, the first man and the first prophet, and concluding with the revelation of the Quran to the Prophet Mohammad. As noted by Rubin, God began to send prophets and messengers 'after humankind became separated [from Paradise] and moral corruption began'.[188]

The era of prophets was punctuated by God's repeated interventions – not only as the selection of prophets and messengers, but also as punishment for the failure of mankind to be faithful to God's covenant and adhere to the 'straight path' of righteous behaviour. God's interventions in this era nonetheless lacked fulfilment, as man was repeatedly disobedient. The emphasis of God's *Sunna* on denoting 'God's way of dealing with the as-yet unbelieving people of the world' or 'the behavior of those rebellious unbelievers who refuse to comply with divine institutions by declining to submit to divine messengers'[189] should thus be seen in the context of the long pre-Islamic history of faithlessness to God's repeated exhortations. The era of prophets had a certain directionality – the gradual yet inexorable unfolding toward the last revelation of God to the last of the prophets, Mohammad.

The revelation of the Quran to the Prophet Mohammad was a moment of Divine fulfilment, a unique moment in its finality – the last opportunity for mankind to embrace God's covenant, to adhere to the 'straight path'. The revelation of the Quran was also a pivotal moment that divided the era of prophets, characterised by the unfolding of God's final covenant, from the era of kings, characterised by God's repeatedly unheeded exhortations to adhere to the last covenant. Pre-Islamic history was teleological, organised around 'presag[ing] the appearance of the Islamic policy under the leadership of Muhammad'.[190] The Quran as revelation was the proof of the pre-Islamic cycle of prophecy, its fulfilment and completion. Mohammad, the seal of the prophets, was the bearer of the final, complete, and eternally valid Divine intervention. Mohammad served as the pivot, the hinge, expressed as adherence to the Prophet's *Sunna* that divided the period of revelatory promise from the period of faithlessness to the last covenant. Mohammad represented the sacred promise of eschatological fulfilment.

---

902) *Tarikh Bad' al-Khalq wa Qisas an-Anbiya* (*History from the Creation through the stories of the Prophets*). See Khalidi, *Arabic Historical Thought*, 71.

[187] On Abbasid chronicles of Iran, see Hoyland, *The 'History of the Kings of the Persians' in Three Arabic Chronicles*, 1–23. On Tabari, see *History*, vol. IV.

[188] Rubin, 'Prophets', 256.

[189] McAuliffe (ed.), *Encyclopedia of the Qur'an*, 164.

[190] Robinson, *Islamic Historiography*, 137.

The era of kings began with the death of the Prophet Mohammad – the end of Divine guidance, of direct Divine intervention via prophet or messenger. It is not that God ceases to interact with mankind after the revelation of the Quran, but that interaction is more limited and oriented primarily towards punishment and/or reward (in this world and the hereafter). With the death of the Prophet Mohammad, the emphasis in history shifted away from the unfolding of God's promise, to its fulfilment; from God's *Sunna* as revealed in history, to obedience to the Prophet's *Sunna*. 'To Sunnis', Robinson explains, the Prophet's model 'came to represent God's last detailed communication to man before the Day of Judgment' – a 'blueprint for society'.[191] Thereafter, fidelity to Gods' covenant, the eschatological march on the 'straight path', was measured by the yardstick of adherence or deviation (*bid'a*) from Prophetic *Sunna* as precedent.

Precedent was the central organising grammar of Abbasid historical tradition and operated on two levels, determining both content and method. Rulers and dynasties were organised sequentially and linearly, each the inheritor of the last, each the continuer of the precedent established by the Prophet Mohammad. As each ruler took up the mantle of the Prophet, he derived his legitimacy according to his adherence to God's covenant – measured by deviation from or adherence to the Prophetic *Sunna*. Temporality followed a constructed continuum, implying the possibility of the repeatability of precedent as parable, regardless of the passage of chronological time and thus antithetical to the notion of ruptures between 'civilizational' epochs – what Khalidi terms 'the eternal presentness' of Quranic time.[192]

Precedent was an enduring reference point, regardless of the passage of time, transcending context and thus effectively ahistorical. Precedent, denoting the eternal relevance of repeatability and replication of Prophetic *Sunna*, permeated Abbasid historiography. The past remained the principle reference point – it legitimised precedent and the adherence to and upholding of tradition. Legitimacy relied on claims to adherence to prior, established and eternally valid precedent.

Parable and the Imperative of Precedent

The concepts of precedent and parable are deeply entwined in Islamic historical epistemology. Precedent is implied by the predominance of parable in the Quran, and subsequently deployed in the Abbasid historical tradition. Parable functions as analogy (*qiyas*), linking two moments as participating in the same meaning.

Although we know that the term '*Sunna*' was used in the pre-Islamic period, we can only speculate when it became a powerful legitimising term. We may confidently assert that by the mid-ninth century, Prophetic prec-

---

[191] Robinson, *Islamic Historiography*, 89.
[192] Khalidi, *Arabic Historical Thought*, 9.

edent as conveying content, together with precedent as method (repetition), had emerged as powerful legal imperatives.¹⁹³ Abbasid historiographical claims that precedent was clearly understood to denote Prophetic *Sunna* immediately upon the Prophet's death must be read as belonging to a later Abbasid reconstruction that claimed unbroken continuity of the Prophetic *Sunna*. The accounts of precedent as an animating concept in the Rashidun period likely reflect not so much an 'accurate' rendering of historical events as a powerful validation of the legal concept of precedent from a subsequent, Hadith-oriented Abbasid historical perspective. To take one oft-cited example, Juynboll recounts a story that appears in both Tabari and Ya'qubi. In Juynboll's paraphrasing:

> Then, in the course of the deliberations of the *shura*, after Umar's death, Ali was enjoined to observe (the rules laid down in) God's book the *sunna* of His messenger and – in the same breath – the *sira* (. . . virtually synonymous with *sunna*) of Abu Bakr and Umar. Ali is alleged to have answered: 'I'll do what I can.' After Uthman has been put to the same test, he is said to have replied with a simple 'Yes' and, seemingly as a consequence, received the nomination.¹⁹⁴

Juynboll concludes from this example that 'the emphasis of the *Sunna* of the first three caliphs is still unmistakable'.¹⁹⁵ Yet if we appreciate the use of parable here, and take into account the legal imperative of locating the concept of *Sunna* as adherence to precedent in the Rashidun period, then we must read this as an Abbasid construction, designed to authorise and define later understandings of *Sunna*. As El-Hibri points out, 'Viewing the Companions as exemplars of the proper practice of the ritual and the law was a crucial matter for religious writers, who relied on the Companions as transmitters of *hadiths* and as individuals who knew best the ways, or "*Sunna*," of the Prophet.'¹⁹⁶

The concept of the *Sunna* of the Prophet and the imperative of establishing precedent became more and more powerful over time with the growing need for actionable precedent as the basis for jurisprudence and law.¹⁹⁷ As Khalidi

---

¹⁹³ Juynboll, 'Some New Ideas on the Development of *Sunna*', 107–9. See also Brown, *The Canonization of al-Bukhari and Muslim*, 3–19.

¹⁹⁴ Juynboll, 'Development of *Sunna*', 102. For the account in Tabari, see *History*, vol. XIV, 159. El-Hibri offers an alternative reading of the narrative of Uthman and Ali discussed above, pointing out that Uthman's affirmation of his commitment to adhere to precedent – here denoting not only that of the Prophet, but of his caliphal forebears, 'confirmed in the best Sunni form the status of the first two caliphs as supplementary models for prophetic Sunna'. El-Hibri, *Parable and Politics*, 70–1.

¹⁹⁵ Juynboll, 'Development of *Sunna*', 102.

¹⁹⁶ El-Hibri, *Parable and Politics*, 8.

¹⁹⁷ Goldziher maintained that 'the endeavor to raise the *sunna* to a position of equality with the sacred book in establishing the law comes more and more into evidence', *Muslim Studies*, 31. Similarly, he noted that '*bid'a* (innovation, deviation) is the

explains, 'The shadow of the Prophet ... proceeded to lengthen in the eyes of his followers.'[198] The development and systematisation of Hadith studies, jurisprudence and theology in the Abbasid period, all of which were primarily guided by concepts of Prophetic precedent, led to a winnowing down of the definition of Prophetic *Sunna* – 'the way of the Prophet', which became 'a', if not 'the', principal tool of Quranic exegesis and jurisprudential methodology. This definitional narrowing was a function of the emergence of a Sunni scholarly consensus that legitimised particular understandings. This process of solidification of consensus was further reinforced by the writing back of *Sunna* into earlier Islamic history in order to construct it as an unbroken line of continuity with the period of the Prophet.[199]

Powerful Sunni jurisprudential imperatives lay behind the identification of Prophetic precedent and the construction of the Rashidun period as an extension of Prophetic *Sunna*. The Rashidun caliphs, it was argued, in their capacity as close and early Prophetic Companions, knew and adhered to Prophetic precedent.[200] They were understood to have replicated the *Sunna* of the Prophet. This meant that their actions replicated those of the Prophet and could be considered a further, if indirect, source of Prophetic precedent. The Rashidun thus emerged as an extension of Prophetic precedent, as illustrated in the name given to these caliphs – the 'Rightly-Guided' – which should be read less as a description than as a claim to embody Prophetic precedent, despite being one step removed from Divine guidance. Just as biblical prophets were 'purged' of error in the doctrine of *ismat al-anbiya* (the infallibility of the prophets), so too were the Prophet's companions shielded from any blame for the conflicts which plagued the community in the doctrine of *adalat al-sahaba* (the justice of the Companions).[201]

The replication of Prophetic precedent by Rashidun caliphs reinforced the idea of the Rashidun as a distinct period – a period of precedent – which could only include the period of governance by the Prophet's earliest companions. Precedent, according to this diffusionist conception, required limitation to a discrete period of time and required the period to constitute a unified whole. The admission of the Rashidun as a period of contradiction or conflict would undermine legal claims that it mirrored Prophetic *Sunna*.[202]

opposite of *sunna*', *Muslim Studies*, 33. Van Ess also cites the practical imperative of law as the reason for the ossification of *kalam*. He also notes that it was not a foregone conclusion 'that jurisprudence would prevail'. See van Ess, *The Flowering of Muslim Theology*, especially 4–33. For a discussion of Western and Islamic Hadith scholarship, see Brown, *Canonization*.

[198] Khalidi, *Arabic Historical Thought*, 14.
[199] El-Hibri, *Parable and Politics*, 71. See also Khalidi, *Arabic Historical Thought*, 44–7.
[200] See Bulliet, *Islam: The View from the Edge*.
[201] El-Hibri, *Parable and Politics*, 8.
[202] The fact that insufficient attention has been paid to the Abbasid construction of the Rashidun only reinforces the extent to which modern scholarship has been remiss in 'questioning' the Abbasid narrative. See El-Hibri, *Parable and Politics*. For

Abbasid (Sunni) legal imperatives concerning the *Sunna* may have necessitated the construction of the Rashidun period, a coherent period that could serve as viable precedent, but the epistemological concept of historical precedent not only sustained, but enabled, these claims.[203]

Islamic History Reimagined: From God's *Sunna* to God's Intent

The classical Islamic historical tradition revolved around the concepts, and methods, of pattern and parable. God's *Sunna* animated all of history for all time and drew mankind into the Abrahamic cycle of prophets and kings. In this historical vision, God was immanent – the immediate cause of all things great and small – holding out the eternal promise of punishment and reward for fidelity to the covenant. God's *Sunna* was most visible in the Prophet's *Sunna*, the last, perfect manifestation of the Divine covenant with mankind. As such, Prophetic *Sunna* cast an infinitely long shadow – as enduring precedent against which all subsequent practice could be measured. Adherence to the straight path, the *sirat al-mustaqim*, depended on faithfulness to precedent – it was eternal, transcendent and ahistorical.

For Abbasid historians, history was the domain of God's *Sunna*, a canvas upon which to discern the patterns of God's behaviour. Foremost among their concerns was to understand the causes of disunity of the community – of the emergence of *fitna* (rebellion, strife) and sectarianism. Was Abu Bakr's assumption of the caliphate in accordance with God's will? How should succession be determined? What were the characteristics of just rule? If a ruler was unjust, was it legitimate to disobey him?[204] Historians worked through various possible interpretations of events and problems, less sure of answers than of the multiple possibilities that their narratives enabled.[205] Yet these questions, and the historical interpretations that sought to address them, firmly linked Abbasid historians with their contemporary audiences.

Islamic modernist historians were no less connected to their audiences and, like their classical forebears, sought the answers to the urgent questions of the day in the workings of history. The pressing question regarding the causes of the increasing power disparity between Europe and Islamic lands animated Islamic modernist historians and their audiences.

Islamic modernist histories circled around the concepts and methods of

---

some thoughts on the construction of the Rashidun that place more emphasis on Alid/Shia historical interpretations, see Borrut, 'Vanishing Syria: Periodization and Power in Early Islam', 37–68, and his book *Entre mémoire et pouvoir*.

[203] Although outside the scope of this project, I also do not see as coincidental that the historical concept of analogy (*qiyas*), implicit in parable, emerged as a central jurisprudential method.

[204] For the central questions that animated Abbasid historiography, see El-Hibri, *Parable and Politics*, esp. 5, 28–9, 140, 148. See also Donner, *Narratives*, 129, 184, 186.

[205] El-Hibri, *Parable and Politics*, 300.

essence and context. They imagined history as universal, measured by the yardstick of comparative movement along a continuum of progress and civilisation. Rather than the cycles of history that animated Abbasid-era historiography, Islamic modernists imagined the advance and stagnation of 'progress' to be like the torch of civilisation – always carried forward, but by different societies at different times. Despite their commitment to the empirical, scientific production of historical knowledge, Islamic modernists retained a deeply eschatological conception of history. History was the progressive movement towards greater and greater consciousness of the nature of God – the gradual unveiling of God's intent.

For Islamic modernists, natural and historical laws replaced Divine immanence implicit in God's *Sunna*. God remained the architect of the world, but did not engage in day-to-day operations. For Abbasid historians, God, while elusive and unpredictable, was merciful and compassionate. For modernists, the laws of nature and history were predictable, but also intractable.

History as a space of meaning allowed Islamic modernists to identify and extract Islamic essence from historical context. They concurred that essence expressed the ideas of liberty, equality, fraternity and justice. Islamic history demonstrated that Islam as essence had and could again serve as a motor of progress. However, the key to progress was the proper implementation of essence in context. Pre-Islamic history demonstrated that without application, truth was unable to withstand the forces of primitivism – civilisational progress required the alignment of institutions with ideals. The Prophet was the perfect exemplar of the possibilities inherent in Islamic essence. With the benefit of Divine guidance, the Prophet successfully negotiated Islamic essence – as the eternal ideals, as God's intent – within the limits of his own particular historical context. The Prophet's precedent thus was recast by Islamic modernists. It no longer consisted of specific practices, embodied in the *Sunna*. Rather, it was understood as the Prophet's divinely guided capacity to harmonise essence in context.

The Rashidun period, following Islamic historical tradition, had long been constructed as a special time – a time when the Prophet's *Sunna* had been followed. Islamic modernists retained the Rashidun as a unique period, but for them it did not exemplify continuity of practice, so much as continuity of intent. Just as the Prophet, through Divine guidance, fully comprehended God's intent, so the Rashidun, through proximity to the Prophet, also comprehended the Prophet's intent. The Rashidun caliphs thus were reshaped from conveyors of Prophetic practice, into vessels of God's intent as diffused via the Prophet. Modernists thereby retained a commitment to precedent, but a precedent firmly detached from content or imitation as method. Progress as God's intent lay not in the replication of precedent as content, but in the replication of precedent as harmony between essence and context.

Jahiliyya was recast by modernists not as a specific, pre-Islamic time period, but as the inertia of primitivism. *Jahiliyya* thus emerged as a metaphor for the perpetual dialectic between progress and inertia, light and darkness. The residual primitivism of pre-Islamic practices and ideas continued to challenge the civilisational force of Islam over the course of history. It had been successfully staved off by the Prophet and the first two Rashidun caliphs, Abu Bakr and Umar, but reasserted itself in the context of the challenges presented by the conquests. Islamic modernists suggested that the fragility of the fledgling Muslim community was a result of external forces, not inherent weakness on the part of the latter two Rashidun caliphs, Uthman and Ali.

Following Islamic historical tradition, the individual characters of the Rashidun caliphs remained inviolable. Their intentions were pure, their commitments sound, despite variability in their leadership. Umar retained his traditional historiographical centrality as the Rashidun caliph who best exemplified leadership. For Ali, however, it was not Umar as the pragmatic leader and lawgiver that he admired. Rather, it was Umar's particular capacity to negotiate the ideals of Islam within the parameters of new circumstances. Umar recalibrated institutions to align with both God's intent and what Ali termed the 'circumstances of the age'.[206]

Modernists' construction of the arc of Islamic history, their exploration of the internal and external dynamics that, combined, had historically both facilitated and obstructed progress, was integral to their reconstruction of Islam's place in the universal story of civilisational progress. The history of the Umayyad and Abbasid periods aptly demonstrated the centrality of institutions based on Islamic ideals. This explained the ongoing civilisational progress that accompanied the Damascene Umayyads compared with their Byzantine and Sasanian predecessors. It was not until the Abbasid period, however, that Islamic ideals were fully in harmony with their manifestation in context. The Golden Age of the Abbasids served as empirical proof of the civilising potential of the essence of Islam.

The writing of new Islamic histories, as the account of the interaction between context and the essence of Islam over time/place, revealed the causes of present 'backwardness' even as it provided the solutions. Islamic modernists' diagnosis of the problem and prescription for the remedy were grounded in history and thus claimed scientific authority – as impartial, rational and empirically verifiable. It was evident that Islam was not the cause of contemporary Islamic turpitude and 'backwardness' vis-à-vis European powers. Rather, Islamic modernists argued that it was the dissonance between this essence and its manifestation in context that contemporary Islamic societies suffered from. It was imperative, they believed, now that they had determined Islamic essence, to rescue it from the shackles of tradition – essence had to be decontextualised from the past and recontexualised in the present in order to restore harmony between essence and contemporary context – 'the circumstances of the (modern) age'.[207] Only then, modernists believed, could 'the gloom of night' be dispelled and the

---

[206] Ali, *Life and Teachings of Mohammed*, 234, 235.
[207] Ali, *Life and Teachings of Mohammed*, 234, 235.

torch of progress once again be carried forward by Islamic societies.[208] The next chapter takes up Islamic modernist understandings of the emergence and solidification of Islamic tradition and traditionalism, alongside the ways in which history demonstrated the Islamic origins of modernity and confirmed the imperative of religious reform.

---

[208] Ali, *Saracens*, 398–9.

CHAPTER

3

THE ISLAMIC ORIGINS OF MODERNITY

Think of the child as European knowledge whose father is Greek knowledge, and whose Arab mother contributed also to the nurturing, yet only the father is appreciated.[1]

Imam Bayezidof, 'Islam and Civilization' (1892)

Such is this great philosophical ensemble, which is commonly called Arab, because it is written in Arabic, but in reality it is Greco-Sassanid. It would be more accurate to say Greek; because the truly fertile element of all of this came from Greece ... The superiority of Syria and Baghdad over the Latin West came solely from the fact that the Greek tradition touched them more closely.

Ernest Renan, 'Islam and Science' (1883)

Introduction: The Dissonant Present

Islamic history, as the arc of time and place that stretched from the revelation of the Quran to the Prophet Mohammad in western Arabia through the vast Abbasid empire, illustrated Islamic modernists' understanding of the past and Islam's place in it. Islamic history was the unfolding of Islamic essence in context, governed by the laws of progress, which explained change over time, and the oscillation between periods of harmony and periods of dissonance.

---

[1] Bayezidof, *Islam ve Medeniyet* (*Islam and Civilization*), 12. Bayezidof's refutation of Renan together with his article 'Islam'in Ilimlerle Ilişkisi' (Islam's Relationship to Science), were translated from Russian to Ottoman by Olga de Lebedeva and published in the Ottoman journal *Tercüman-i Hakikat* in 1892 by managing editor Ahmet Cevdet. For a recent translation of Bayezidof's *Islam ve Medeniyet*, see Baiazitov, *A Tatar Akhund's Refutation of Ernest Renan's Lecture on Islam & Science (1883)*. All translations to English are my own, unless otherwise noted.

Islamic modernists' quest to identify the laws of progress, and to chart Islamic history as its expression through time, was equally an attempt to understand the causal relationships between harmony and progress, dissonance and decline. They sought to account for ways in which the relationship between essence and context either promoted or hindered civilisational progress. Islamic history was a site of the exploration of the past and its intersection with the future. If Islamic modernists could understand the causes of civilisational progress in Islamic history, they could use this understanding to evaluate the very real problems of civilisational 'decline' that they observed in their own nineteenth-century context. Deeply embedded in modernists' description of Islamic history were prescriptions for alleviating the challenges of the present.

Above all, modernists grappled with the thorny question of comparative development. If Islam was indeed superior to Christianity, as they insisted it was, then what accounted for the contemporary torpor of Islam and Islamic societies' 'backwardness' vis-à-vis European powers? Were Islamic achievements in the past really due to Islam, or was progress achieved despite Islam, as European scholars of Islamic history averred? If, as Islamic modernists countered, Islam as essence was not the cause of the present backwardness of Muslim societies, then what accounted for it? As Afghani succinctly demanded: 'What is the cause of the . . . distress of the Muslims, and is there a cure . . . ?'[2]

Islamic modernists, like other religious modernists, were caught between a commitment to the enduring validity of Islam, and a need to account for the contemporary stagnation and inertia of Islamic institutions (scholarship, law, education) and practices (rituals, worship). They were determined to demonstrate the truth of Islam and to 'rescue' this truth from the misperceptions that surrounded it – to extract Islam as essence from history as context and by so doing, to regenerate Islam and reclaim the torch of progress. Islamic history became the medium that modernists employed to answer these questions, as well as to articulate possible solutions.

Historicism and the rewriting of Islamic history enabled modernists to carry this programme forward. Islamic history provided a compelling explanation of the causes of civilisational progress, an explanation that enabled modernists to insist that contemporary 'backwardness' was neither inevitable nor necessary. Islamic history illuminated the elaboration of 'Islam' as essence over time manifest in institutions, ideas and practices, and revealed the conditions in which these practices had been both productive and prohibitive of progress. Only by understanding the contours of a particular context could scholars evaluate the efficacy of Islamic institutions *in situ* as manifestations of Islamic essence.

As discussed in Chapter 2, historicism, as the premise of context, lay at the heart of Islamic modernists' construction of Islamic history and in the laws

---

[2] Afghani, 'Commentary on the Commentator', 127.

of progress that governed it. Historical context both defined and reflected societies at particular levels of civilisation. Context was both particular – the unfolding of Islamic essence in a series of specific historical contexts – and universal – the location of this 'unfolding' within human civilisational progress. Modernists defined Islam in relationship to context, as an essence; neither a product nor cause of context, but transcendent and ahistorical. The genius of the Prophet lay in his ability to appropriately articulate essence in context – to put Islamic ideals into practice via particular laws and prescribed behaviours. Yet these practices were themselves necessarily contextual, and thus contingent. They reflected their context and were constrained by it. As context changed, practices demanded recalibration and rearticulation. Harmony and dissonance, thus, were the products of these calibrations and articulations – the motors, or alternately, obstacles, of progress.

For Islamic modernists, Islamic history clearly demonstrated that it was not Islam, as essence, that was to blame for periods of harmony or dissonance, but rather whether or not the enactment of Islamic essence was appropriate for particular historical circumstances – in other words, whether essence operated in harmony with context. The issue then, was to evaluate how and why practices began to diverge from the ideals embedded in Islamic essence – when and why did dissonance replace harmony? What prevented practices from being rearticulated and reworked in new contexts? How could the disparity between the triumphs of the Abbasid period and the failures of the present be accounted for?

The diagnosis, according to modernists, was complex. At the concrete level, the 'Golden Age' of Abbasid harmony came to an end with the Mongol conquests. The demise of the Abbasids spelled political ruin accompanied by economic, cultural and intellectual decimation. Yet the fall of the Abbasid dynasty was, in and of itself, insufficient to account for the modernist perception of a 'backward' present.

It was not the passage of chronological time, per se, that led to dissonance following the Abbasid period up to and including the present, but rather the passage of historical time – of civilistional levels. Had the world remained at the Abbasid-era level of civilisation, the solution would be to restore Abbasid institutions. Yet the world had not remained civilisationally static. Modernity, understood as a civilisational level, had been ushered in by Europe. A new civilisational threshold had been breached, yet Islamic societies retained institutions that had been calibrated according to an earlier, more primitive, civilisational level. Practices, once harmonious, had become dissonant, not necessarily through their decline or dissolution, but from their inability to change apace with civilisation. The challenge, thus, was to become modern – to generate modern civilisation – to recalibrate practice in light of modern context.

The most pernicious obstacle to such a recalibration, Islamic modernists believed, was Islamic 'tradition'. In their view, the predominance of dogmatism and its ossification into tradition foreclosed possibilities of intellectual freedom, interpretation and reinterpretation. The power of orthodoxy and the methodology of precedent that it enshrined, inhibited the hermeneutic, interpretive and institutional flexibility that was necessary to accommodate changing contexts. As Jamal al-Din al-Afghani explained, progress, like science, was never ending: 'just as the germs of plants and animals are transformed from a state of imperfection to perfection', so too must philosophy and science continue to develop.[3] Islamic essence had been prevented from adapting to different contexts, which in turn led to an ever growing disparity between Islamic essence and its institutional enactment. For Islamic modernists then, the shackles of tradition were the root cause of present-day Islamic intellectual stagnation.

This chapter focuses on Islamic modernists' deployment of history – as scientific method and empirical (historical) evidence – in order to achieve two related objectives. First, to demonstrate the imperative of religious reform. From their exploration of the historical causes of dissonance, Islamic modernists concluded that the problem centred around the emergence and ossification of tradition. Only Islamic reform could free Islam from the bondage of the past and allow it to be recontextualised into the present. The harmonisation of eternal ideals with the circumstances of the age involved the reformulation of Islam.

Second, to insist on the possibility of an indigenous, Islamic modernity. Islamic modernists rejected European claims to have generated modernity, instead offering an alternative genealogy of the modern. By constructing an argument for the Islamic origins of modernity, Islamic modernists rejected the imitative model of modernisation as westernisation, and imagined an authentic modernity, one not defined by Europe.

The Ossification Argument

Islamic modernists' identification of intellectual freedom, and conversely, intellectual stagnation, as the root cause of contemporary power disparity with European great powers was an interpretation they shared with Orientalist scholars, such as Armand-Pierre Caussin de Perceval, William Muir, Edward Gibbon, Louis-Amélie Sédillot, Ernest Renan and Gustav Le Bon.[4] Some European scholars suggested that the anti-intellectualism of

---

[3] Afghani, 'The Benefits of Philosophy', 116.

[4] Syed Ameer Ali relied on many European scholars, in addition to Islamic 'primary' sources including al-Tabari (d. 923), Ibn Ishaq (d. 767) and Ibn Sa'd (d. 845). See Armand-Pierre Caussin de Perceval, *Essai sur l'histoire des Arabes avant l'Islamisme, pendant l'époque de Mahomet*, 3 vols (1847–9); William Muir, *The Life of Mohammad From Original Sources*, 4 vols (1861); Edward Gibbon, *The History of the Decline and Fall of the Roman Empire* (1776–89); Louis-Amélie Sédillot, *Histoire des Arabes* (1854). Bayezidof cited Gustave Le Bon extensively on the achievements of the Abbasid period: Le Bon, *La Civilisation des Arabes* (1884), cited in Bayezidof, 'Islam in

Islamic societies was innate to Islam, others that it was simply a historical phase that could, in principle, be overcome. In either case, however, Europe was claimed as the origin and originator of modernity. Sole heir to the unique combination of Hellenic civilisation and Christianity, Europe, exceptionally, had generated modernity; non-European societies were doomed to imitation, and thus replication, of European modernity. At best they could produce derivative modernities. At worst, they would remain stagnant, forever stationary and increasingly left behind, as modernity moved forward. This, very succinctly, was an argument for European exceptionalism.

Despite their common identification of Islamic tradition as responsible for contemporary power disparity between Christian Europe and Islamic societies, Islamic modernists and Orientalists differed greatly in their explanations of how and why Islamic tradition developed. For Islamic modernists, Islamic history, and the Abbasid period in particular, served as empirical evidence that Islam, as essence, had historically served as a motor of progress. Intellectual stagnation was not inherent in Islam, they argued, but a casualty of the emergence and subsequent ossification of tradition. It followed therefore that the present-day power disparity was neither necessary nor inevitable. Islamic essence could, they insisted, be rescued from tradition.

Islamic modernists, despite important differences amongst themselves, largely concurred with European scholars who posited that the gradual decline of intellectual and cultural fluorescence of the Abbasid period was primarily due to the emergence and gradual ossification of Islamic tradition. Science – as method and content – ground to a halt with the triumph of tradition – also understood to consist of both method and content. According to both Syed Ameer Ali and Afghani, the zenith of the Abbasid Golden Age was enabled by the harmonisation of Islamic essence and the manifestation, or expression, of this essence in Islamic institutions. Over time, the harmony of essence and context gave way to dissonance as a consequence of the emergence and solidification of tradition. The rise of tradition was not identified as primarily responsible for the downfall of the Abbasids – that dishonour fell to the Mongols – but increasing dissonance was indirectly responsible for the subsequent inability of Islamic societies to reclaim harmony. Tradition was the anchor that prevented change and adaptation to new contexts – it fixed institutions in an increasingly anachronistic context, preventing progress, and leading inevitably to the present state of 'backwardness'.

Ilimlerle İlişkisi', 51–5. Arguments concerning the ossification of Islamic tradition were first articulated by nineteenth-century European scholars of Islamic history and later reinforced by scholars of Islamic law, e.g. Ignaz Goldziher (b. 1850) in *Muhammedanische Studien*, Joseph Schacht (b. 1902) in *Origins of Muhammadan Jurisprudence* (1950), and, a generation later, Joseph van Ess (b. 1934), *The Flowering of Muslim Theology*. This narrative remains hegemonic to this day, although work on the impact of colonialism on Islamic law is beginning to destabilise it. See Hallaq, *Shari'a: Theory, Practice, Transformations*.

Historical explanations of the emergence of Islamic tradition varied amongst Islamic modernists. Two of the most salient accounts were put forward by Ali and Afghani. Ali embedded the emergence of Islamic institutions within his larger paradigm of the perpetual battle between backwardness and civilisation. For him, this dichotomy explained the variant understandings and applications of Islam. Unsurprisingly, he dated the beginning of the institutionalisation of Islam to the Umayyad period. In a rendition that resonated with his Shiite background, he described Caliph (and first Shiite Imam) Ali b. Abu Taleb as the champion of the ideals of Islam – a beacon of rationalism and enlightenment in the darkness of irrationality and ignorance. Rationalism, he insisted, was the hallmark of the true Islam of the Prophet, juxtaposing its antithesis as 'false' – a deviation. Although Islamic institutions of law and theology began to form in the Umayyad period, they were only fully developed in the Abbasid era.

Syed Ameer Ali: The Hijacking of 'True' Islam

According to Syed Ameer Ali, 'conformity' and 'casuistry' were neither necessary nor inevitable results of the development of Islamic institutions, but were products of particular historical forces. 'The insistence of a church upon conformity,' he stated, 'varies in proportion to the forces with which it has to contend.'[5] Accordingly, what he called 'the superstructure of the great Sunni School' was a product of the 'formation of a hierarch whose preponderating [sic] influence under weaker [Abbasid] monarchs stifled growth and barred all avenues of progress'.[6] These institutions only solidified in the Abbasid period.

Ali recounted that Ma'mun's (Abbasid) caliphate, which he deemed 'the most glorious epoch in Saracenic history', was distinguished by 'liberty of conscience and freedom of worship'. This was the high point of civilisation, the apogee of Islamic intellectual creativity and production. Ma'mun, described as 'the grandest and most liberal-minded of the Saracenic sovereigns, and one of the most farseeing monarchs of any age', supported the Mu'tazilites, whom Ali defined as 'Rationalists, Utilitarians and Evolutionists'.[7] Ma'mun and his two successors championed this methodology and attempted

---

[5] Ali, *Saracens*, 252.
[6] Ali, *Saracens*, 252.
[7] According to Ali, Mu'tazilites were 'decided Rationalists, on account of the great predominance they allow to Reason, in every question regarding the progress of man; they are Utilitarians, in adopting the doctrine of general usefulness and the promotion of happiness of the many, as the criterion of right and wrong; they are Evolutionists, in regarding every law that regulates the mutual relations of human beings'. See Ali, *Life and Teachings of Mohammed*, 305–6.

to infuse this rationalistic spirit which animated them and a portion of their subjects, into the whole Moslem world. Unfortunately for Islam it was found ... that the Jurists of Bagdad were more powerful than the Caliphs; and the triumph of patristicism [sic] under [Caliph] Mutawwakil, was one of the chief causes of the downfall of the Caliphate.[8]

With the demise of rationalism, Islam now approximated 'the spectacle of orthodox Christendom'.[9]

Ma'mun's caliphate witnessed the highpoint of rationalism, but it also marked the beginning of the degeneration of Islamic institutions into a self-perpetuating state of dogmatism and intransigence. The 'genius' of Caliph Ma'mun was in foreseeing the development of dogma and rigidity of 'the Church'. Ma'mun understood that 'adherence to those doctrines was worse than treason, for their tendency was to stifle all political and social development, and end in the destruction of the commonwealth. He foresaw the effect of swathing the mind of man with inflexible dogmas.'[10] Dogmatism was both unable and unwilling to accommodate changing contexts.

The problem, as Ali understood it, was that the development of Islamic institutions fell victim to the triumph of formalism and traditionalism over rationalism. 'It has been justly remarked', he asserted,

> that as long as Islam retained its pristine character it proved itself the warm protector and promotor of knowledge and civilization – the zealous ally of Intellectual freedom. The moment extraneous elements attached themselves to it, it lagged behind in the race of progress. Let us hope that the time is approaching when Islam, freed from the blind idolatry of letters and apotheosis of dead men, will regain her true character and, joining hands with the Christianity of the devoted Prophet of Nazareth, will march on together in the work of Civilization.[11]

As a consequence of the defeat of rationalism, Islam became trapped in the institutions that emerged to articulate it – Islam as essence thus was unable to develop or evolve to suit new contexts. It became a prisoner of traditionalism, restrained within particular institutions which emerged in a particular context.

---

[8] Ali, *Life and Teachings of Mohammed*, 306–7. Ali, in noting the triumph of the imperatives of law over theology, prefigures Islamicist Joseph van Ess' theory that 'the kalam phenomenon reached its zenith very early; its most creative period did not occur after it had come of age, but well before, at a time when signs of tedium and paralysis had not yet appeared'. See van Ess, *The Flowering of Muslim Theology*, 4.

[9] Ali, *Life and Teachings of Mohammed*, 647.

[10] Ali, *Saracens*, 275.

[11] Ali, *Life and Teachings of Mohammed*, 345–6.

Ali, by providing the historical context of the emergence of Islamic tradition, sought to explain current intellectual 'stagnation' which he and many other modernists agreed was the root cause of contemporary power disparity between Islamic societies and Europe. The solution to dogmatism in Ali's view – 'secularising the state and emancipating the human intellect from the shackles which doctors and jurists [had] placed upon it'[12] – was embedded in his account of Islamic history. These 'shackles', evocative of Renan's 'iron band', were products of historical development – neither necessary nor intrinsic to Islam, and certainly not representative of the Islam of the Prophet Mohammad – the 'true' Islam.

Ali clearly distinguished between the development of dogmatism and 'true' Islam, insisting that the latter was inherently liberal and rational. He situated the 'established Church', Islamic canon, orthodoxy and the institutions that sustained them, in contradistinction to 'human reason' and 'in direct conflict with the teachings of the Koran [sic] and of the Prophet'.[13] Some Islamic schools of thought maintained the 'truth' while others diverged from it. The history of Islamic schools of thought was a history of the battle between forces of rationalism and irrationalism, progress and backwardness. Sometimes the rationalists were dominant. Other times they lost ground to the forces of irrationalism, dogmatism and orthodoxy.

Ultimately, due to particular historical circumstances, the forces of dogmatism triumphed, and 'rationalists were expelled from public offices, and lectures on science and philosophy were interdicted'.[14] As a consequence, the intellectual brilliance that rational thought generated, which had produced religious tolerance, scientific and cultural achievements and civilisational progress, dimmed. 'Conformity was insisted upon as essential to orthodoxy', Ali explained, which 'imparted a rigidity to the dogmas of the Church' that 'hampered efforts at reform in later times'.[15] For him, the inherent rationalism of Islamic essence was overwhelmed by both the legal imperatives of governance, and the incapacity of the general population to grasp rationalism – as either content or method. Law was essential, but dangerously prone to ossification. Ali was caught between insisting on the centrality of law as the genius of the Prophet, and on law's historic role in inhibiting change.

Al-Afghani: Dogma as an Intellectual 'Cage'

Jamal al-Din Al-Afghani offered a somewhat different account of the emergence, and subsequent ossification, of Islamic tradition. For him, religion as faith was fundamentally inimical to science as reason. Taking a phenomenological position, Afghani posited that

---

[12] Ali, *Saracens*, 275.
[13] Ali, *Saracens*, 276.
[14] Ali, *Saracens*, 289.
[15] Ali, *Saracens*, 306.

religions, by whatever names they are called, all resemble each other. No agreement and no reconciliation are possible between these religions and philosophy. Religion imposes on man its faith and its belief, whereas philosophy frees him of it totally or in part.[16]

Yet historically, Afghani believed, this 'imposition of faith' initially had produced salutary effects.

In his refutation of Renan's 'Islam and Science' article, Afghani described the emergence of orthodoxy as a natural outgrowth of religion, one that was initially productive of progress. He explained that 'obedience that was imposed in the name of the supreme Being to whom the educators attributed all events, without permitting men to discuss its utility or its disadvantages' enabled civilisational evolution out of an era of primitivism. 'Whether it be Muslim, Christian or pagan', he wrote, 'all nations have emerged from barbarism and marched toward a more advanced civilization.'[17] Orthodoxy, as the limitation of possible interpretations, was buttressed by the emergence of canon, both of which were perpetuated and replicated in educational institutions. Afghani concurred with Syed Ameer Ali that the gradual institutionalisation of Islam offered a degree of normativism in theology and law, which served social and legal needs, but that invariably also led to the solidification and ossification of Islamic tradition.

Over time, according to Afghani, the costs of orthodoxy began to outweigh the benefits. Institutions designed to sustain and perpetuate orthodoxy were unable to accommodate change. As contexts changed over time, the dissonance between institutions and context grew. While initially progressive, the nature of orthodoxy inhibited change. 'Obedience' to dogma, as tradition, became an intellectual cage, restraining 'free investigation' and 'philosophy' that lay at the heart of 'science' – science both as fields of knowledge, but more importantly, as scientific method. The gradual ossification of Islamic tradition narrowed the possibility of intellectual criticism and traditionalism, and the maintenance of precedent became hegemonic. Islam transitioned from an avenue of promoting science and thus civilisation, to a roadblock that hindered it. Tradition prevented adaptation to new contexts and thus, inhibited evolution. Religion, described by Afghani as a 'a slave to dogma', relinquished its ability to serve as a motor of progress.

Islamic modernists were concerned to refute European assumptions concerning the immutability of Islamic tradition. They firmly maintained that the rejection of tradition (as content, and traditionalism as method), with the concomitant firm embrace of modernity (as content and method), were both possible and necessary.

---

[16] Afghani, 'Answer ... to Renan', 187.
[17] Afghani, 'Answer ... to Renan', 183.

Comparison as a Method of Refutation

Comparison with Europe was unavoidable, and not surprisingly, ubiquitous, in Islamic modernists histories. Islamic modernists drew on European scholarship on Islamic history, as well as on Christian and European history more generally. Moreover, they deployed comparison between Christianity and Islam extensively and systematically in their works on the Prophet Mohammad and Islamic history. There were three, intersecting reasons for their extensive use of comparison. First, the adoption of a comparative framework was a natural outcome of the universal, phenomenological and inherently comparative epistemology of historicism. Islamic modernists, in seeking to locate Islam in the universal taxonomy of essentialised religions, were necessarily and explicitly comparative. Likewise, any exploration of the essence of Islam in history and its capacity to generate progress and civilisation involved comparison with the capacity of Christianity in history to do the same.

Second, as a result of the increasing power disparity between European great powers and other countries in the world, Europe was widely perceived as having achieved 'modernity' – of having 'become modern'. European great powers provided empirical proof of the capacity of modernity to generate power, and thus served as possible models of modernity. Third, European historical and religious studies scholarship, operating within a dominant Protestant paradigm, claimed that European modernity was the exclusive consequence of European (implicitly Christian) agency.

These three imperatives intersected with and reinforced each other. Islamic modernists, in order to assert Islam's capacity to serve as a motor of civilisation and progress cum modernity, were bound to refute European exceptionalism. Islamic modernists' deliberate use of comparison as refutation enabled them to destabilise European claims to exclusive ownership of modernity, and to assert an alternative Islamic genealogy of modernity.

The depth and breadth of engagement with European scholarship varied amongst Islamic modernists. All evinced familiarity with European claims to superiority, whether expressed in European scholarship and/or by way of political, economic and cultural contacts. Islamic modernists themselves were deeply engaged with European Christian (largely Protestant) scholarship and frequently compared Christianity with Islam as well as Christian with Islamic history. Their profound awareness of the political power disparity, of European claims to modernity and of the consequent urgency of religious reform, animated their scholarship.

Namık Kemal frequently cited European scholarship in his *The Complete History of Islam* (*Büyük Islam Tarihi*) in order to substantiate his claims to Abbasid civilisational achievements. Imam Bayezidof, in his two essays on Islam, alluded to Ernest Renan's works, suggesting a familiarity which extended beyond Renan's 'Islam and Science' article, which Bayezidof explicitly refuted. Jamal al-Din Al-Afghani too, as a result of his extensive peregrinations, evidenced a familiarity with European and Muslim scholarship ranging from the central Middle East, to Egypt, Central Asia, Russia and the Indian subcontinent. None of the Islamic modernists dealt with in this book, however, were more familiar with European scholarship than Syed Ameer Ali.

Ali was widely read and broadly educated. In his works he drew heavily on 'canonical' Islamic sources on Islamic history such as Ibn Ishaq, al-Tabari, Ibn Athir, ibn Sa'd and Shahrestani, as well as the Hadith (to a limited extent) and the Quran (to a large extent). Ali also demonstrated an extensive and wide-ranging familiarity with European 'secondary' scholarship on Islam and Islamic history, as well as Christian history. His use of comparison as refutation was systematic and extensive. Comparing and contrasting the Prophet with Jesus, Islam with Christianity, and Islamic history with Christian history was an integral component of his inquiry into universal religious evolution as civilisational progress, and his assertion of the possibility of an Islamic modern.

Christianity and Christian history were not a simple foil to Islam and Islamic history, but at a more profound methodological level, symptomatic of Ali and other Islamic modernists' firm embrace of historicism. The laws of progress were universal. Truth was universal. Comparison is implicit in the modern intellectual epistemology of historicism. The premise of historicism, that history is made up of sequences of discreet, self-reflexive contexts, together constituting the universal civilisational progress of mankind, itself begs comparison. The epistemology of historicism, therefore, was inseparable from historicism as method – of the historicisation of context, and its location in universal history. Civilisational progress was always measured comparatively and relatively. This also meant that the nature and concept of comparison was bound up with notions of history, time and civilisational progress. Ali and other Islamic modernists focused their comparisons on two distinct historical periods: antiquity and the Abbasid period – the 'Golden Age' of Islamic civilisation.

Antiquity

Antiquity, while not delineated by specific chronological brackets, was conceived of as a civilisational level. All societies belonging to that civilisational level were characterised by a similar level of consciousness of the Divine expressed as paganism and similar 'barbarous' practices such as polygamy, slavery, religious intolerance and physical brutality. In Syed Ameer Ali's conception, despite a relatively wide degree of chronological and cultural diversity, early attempts at wrenching antiquity from paganism to monotheism all belong to this same civilisational level. The classical societies of Greece and Rome formed a general canvas on which he painted in the various religious reformers – from Zoroaster to Mohammad – who attempted to move their societies, and mankind more generally, into monotheism. Monotheism constituted a civilisational leap forward.

One after the other, Zoroaster and the Abrahamic prophets attempted to cross a civilisational threshold; to usher their societies from pagan primitivism into the more progressive civilisational age of monotheism. As discussed in preceding chapters, Ali, in *The Life and Teachings of Mohammad* and in *A Short History of the Saracens*, detailed ways in which the laws of progress did and did not permit this divinely ordained civilisational jump. In each case, Divine intervention in the form of revelation to a prophet provided the causal agency necessary for civilisational progress. Yet time and time again, prophets failed to lead their societies out of the primitivism of paganism, or succeeded, but only temporarily – the inertia and power of ignorance, never fully conquered, gradually dragged their societies back into the morass of primitivism.

Antiquity thus was the civilisational origin, and thus location, of the essence of the Abrahamic monotheisms. Comparison of these origins enabled Ali to contrast the essence of each of the three religions with each other. As discussed in Chapter 1, he located Judaism as the least evolved of the three Abrahamic religions, and devoted the majority of his energy to a comparison of the essences of Islam and Christianity in order to assert Islam's superiority.

Ali's extensive comparison between Mohammad and Jesus, discussed in greater detail in Chapter 4, was a comparison of essences – of the essence of Islam, most perfectly expressed by Mohammad, compared to the essence of Christianity, most perfectly expressed by Jesus. In his rendition, the essences themselves were largely equivalent. Unlike Zoroaster and Moses who preceded them, Jesus and Mohammad were both the recipients of a similarly evolved Divinely inspired truth. They shared a comparable essence.

It was not the essence of Christianity, therefore, that was inferior to the essence of Islam, Ali argued, but rather its expression in history, or lack thereof. Jesus' failure to implement the truth bestowed by God meant that the essence of Christianity was never actualised, never manifest in history – it never translated itself into 'a system of positive morality embodied in effectual laws'.[18] Instead, Christianity, following the historical laws of progress, was fatally poisoned by the latent primitivism that Jesus failed to vanquish. Directly quoting European historian Henry Hart Milman, Ali recounted that after Jesus, Christianity 'sank downward into the common ignorance, and yielded to that worst barbarism – a worn out civilization'.[19] The Christianity of history, therefore, was not an expression of its true essence, which was irretrievably lost upon Jesus' death.

Ali seized on Ernest Renan's admission of Christianity's deviation from the truth of Jesus, to argue that the essence of Christianity could never be reclaimed. Citing European scholars in support of his argument, he argued that the essence of Christianity was not retrievable from the Gospels. 'The traditions which record the sayings of Jesus have gone through such a

---

[18] Ali, *Life and Teachings of Mohammed*, 3.
[19] Ali, *Life and Teachings of Mohammed*, 15, quoting Henry Hart Milman, *History of Latin Christianity* (1855), vol. I, 4.

process of elimination and selection', he explained, 'that it is hardly possible at the present moment to say which are really his own worlds and which are not.'[20] Citing Milman he continued, arguing that

> Milman himself admits that the traditions regarding the acts and sayings of Jesus, which were floating about among Christian communities, were not cast in to their present shape till almost the close of the first half of the second century. 'Necessarily, therefore, the ancient collectors and modelers of the Christian Gospels ... must have exercised a discretionary latitude in the reception of the traditions' ... Hence a great many additions were made, though unconsciously, to the sayings and doings of Jesus.[21]

Although both Jesus and Mohammad had been enlightened via Divine revelation, only Mohammad managed to translate that essence into practice. Indeed, Ali went some way towards claiming that Islam was closer to the essence of Jesus, than Christianity ever had been. 'The glory of Islam', he insisted, 'consists in having embodied the beautiful sentiment of Jesus into definite laws.'[22] It was only with the Prophet Mohammad, he asserted, that monotheism as a more advanced level of civilization, prevailed. The Prophet was the torch-bearer of universal civilisational progress.

The practices enjoined by Mohammad, expressed as prescriptions of piety and law, carried forward the ideals of Islam and were able to shape both the level of religious consciousness and the associated religious and cultural practices, such that Islamic society achieved a civilisational jump from pagan 'barbarity' to the more advanced level of monotheism. Islamic laws and practices served as the motors of civilisational progress and managed to protect civilisational advances, although not entirely, from the perpetual challenge of 'forces of primitivism' and 'ignorance'. Laws were barricades against the perpetual tide of primitivism.

According to Ali, the history of Christianity was not the expression or manifestation of Christian essence in history; the Christianity of history had no essence to harness as the motor of progress. Rather, Christianity was the ongoing expression of unvanquished primitivism. As revealed in the comparison between the Christian 'Dark Ages' and the Islamic Abbasid 'Golden Age', Christianity actively hindered progress whereas Islam carried forward the torch of progress and civilisation ignited by Mohammad.

The Abbasid 'Golden Age' Versus the European 'Dark Ages'

Just as comparison between the origins of Christianity and Islam in antiquity revealed their respective essences, comparison between the Abbasid

---

[20] Ali, *Life and Teachings of Mohammed*, 272.
[21] Ali, *Life and Teachings of Mohammed*, note II to Chapter XVI, 286.
[22] Ali, *Life and Teachings of Mohammed*, 183.

Golden Age and the European Dark Ages revealed their respective histories – the impact of essence in historical context. Islamic modernists consistently emphasised the superiority of the Islamic Abbasids compared to their European contemporaries who were mired in the 'Dark Ages'. The Abbasids ushered in a Golden Age, the zenith of Islamic civilisation, and they did so as a result of Islam, not despite it.

European scholars of Islamic history largely concurred that the Abbasid period experienced a civilisational 'Golden Age', and were extensively cited by Islamic modernists as further attestation of the superiority of the Abbasids to their European contemporaries. European scholars, however, suggested that Abbasid cultural and scientific fluorescence had occurred before the 'ossification' of Islamic tradition, and thus could never be repeated. They also predominantly maintained that despite the achievements in culture and science under the Abbasids, the Abbasids had primarily been caretakers of the Greek scientific tradition, not innovators or contributors in their own right. European scholars recognised the Abbasids as transmitters of classical Greek texts and knowledge, but suggested that it was only in the hands of Europeans that this knowledge developed into 'modern' sciences. Europeans acknowledged the Abbasids for their safekeeping of classical heritage, but refused to recognise their contributions to knowledge itself. In so doing, Europeans jealously guarded 'classical heritage' as their own patrimony, rather than acknowledging a shared classical heritage and their debt to Abbasid scholars. Christian exceptionalism, as the innate capacity to generate modernity, was articulated despite the Abbasid scholarly and scientific contributions, a historical interpretation that Islamic modernists adamantly contested.

Islamic modernists deployed historical arguments to refute assertions of Christian exceptionalism. For Namık Kemal, Jamal al-Din al-Afghani, Imam Bayezidof and Syed Ameer Ali, to mention only a few, Abbasid history demonstrated that Islam was intrinsic to civilisational progress not incidental to it. One of the most vehement articulations of European exceptionalism was expressed by Renan, an important religious studies scholar and a committed Catholic modernist. Presumptions of Christian exceptionalism undergirded Renan's *Life of Jesus*, but were most infamously articulated in an 1883 lecture he delivered at the Sorbonne entitled 'Islam and Science' which was published in the Parisian *Journal des débats politiques et littéraires* shortly thereafter.[23] Islamic modernists were sympathetic to Renan's historicist project of the revivification of religion and his commitment to religion's centrality in the modern. Ali, Afghani, Bayezidof and Namık Kemal all demonstrated familiarity with Renan's scholarship. Despite, or possibly because of their advocacy of comparable religious modernist projects, they took umbrage with Renan's arguments for Christian exceptionalism and penned refutations to Renan's 'Islam and Science' article.

---

[23] Renan, 'Islam and Science', *Journal des débats politiques et littéraires*, 30 March 1883.

Renan was not alone in insisting that European progress was a product of historical development (as changing context) together with the causal agent of 'the essence of Europe' – itself a unique combination of Christianity tempered with Indo-European 'Aryan' creativity. Renan, following accepted philological theories, attributed this creativity to a semi-racialised notion of language that had emerged in the scholarly field of philology. Languages were indicative of the essence, the 'genius of each people'.[24] Indo-European languages, philologists insisted, were, by dint of their grammatical structures, inherently conducive to creativity and rational thought which in turn enabled intellectual, religious and scientific progress. Non-Indo-European languages (and here Semitic languages played the principal role of the dichotomous 'Other') were less flexible and doomed their users to dogmatism, inflexibility and passivity.[25]

In 'Islam and Science', Renan argued that Islam was a metaphoric 'iron band' crowning the heads of Muslims that prevented rational and scientific thought and which therefore accounted for Islamic societies' backwardness vis-à-vis Europe.[26] He stated:

> Liberty has never been more profoundly damaged than by a form of social organization where religion dominates civil life absolutely . . . Islam is the indistinguishable union of the spiritual and the temporal, it is the reign of dogma, it is the heaviest chain that humanity has ever had to bear.[27]

Islam, as inherently inimical to freedom of thought and intellectual inquiry, prevented scientific thought, which was the core ingredient of progress. 'Anyone a little knowledgeable about the affairs of our time', Renan proclaimed confidently,

> sees clearly the present inferiority of the Muslim countries, the intellectual nullity of those races that have received their culture and education solely from that religion. All those who have traveled in the Orient or in Africa have been struck by the fatally enslaved spirit of the true believer, by that sort of iron band that encircles his head, rendering it completely closed to science, incapable either of learning anything or of working with any new idea.[28]

---

[24] Étienne Bonnot de Condillac (1715–80), French philosopher and epistemologist, connected language to the essential character of a 'people'. See Olender, *Languages of Paradise*, 5–6.
[25] On the role of philology and other 'classificatory sciences' on the construction of the European self and related civilisational taxonomy of difference, see Masuzawa, *The Invention of World Religions*.
[26] See Ringer and Shissler, 'The Al-Afghani-Renan Debate, Reconsidered', xxviii–xlv. See also Norman, 'Disputing the "Iron Circle"', 693–714.
[27] Renan, 'Islam and Science'.
[28] Renan, 'Islam and Science'.

Succinctly summarised, Renan's argument hinged on two assertions. First, that Islam was innately and inherently incompatible with science as intellectual creativity; and second, that Abbasid cultural, political and scientific achievements had occurred despite, not because of Islam. He concluded, on the basis of these twin assertions, that Islam had been and would always remain incapable of serving as a motor of progress and civilisation. Contemporary Islamic societies were not capable of modernity.

Islamic modernists concurred with Renan concerning the centrality of science to modernity. Science, in their understanding, consisted of scientific method, which was productive of sciences as content (as in the specific fields of scientific endeavour and inquiry). Sciences included not only what today we might term the 'hard' sciences, but also history, which Islamic modernists believed applied similar methods of rationalism and empiricism. History – the determination of laws of progress in context over time – was scientific in method and content. For them, historicism was a scientific method, and the findings of history were scientifically valid. They concurred with Renan that creativity, vibrancy, innovation and strength all derived from the building blocks of science. For Islamic modernists, science as method and content was the *sine qua non* of modernity.

Science, according to Islamic modernists, was one crucial element in a cluster of characteristics or values that were central to modernity and that characterised modern civilisation. Islamic modernists consistently identified these ideals as: women's rights, religious tolerance, the equality of subjects regardless of race, the discouragement of polygamy and slavery, as well as political unity, representative government, and so forth. Islamic modernists measured civilisation – past and present – according to these 'modern' yardsticks, and in so doing, claimed these yardsticks as universal, eternally applicable, and transcendent of time and place – ahistorical.

At the same time, these 'modern' and universal ideals were the very same that many Islamic modernists claimed comprised the essence of Islam. They asserted that modern ideals – the banner of *Liberté, Égalité, Fraternité* – were quintessentially Islamic (the same Islamic ideals that animated Ali's *Rashidun* 'Republic'), as well as quintessentially modern and universal. The ideals of the French Revolution of 1789, claimed as defining European modernity, were also claimed as synonymous with Islamic essence.

Islamic modernists marshalled historical evidence to demonstrate that modern values, consistent with Islamic essence, had led to the civilisational achievements of the Abbasid period – the Abbasid Golden Age. Islam, in their analysis, did not inhibit science, but was productive of it. For Islamic modernists, the undisputed scientific and cultural fluorescence of the Abbasid Golden Age unequivocally demonstrated that Islam was intrinsically 'modern' and could again be harnessed to achieve modernity.

The question of whether Islam promoted or hindered science was at the heart Islamic modernist and European scholars' contested claims to the modern. For Islamic modernists, the ideals of Islam were directly responsible for civilisational progress. It was not simply that Islam was 'compatible' with science, cultural progress and intellectual achievements (not to mention their derivatives of political power, just rule and proper governance), but that Islam enabled these achievements by animating Islamic institutions. Islam was the motor of civilisation and progress.

After all, Islamic modernists argued, it was the revelation of the Quran to the Prophet Mohammad that had enabled Muslims to reject the primitivism of the *jahiliyya*, and to effect the civilisational jump from paganism to monotheism. Namık Kemal described how Islam, which he defined as a set of religious precepts based on the Quran, wrenched Arabian society out of the shackles of paganism. Like Ali, Namık Kemal adopted an evolutionary conception of history as denoting civilisational progress over time. He explained that Islam 'showed people the correct path' and that as a result, society abandoned uncivilised practices of 'idol worship, theft, adultery, slander and the burial of infant daughters' and instead 'committed to telling the truth and being trustworthy'.[29]

Bayezidof, in a pair of articles entitled 'Science and Arts in Islam' and 'Islam and Civilization', similarly contended that the adoption of Islam as a set of moral and legal precepts had generated civilisational progress. He explained that

> in the *jahiliyya* period there was continuous warfare and conflict. The Prophet changed everything; brought peace and an end of conflict; cleansed the entire Arabian desert of idols and their sites of worship; inaugurated a new era; the Prophet's religious message brought everyone together as fellow countrymen.[30]

In similar ways, Islam was the motor of progress in the Abbasid period. The Abbasid empire's capacity to draw on, engage with, and ultimately produce new cultural, artistic and intellectual achievements was a direct consequence of the implementation of Quranic precepts. The 'Abbasid caliphs', Bayezidof explained, 'made every effort to further civilization, and [established] religious centers of learning in several cities, where youth would be trained in sciences'.[31] Caliphs 'worked to spread and expand Islamic governance and civilization in Iraq, Syria and Iran ... [resulting in] the establishment of universities, madrasas, mosques, *vaqfs* (foundations), and hospitals'.[32] 'If we follow the last ten centuries of Arab literary and intellectual progress', Bayezidof noted, 'we will be obliged to recognize how [high] their degree of humanitarianism and excellence [was]. On the issue of the furthering of politics, piety, and thought, the Arabs, following in the way shown by the Prophet, took many scientific and artistic questions in hand and spread

---

[29] Kemal, *Büyük Islam Tarihi*, 31.
[30] Bayezidof, 'Islam'in Ilimlerle Ilişkisi', 46.
[31] Bayezidof, 'Islam'in Ilimlerle Ilişkisi', 47.
[32] Bayezidof, 'Islam'in Ilimlerle Ilişkisi', 49.

Arab-Islamic literature throughout the Islamic world.'³³ For Bayezidof, Islam was instrumental, not incidental, in the process of generating civilisation:

> [Islam is] one of the most rational theological systems, or religious forms, available to the human mind at various stages of its development. Islam, more than any other system, reconciles within itself the spiritual needs and physical nature of man.³⁴

Bayezidof and Namık Kemal both cited numerous passages of the Quran and Prophetic hadiths as evidence that the essence of Islam (and the Prophet's understanding of this essence), valued intellectual inquiry and the pursuit of science.³⁵ Bayezidof argued that 'from the examples of the history of Arab civilization, Quranic verses, hadiths and passages taken from Arabic literature, it is clear that Islam was not an obstacle against the teaching of civilization and intellectual advancement. Quite to the contrary, it encouraged and widened them.'³⁶ Islamic modernists located the 'essence' of Islam in the Quran, an essence which was understood and manifested by the Prophet in his speech and actions. The cause of Abbasid greatness was the essence of Islam, properly manifest in Islamic institutions.

Renan, in 'Islam and Science', insisted that the very real intellectual accomplishments of the Abbasid period had not, in fact, derived from Islamic precepts. The great scholars of the period could not in good conscience, he insisted, be considered Muslim. According to Renan, Caliph Ma'mun and the luminaries of the Abbasid period were only nominally Muslim – their intellectual capacity was a product of their Aryan Persian, Christian or pagan background. It would be a mistake, Renan asserted, to assign any credit for Abbasid achievements to Islam.

In response to Renan's assertion, Namık Kemal and Bayezidof argued that Renan's racially essentialist position distorted the historical evidence. They insisted that it was precisely Islam's message of universalism and equality that enabled the participation and interaction between many cultures and peoples. The Abbasid *pax Islamicus* accurately expressed the 'ideals' of Islam in institutions of political unity, assimilation and inclusion, and produced the intellectual and cultural fruition of the Abbasid period. Islam enabled the creation of an ethno-linguistic melting pot – the absorption and assimilation of many peoples and traditions. In so doing, it facilitated cultural and intellectual synthesis, creativity and innovation.

In a passage that reads as a refutation of Renan's characterisation of Islam as inescapably Semitic, Namık Kemal explained:

---

[33] Bayezidof, 'Renan-a Reddiye', 12.
[34] Baiazitov, 'A Refutation', 23.
[35] Baiazitov, 'A Refutation', and Kemal, *Renan Mudafaanamesi*.
[36] Bayezidof, 'Islam'in Ilimlerle Ilişkisi', 51.

It should have become apparent by now, that Islamic civilization means Arab, Turkish and Iranian civilization. Or it would be true to say that besides these, Byzantine and Nestorian [Syriac] and other civilizations also contributed to it. In today's widening world, we are not able to think of a civilization that is unaffected by interaction with others. Islamic civilization, from the standpoint of law, was established as a system of indulgence and tolerance, and shows respect for the principles of religion and society ... the religious principles of fraternity and equality held closely, became a standard that within a short period of time, opened the way for an expansion from the borders of India, to the Atlas ocean.[37]

Bayezidof similarly contended that Islam facilitated the productive and creative cross-fertilisation of many cultures. He explicitly denounced European claims to be the sole heirs of classical knowledge, arguing that Islamic science was not simply a conveyor belt for transmitting classical knowledge to Europe, but had been a significant contributor to new knowledge. Sciences build on one another, Bayezidof wrote of Abbasid scientific progress, and share Greek, Iranian, Indian and other roots. Offering up an unusual metaphor, Bayezidof urged his readers to imaging knowledge as having both a mother and a father:

> are we not able to declare that Greece serves as the father of the intellectual sciences, while Arabia, or Islam, takes the place of their nurturing mother? If we admit this comparison is apt, then we can conclude that Europe owes a great debt of gratitude to Islam.[38]

Prefiguring the 'Sabra thesis', Bayezidof and Namık Kemal both insisted on recognising Islamic science as a full-fledged contributor to Greek science.[39] They both also extended the genealogy of 'modern' science to include Persian and Indian contributions, further problematising European constructions of a linear genealogy hailing directly and uniquely back to the Hellenic past. As Bayezidof explained:

> Truly, all honor belonging to the initial form of these sciences should be bestowed not only upon the Greeks, but also to Egypt and India, from whence came the wave of Reason. But why deny the existence of Arab or Muslim sciences during that seven-century period of great intellectual progress?[40]

According to Islamic modernists, a historical comparison of the Islamic Abbasids with their Christian European contemporaries demonstrated

---

[37] Kemal, *Büyük Islam Tarihi*, 462.
[38] Baiazitov, 'A Refutation', 33.
[39] Sabra, 'The Appropriation ... of Greek Science in Medieval Islam', 223–43.
[40] Baiazitov, 'A Refutation', 25.

unequivocally that the Abbasids had championed 'modern' ideals. Ali, Afghani and Bayezidof directly inverted European claims to modernity, suggesting that it was Christianity, not Islam, that had hindered science, progress and civilisation. Ali cited European scholarship to demonstrate that Christianity, not Islam, had continually transgressed 'modern' values of religious tolerance, women's rights and rational governance. He contrasted Christianity with Islam regarding their positions on women, noting that Christianity taught that women were inferior, 'a necessary evil', whereas Islam included 'respect for women [as] one of the essential teachings of the creed'.[41] Bayezidof concurred – women's rights and religious tolerance figured prominently in his characterisation of the 'essence' of Islam. He wrote:

> If we construct a parallel between Christian Europe and Asiatic Islam during the time that Renan discusses, we will see a strange contrast. On the one hand, Islam searched everywhere for philosophy and sciences, and the Caliphs generously awarded scholars. On the other, Christian Europe stood idly by during the intellectual movements of the Arabs and was completely disinterested in these movements of thought ... Islam in its incipient form searched everywhere for science while science was searching for Catholic Europe and found it only with difficulty through the Muslim Arabs.[42]

Refuting Christian claims that Islam was inherently inclined to violence and persecution, Ali argued that Islam had long been the champion of tolerance and reason, in direct contradistinction to the historical record of the Christian church:

> Islam 'grasped the sword' in self-defense; Christianity grasped it, in order to stifle freedom of thought and liberty of belief. With the conversion of Constantine, Christianity had become the dominant religion of the western world. It had thenceforth nothing to fear from its enemies; but from the moment it obtained the mastery, it developed its true character of isolation and exclusiveness. Wherever Christianity prevailed, no other religion could be followed without molestation. The Moslems, on the other hand, required from others a simple guarantee of peace and amity, tribute in return for protection, or perfect equality – the possession of equal rights and privileges, on condition of the acceptance of Islam.[43]

Persecution was not simply contingent to Christianity as expressed by Christian tradition, Ali suggested, but inherent in it – an intrinsic, immutable component of the Church's failure to correctly manifest the truth of Jesus:

---

[41] Ali, *Life and Teachings of Mohammed*, 244.
[42] Baiazitov, 'A Refutation', 30.
[43] Ali, *Life and Teachings of Mohammed*, 216.

Every act of violation was sanctified by the Church ... From the first slaughters of Charlemagne, with the full sanction of the Church, to the massacre and enslavement of the unoffending races of America, there is an unbroken series of the infringement of international duties, and the claims of humanity. This utter disregard of the first principles of charity led also to the persecution of those followers of Jesus who ventured to think differently from the Church. The rise of Protestantism made no difference.[44]

In contrast, 'the spirit of Islam', Ali explained,

is entirely opposed to isolation and exclusiveness ... By the laws of Islam, liberty of conscience and freedom of worship were allowed and guaranteed to the followers of every other creed under Moslem domination. The passage in the Koran, 'Let there be no forcing in Religion', is the grandest testimony to the principle of toleration and charity ... Mohammad did not merely preach toleration; he embodied it into a law.[45]

Christian Europe, Ali suggested, could not claim to have originated 'modernity'. Rather, it was the civilisational influence of the Islamic Abbasids, which gradually, over time, succeeded in effecting Christian Europe. In addition to the 'modern' values of toleration and respect, Ali declared that Islam had generated 'modern' sciences. 'The Saracenic race', by which he meant Arabs,

by their elastic genius as well as by their central position – with the hoarded treasures of dying Greece and Rome on one side and of Persia on the other – and India and China far away sleeping the sleep of ages – were pre-eminently fitted to become the teachers of humanity. Under the inspiring influences of the great Prophet, who gave them a code and a nationality, and assisted by their sovereigns, the Saracens caught up the lessons of wisdom from the East and the West, combined them with the teachings of the Master, and started from soldiers into scholars.[46]

Despite European claims to the contrary, Ali credited the Abbasids with having generated 'modern' scientific methods. 'The deductive method, hitherto proudly regarded as the invention and sole monopoly of modern Europe, was perfectly understood by the Moslems', he insisted.[47] Similarly,

---

[44] Ali, *Life and Teachings of Mohammed*, 205, citing Milman, *History of Latin Christianity*, vol. I, 352, and William Edward Hartpole Lecky, *History of the Rise and Influence of the Spirit of Rationalism in Europe*, first published in 1865, 'chapter on persecution'.

[45] Ali, *Life and Teachings of Mohammed*, 206–7, citing the Quran 2:256: 'There is no coercion in religion.'

[46] Ali, *Life and Teachings of Mohammed*, 296. Ali does not give the specific reference of who he is quoting.

[47] Ali, *Life and Teachings of Mohammed*, 323.

he argued that 'the Moslems certainly deserve the gratitude of the modern world, for having introduced the method of experimentation into the domains of the exact sciences in place of the theorizing of the Greeks'.[48] Along the same lines, Ali noted that 'the science of historic evidence, unknown or at least unappreciated in Europe till the middle of the last century, was perfectly known to the Moslems'.[49] Islam deliberately promoted science, both in content and method:

> While Christian Europe had placed learning under the ban of persecution ... the Vicegerents of Mohammad allied themselves to the cause of civilization, and assisted in the growth of Freethought and Free-enquiry – originated and consecrated by the Prophet himself ... The cultivation of the physical sciences, – that great index to the intellectual liberty of a nation, – formed the day-dream of the whole life of the Moslems.[50]

A more accurate historical perspective, Ali insisted, would rectify European claims to have originated modern science, and modern values more generally – to have carried forward the torch of civilisation. He described a grand sweep of history, which bears quoting at length:

> Moslems went out into the world, not to slaughter like the Israelites of old, but to teach and elevate, to civilize and refine. Afflicted and down-trodden humanity awoke to new life. Whilst the barbarians of Europe, who had overturned an effete empire, were groping in the darkness of absolute ignorance and brutality, the Moslems were occupied in the task of civilization. During the centuries of moral and intellectual desolation in Christian Europe, Islam led the vanguard of intellectual progress ... Christianity had established itself on the throne of the Caesars, but it had utterly failed in the object of regenerating the nations of the earth. From the fourth century of the Christian era to the twelfth century, the darkness of Europe grew deeper and deeper. During these ages of ignorance Ecclesiasticism barred every access through which the light of knowledge, represented latterly by Moslem civilization, could stream in. But though jealously shut out from this land of fanaticism, the benignant influences of Islam in time made themselves felt in every part ... The first outburst of Rationalism in the West, occurred in the province most amenable to the power of Moslem civilization. Ecclesiasticism crushed this fair flower with fire and with sword, and threw back the progress of the world for centuries. But the principles of the Liberty of Thought, so strongly impressed on Islam, had communicated their vitality to Christian Europe.[51]

---

[48] Ali, *Life and Teachings of Mohammed*, 328.
[49] Ali, *Life and Teachings of Mohammed*, 337.
[50] Ali, *Life and Teachings of Mohammed*, 341.
[51] Ali, *Life and Teachings of Mohammed*, 338–9.

Ali, Bayezidof and Namık Kemal, in equating Islamic essence with the generation of 'modern' scientific method, proffered an alternative genealogy of modernity – one that originated in Islamic lands, not Europe. 'Islam', Ali asserted, 'introduced into the modern world civilization, philosophy, the arts and the sciences, everything that ennobles the heart and elevates the mind. It inaugurated the reign of intellectual liberty.'[52] He even went so far as to posit that while Islam was generative of 'modernity', Christianity had actively hindered it. 'The two failures of the Moslems, one before Constantinople, and the other in France', Ali declared, 'retarded the progress of the world for ages . . . The Renaissance, Civilization, the growth of intellectual liberty would have been accelerated by seven hundred years.'[53] Had Islam triumphed, he continued, the world would have been spared the Inquisition, the 'massacres of the poor Aztecs and Incas', the Thirty-Years War and other religiously sanctioned violence. Indeed, even 'the reformation of the Christian Church would have been accomplished centuries earlier'.[54]

Universalising Islam – Becoming Modern

Namık Kemal, Imam Bayezidof, Jamal al-Din al-Afghani and Syed Ameer Ali explicitly contrasted Abbasid civilisation with the European Dark Ages in order to emphasise the former's comparative superiority. At the same time, they also implicitly compared Abbasid civilisation to contemporary European civilisation. Their measures of civilisational progress were those of their own modern time period: women's rights, religious tolerance, political unity, representative government, and so forth. Modernists assessed civilisation according to 'modern' yardsticks, and in so doing, claimed these yardsticks as eternally applicable and transcendent of time and place. In this way, the ideals of *Liberté, Égalité, Fraternité* – those very Islamic ideals that animated Ali's 'Republic' – were universalised. The ideals of the French Revolution of 1789, hailed as the beating heart of European modernity, became synonymous with eternal, ahistorical Islamic ideals. In equating the essence of Islam with universal modern ideals, Islamic modernists thereby proposed an alternative genealogy of modernity, one that originated in Islam, not in Europe.

According to this genealogy, modern values originated in Islam, and only later were adopted and developed in Europe. The Spanish Umayyads, and to a greater extent, the Abbasids, as expressions of the most advanced civilisations of their time, reclaimed their place as the crucible of subsequent European progress. European modernity, rather than the child of Christian and classical Greek parents, Ali stated, had actually been fathered by Islam.

---

[52] Ali, *Life and Teachings of Mohammed*, 345.
[53] Ali, *Life and Teachings of Mohammed*, 343.
[54] Ali, *Life and Teachings of Mohammed*, 345.

The claim to an Islamic origin of modernity was simultaneously a claim to agency – an argument for the capacity of Islam to generate progress and civilisation and to participate in the modern on its own terms. This permitted more than the construction of an alternative authentic modernity, it enabled modernity itself to be claimed as indigenous.

In Ali's rendition, European modernity was derivative – it was dependent on having been infused with Islamic essence. Islamic modernists turned claims to European exceptionalism on their head, marshalling historical evidence that while Islam had generated progress, Christianity had actively resisted it. Europe had become modern not because of Christianity, he maintained, but despite it. Christianity was the 'iron band' that inhibited modernity. The development of modernity in Europe, therefore, was the story of the suppression of the Christian Church, the forcing of Christian dogma and tradition into submission by a secular state. In making this assertion, Ali clearly distinguished between the 'essence' of Christianity as found in Jesus, and the Christianity of history, which, he argued, preserved very little, if anything, of its original essence. Islamic history revealed the essence of Islam, which could be recontextualised into the present: the essence of Christianity was forever lost.

The Abbasid Golden Age provided empirical evidence that Islam had and could again serve as the motor of progress and civilisation. A historicisation of Islamic history confirmed that the current state of 'backwardness' prevalent amongst contemporary Islamic societies was historically contingent, not the inevitable consequence of the 'essence' of Islam. Contemporary dissonance between the inherently 'modern' essence of Islam and the methods, values and content expressed in Islamic societies was due to the emergence and subsequent ossification of tradition. Tradition limited the possibility of adapting to the changing 'circumstances of the age'. Tradition was the anchor holding society back even as civilisation sailed forward.

The descriptions of the emergence of Islamic tradition and the rise of traditionalism as methodology that lay at the heart of modernist Islamic histories must be read as prescriptions for the rejection of tradition and the embrace of modernity. Islamic modernists argued that Islam was not only compatible with modernity, but necessary to it. They firmly believed that the essence of Islam, cleansed of tradition, could be replanted in the 'moral desert' of present backwardness to regenerate the 'garden' of modernity.[55]

For Islamic modernists, historicism enabled them to determine the contours of particular historical contexts. Yet historicism – as contextualisation – did not primarily conceive of time chronologically. Historical time was quintessentially civilisational. The evolution of humanity occurred in chronological time certainly, but was located, imagined and expressed as the

---

[55] Ali noted in reference to the effect of Islamic governance of Umayyad Spain, 'What had once been a moral desert, was transformed into a garden.' See Ali, *Life and Teachings of Mohammed*, 149.

passage of civilisational time. Modernity was conceived of as a civilisational level, with associated religious, intellectual and institutional characteristics. The presumption of modernity having 'arisen' or 'begun' did not hinge on the existence of a precise date or watershed moment, but on the march of civilisational progress.

History, as the story of civilisational progress, was recalibrated and no longer coterminous with chronological time. The rupture of chronological time from historical time meant that societies were conceived of in relation to civilisational progress, regardless of their location in chronological time. The equation of historical time with civilisational development led, as Reinhart Koselleck noted, to the non-contemporaneity of the contemporaneous, and vice versa.[56] In other words, comparable civilisational levels could be achieved at different chronological moments, whereas in the same chronological time, different societies exhibited different levels of civilisation.

Modernity, like antiquity, was a civilisational level, with associated religious, intellectual and institutional characteristics. Just as paganism was the religious expression of primitivism, modern Islam was the religious expression of modernity. There were several crucial implications of this deeply historicist conception of the modern. First, that just as not all societies in pagan antiquity were identical, not all societies in modernity were identical. Participation in a civilisational level entailed the sharing of certain essential characteristics indicative of a similar level of consciousness of the Divine, but did not necessitate identical cultures. There were many possible moderns; being modern was firmly disassociated from imitation or replication of European modernity.

Second, conceiving of modernity as a civilisational level meant that it was, in principle, universal. Modernity, like paganism, was not circumscribed to one place or owned by one society. Modernity was not, as some European Christian Orientalists argued, the exceptional expression of European progress – the unique combination of Christianity and classical Greek culture as united and nurtured in Europe. In asserting that Islam was 'incapable of transforming itself or including any element of civil or profane life', Renan doomed Islamic societies to a future of imitation – the adoption of European models.[57] Renan effectively associated particularism, passivity and historical

---

[56] Here I am following Koselleck's notion of the disconnect between historical time and natural time. I believe that the concept of chronological time, however, best describes this phenomenon, since natural time suggests natural rhythms (sunrise, sunset, seasons) which I do not believe are disengaged from concepts of historical time the way that chronological time (suggestive of the sequence of dynasties or rulers that was the stuff of much pre-modern history) was. Koselleck, *Futures Past*, 95. Some translators have preferred the terms 'simultaneous' and 'non-simultaneous', but I prefer 'contemporaneous' and 'non-contemporaneous'.

[57] Renan, '*Averroès et L'Averroïsm*', vol. 111, 13.

contingency with the Orient, and linked the European 'Self' with universalism, agency and a historically transcendent essence. In the view of Islamic modernists, however, modernity was universal, not culturally contingent. Modernity was severed from any exceptionalist claims and accessible to all who could cross the civilisational threshold. Islamic societies, if they could reinstitute harmony and regenerate Islam as a motor of progress, could affect the civilisational leap to the modern, not via imitation of Europe, but as a return to an indigenous origin – the return to 'true' Islam.

At a theoretical level, claiming modernity was not a chronological claim to exist in the present, but an assertion of participation in modern civilisation – a civilisation which not all contemporary societies could lay claim to. To be modern was to adopt a set of values, intellectual methods and sociopolitical commitments, and to reject the values, methods and commitments associated with tradition. Crossing the civilisational threshold necessitated a civilisational rupture – a rejection of the dissonant present and the concomitant embrace of the modern future.

This rupture was negotiated via language, with the emergence of definitions of modernity and its antithesis – tradition. Islamic histories defined and constructed tradition in a binary relationship with modernity, the one shaping and necessitating the other. Tradition was the source of dissonance and backwardness; modernity the possibility of harmony and civilisational progress. Modernity and tradition were each other's 'Other' – their necessary constitutive binaries. Definitions of 'tradition' and 'modernity' signalled the claims themselves. The emergence of the Ottoman terms for 'progress' (*terakki*) and 'civilisation' (*medeniyet*) as well as their Arabic, Persian and other linguistic synonyms, was symptomatic of the assertion of this civilisational rupture, symptomatic of claiming modernity which was integral to 'becoming' modern.

Claiming participation in the modern depended on the existence of a rupture between modern and pre-modern 'eras' as civilisational levels, and a successful transition from one to the other. Dividing human history into three distinct breaks – between past harmony, present dissonance and future (modern) harmony – added value to these ruptures and posited them as civilisational thresholds. The present became a discrete period of time, sandwiched between periods of harmony – one which existed in the past, the other as a promised future. It allowed for the 'modern' to set itself apart, historically and by definition, from the non-modern present which was cast as an interregnum, a deviation – the equivalent of the 'Dark Ages' in European historical thought.[58] The path to the modern thus travelled via the past. Modernity was claimed as a resumption or restoration of harmony through a rejection of the dissonant present. Regardless of disputes surrounding precisely where to locate the 'modern' chronologi-

---

[58] On the politics of periodisation in the construction of the European 'Middle Ages', see Davis, *Periodization and Sovereignty*.

cally, the adoption of this tripartite periodisation was a blueprint for entry into the modern; it represented a break with an imagined 'traditional' – the 'backward' present – and the promise of resuming, or reinstating, a period of harmony.

The attempt to position modernity as a rejection of tradition was also an attempt to release the present from its current historical time, to enable it to progress to the next level of civilisation. The terms 'primitive' and 'backward' became coterminous not only with less progressive levels of civilisation, but also with previous historical time. This explains modernity's claim to be somehow further along in time relative to the non-modern, which is rejected as 'backward'. As each historical time was unique contextually, the past also became 'othered' and 'estranged'.[59] The idea of modernity as the speeding up of time, of the rapid movement through history as time, was experienced as ruptures in time, a temporal and historical distancing of the present from the past. The acceleration of history can be understood as claims to the increasing frequency of civilisational cum historical ruptures.[60] Modern history embraced this project of accounting for how and why societies did nor did not progress, as well as for how and why the torch of civilisational progress moved from one society to another.

At a concrete level, to become modern was to embrace modern values, commitments, sensibilities and dispositions – the habitus of modernity. Modernity required a subjective 'becoming'– the embodiment and self-consciousness embrace of modern values and practices. In other words, 'becoming modern' was performed through the rejection/embrace of traditional/modern ideas, values and methods, respectively. Islamic modernist accusations that European historians had not accurately or impartially employed historical methods in their interpretation of Islamic history was equally an accusation of their failure to fully embrace modernity. Bayezidof, for example, called Renan to account, insisting that had Renan actually applied scientific methodology to the study of Islam, he would have come to very different conclusions. Bayezidof attributed Renan's scholarly failures to his prejudice against Islam, which made him fall short of applying internationally accepted 'scientific' scholarly methods: 'Why would this educated French man, giving his speech at a gathering of the French Scientific Association ... not wish to use the generally accepted method of impartial and precise analysis of the topic about which he was speaking?' Bayezidof lamented.[61]

Similarly, Ali and Bayezidof highlighted European scholars' frequent tendencies to apply historicism only when it suited their purposes. Bayezidof

---

[59] Zammito, 'Koselleck's Philosophy of Historical Time(s) and the Practice of History', 323.
[60] Zammito, 'Koselleck's Philosophy', 133.
[61] Baiazitov, 'A Refutation', 24.

pointed out that 'to attribute the Arabs' scientific stagnation exclusively to their religion and claim this decline as a result of their religion, while attributing other peoples' decline to non-religious reasons, is not entirely fair'.[62] Ali facetiously decried the hypocrisy of European scholars, whom, he accused, only applied historicism to Christianity:

> The Christian biographers of the Prophet of Arabia, probably under the influence of that fine sentiment called 'Christian verity', have denominated the punishment of criminals, 'assassinations', 'Murders', or 'barbarous deeds', which to the general reader convey such an idea of horror as to revolt him, before he has time to reflect on the candour of the historian . . .[63]

Proposing an alternative, more fully historicist reading, Ali noted that, first, 'this was accepted punishment for criminals' and not 'assassination or murder' and second, 'as to the cruelty of the punishment, he forgot that Christian England hanged men and women for stealing a few shillings up to the middle of the 18th century; he forgot the terrible tortures of the rack and the stake which destroyed myriads of innocent beings in Christian Europe'.[64] We see this too in Ali's noting of European scholarly hypocrisy on religious matters. It was not just that European scholars failed to universally apply historicism, but that even as they insisted on the superiority of Christianity as testified by the miracles of Christ, they themselves evidenced more primitive religious sensibilities. Ali observed that 'Patristic Christianity held, and still holds, to the miracles as a proof of the divinity of Jesus',[65] beliefs which were shared, Ali notes, by many European historians.

These claims were not simply Islamic modernist assertions of historical fallacies committed by the leading European historians of the day, but equally claims to adhere more closely to the strictures of historical scientific method and more advanced conceptions of the Divine than did their European colleagues – proof of their fidelity to modernity. Their greater commitment to historicism than their European counterparts was illustrative of their greater embodiment of modernity.

Claiming the modern thus, was not only a project that depended on a rupture in time and the construction of the civilisational other as 'traditional' – it also required the cultivation of new, modern sensibilities and dispositions. As will be discussed in Chapter 4, Islamic modernists' project was to retrieve Mohammad from historical context, to cleanse him of the distortions of tradition and to showcase him as the modern embodiment of the essence of Islam. Islamic modernists' quest for the historical prophet was essential for the identification, divorce and retrieval of essence from context, of truth

---

[62] Baiazitov, 'A Refutation', 31.
[63] Ali, *Life and Teachings of Mohammad*, 124.
[64] Ali, *Life and Teachings of Mohammed*, 124.
[65] Ali, *Life of and Teachings of Mohammad*, note on 103.

from tradition as the solidification of layers of particular context-bound interpretation. Such decontextualisation paved the way for the final step – the recontextualisation of Islamic essence in the present.

CHAPTER
4

THE QUEST FOR THE HISTORICAL PROPHET

[Islam] is not merely a system of positive moral rules, based on a true conception of Human Progress, but it is also the establishment of certain principles, the enforcement of certain dispositions, the cultivation of a certain temper of mind, which the conscience is to apply to the ever-varying exigencies of time and place.[1]

Syed Ameer Ali (1873)

The great progress in critical thought has been to substitute the category of becoming for that of being, the conception of the relative for that of the absolute, movement for immobility. Previously, everything was considered as existing; one spoke in absolute terms about philosophy, law, politics, art, and poetry. Now everything is considered to be in the process of becoming.[2]

Ernest Renan (1852)

Introduction

Preceding chapters have discussed ways in which Islamic modernists located Islam in the evolutionary taxonomy of universal civilisational progress and explored the historical laws of progress as they provided new meanings to Islamic history. Islamic modernists constructed Islamic history as Islamic essence manifest either in harmony or dissonance within particular historical contexts. In a bid to claim modernity, they demonstrated that there was no inherent contradiction between Islam and modernity. To the contrary, they argued that Islamic essence was not only consonant with modern ideals, but the origin of modernity. The establishment of an Islamic genealogy of modernity was essential to their ability to articulate a possible future modern

---

[1] Ali, *Life and Teachings of Mohammed*, 186.
[2] Renan, *Averroes et l'Averroïsme*, 11.

as authentic rather than adopted. If the identification and retrieval of Islamic essence from history – effectively its decontextualisation – was the first step in a process of religious reform, the reinsertion of essence – its recontextualisation in the present – was the second.

The project of religious reform pivoted on the Prophet Mohammad. The historicisation of the Prophet was crucial to the articulation of a new, modern, methodological path forward – a new hermeneutics of the Quran and the Hadith. The Prophet, in his exemplary capacity, served as the embodiment of the ideal modern Muslim. By historicising the Prophet, Islamic modernists were able to reconstruct him at the nexus of essence and context, the intermediary between God's intent and the limits of possibility of his audience. He was simultaneously the embodiment of Islamic essence, and the primary exemplar of the manifestation of essence in harmony with context. Historicising the Prophet was the necessary prerequisite for religious reform as the decontextualisation of Islamic essence and its recontextualisation in the modern present – the reclamation of eternal truth from the distortions of tradition.

Islamic modernists' quest for the historical prophet was inherently prescriptive. In Islamic tradition, the Prophet Mohammad is exemplary, the ultimate and eternal model of emulation – the perfect man – *al-insan al-kamil*. What he said and did – his 'long shadow'[3] – was transmitted in the Hadith and conceptualised as Prophetic Sunna. The Prophetic Sunna served as the foundation of Islamic precedent, precedent which was a crucial interpretive lens in understanding the Quran, and well as in generating Islamic law and prescriptions for piety.

The quest for the historical prophet was simultaneously the quest for the essence of Islam in its greatest, most perfect historical expression – the Prophet Mohammad. Historicising the Prophet was necessary in order to humanise him and fundamentally reconstruct the concept of precedent. For Islamic modernists, the Prophet was first and foremost the mediator of God's intent. Mohammad was not simply the bearer of God's directives for mankind, but enjoyed a Divinely bestowed consciousness which provided him with knowledge of God's intent. Aided by God, Mohammad translated God's intent into practice. Islamic modernists suggested that it was this act of translation – the art of negotiating the relationship of author (as God) with audience (seventh-century Arabian society) – that constituted the true precedent of the Prophet. It was this mediating role between the eternal and the historically contingent that modernists defined as prophetic precedent – replacing Hadith as content and Sunna as replication, with the concept of translation.

---

[3] I am borrowing this metaphor from Khalidi, *Arabic Historical Thought*, 14.

The Incomparable Man[4]

The Prophet Mohammad embodied a fundamental duality. He was a product of his own particular historical context, and yet via Divine guidance, capable of transcending it. He was embedded in historical context, but freed of its tethers by God. The Prophet was the 'incomparable man' – human yet enjoying Divine knowledge; born of seventh-century Arabia, but transformed by God into the translator of Divine intent on earth.

Prior to the revelation of the Quran, Syed Ameer Ali, largely following earlier Islamic histories, described Mohammad as standing out from his contemporaries. Relying heavily on the principle events narrated in Tabari's classic Abbasid-era chronicle, Ali described Mohammad's ethical character, his concern for the welfare of his community, and his spiritual inclinations. Ali's account of Mohammad prior to the revelation emphasised the esteem in which his own community held him. This was conveyed by the account of the rebuilding of the Kaaba, and of Mohammad relating to Khadija his first, unsettling, experience of revelation. In Tabari's account of this event, Khadija reassures Mohammad that he could not have encountered an evil spirit, since he was a good person and expressed the values of Arabian society at the time: 'Rejoice, for God will never put you to shame, for you treat your kinsfolk well, tell the truth, deliver what is entrusted to you, endure fatigue, offer hospitality to the guest, and aid people in misfortune.' Khadija then brought Mohammad to her cousin, a Christian, who confirmed Mohammad's selection by God as a prophet.[5]

While following the same basic contours of Tabari's account, Ali stressed Mohammad's character and personality traits. 'His kindliness of heart, and his gentleness of manners, combined with his fidelity, his honesty, his truth, and his unsullied character',[6] Ali wrote, led the community to name Mohammad *'al-Amin'* – which Ali translated as 'the True' rather than the more frequently translated 'the Trustworthy'. Ali stressed Mohammad's inner consciousness, and his natural inclination to spirituality and ethics manifest as his concern for the moral uplifting of society. Mohammad's ultimate goals consisted of 'raising the Arabs as well as the surrounding nations from the depth of social and moral degradation into which

---

[4] Renan first described Jesus as 'the incomparable man' in his inaugural lecture delivered upon his assumption of the Chair of Hebrew at the Collège de France in 1862. For an account of the 'fracas' surrounding this lecture, see Priest, *The Gospel According to Renan*, 60–3. 'The incomparable man', as discussed later in the chapter, also accurately conveys Syed Ameer Ali's characterisation of the Prophet.

[5] Tabari (d. 923), *Tarikh al-rusul wa 'l-moluk*, translated as *The History of al-Tabari*, VI, 68–9.

[6] Ali, *Life and Teachings of Mohammed*, 28, following Ibn Hisham's redaction of Ibn Ishaq, *The Life of Muhammad* and Tabari's chronicle, *Tarikh al-rusul wa 'l-moluk*.

they had fallen'.⁷ Mohammad was selected by God to perform a 'duty to mankind'.⁸

Ali's emphasis on the interior spiritual and moral sensibilities of Mohammad is again apparent when we juxtapose his version of the Christian monk Bahira foreshadowing Mohammad's later role as prophet and messenger of God with Tabari's classic account. In Tabari's chronicle, Bahira encountered Mohammad while the latter was on a trading trip in Syria with his uncle, Abu Taleb.⁹ According to Tabari, Bahira had knowledge 'by means of a book which was handed down [by monks] from generation to generation'. Bahira then witnessed a series of miracles. First, Mohammad was 'shaded by a cloud which marked him out from among the company'. Next, when Mohammad and his companions went and stood under a tree, Bahira observed 'the cloud covering the tree and bending down its branches over the Messenger of God until he was in the shade beneath it'. Bahira then approached and closely observed Mohammad's features 'whose description he had found in his book'. The monk's identification of Mohammad as a future prophet was confirmed when Mohammad's responses to Bahira's questions concerning 'certain matters which had taken place both when he was awake and when he was asleep', corresponded to 'the description which [Bahira] had found in his book'. Mohammad, thus, according to Tabari, possessed Divinely bestowed knowledge – only thus could he have answered Bahira's questions regarding what had happened 'when he was asleep'. This oblique reference to Mohammad's knowledge of 'the seen and the unseen' was also physically manifest: 'Bahira looked at Muhammad's back, and saw the seal of prophethood between his shoulders.' In summary, Bahira identified Mohammad from a variety of clues found in a book: miracles, knowledge 'of the unseen' which only God possesses, and a 'mark of prophecy' on Mohammad's body.¹⁰ Tabari's account described this mark as physically visible, yet only recognisable for what it signified by individuals like Bahira, who possessed the requisite (biblical) knowledge. Mohammad's future prophethood was thus confirmed as being foretold in the Bible or

---

⁷ Ali, *Life and Teachings of Mohammed*, 25.
⁸ Ali, *Life and Teachings of Mohammed*, 36.
⁹ The account of Mohammad's encounter with Bahira occurs in Tabari, *History*, VI 'Muhammad at Mecca', 44–7. The Bahira story is only one of many accounts provided by Tabari that indicate foreknowledge by monotheists of the coming of a prophet. Tabari, citing a hadith transmitted by the monotheistic *hanif* Zayd b. Amr, noted that Mohammad was recognised due to the mark of the 'seal of prophethood between his shoulders'. Tabari also provides evidence of Mohammad performing miracles as testimony of his divine calling. See Tabari, *History*, VI, 66–7.
¹⁰ The concept of 'knowledge of the unseen' (*ghayb*), the prerogative of God who reveals it to chosen messengers, appears forty-seven times in the Quran. God is 'the one who knows the unseen and the visible' (Quran 39:46). In addition, see the Quran 6:59, 72:26–8; 3:44.

some other Christian text – Bahira's 'book' passed down from monk to monk.[11]

Ali followed the general contours of Tabari's Bahira account, even as he fundamentally reconstructed its meaning. In Ali's narrative, Bahira, 'who, struck by the signs of future grandeur and intellectual and moral qualities of the highest type on the countenance of the orphan child of Abdullah, recognized in him the liberator and savior of his country and people'.[12] Mohammad, in Ali's rendering, was not identified by any miracles or mark on his body; rather, Bahira recognised in Mohammad 'intellectual and moral qualities'.[13] Mohammad's 'countenance reflected the benevolence of his heart'.[14] Ali translated Bahira's test of Mohammad's 'knowledge of the unseen' into Mohammad's innate sensibilities and dispositions that inclined God to choose him as the vessel of revelation. It would not be until after Mohammad began receiving the revelation, however, that Ali described him as enjoying a heightened consciousness of the Divine, thereby emphasising Mohammad's human limitations and the transformative effects of God's word.

The choice of Mohammad as prophet rested with God, but Mohammad's innate intellectual and morality capacity played a role in God's choice. The mark of prophecy, in Ali's rendition, was the outward expression of his inner character, not a physical mark on his body. Mohammad demonstrated the spiritual, intellectual and moral requisites for prophecy. This stress on Mohammad's character and personality sustained Ali's portrayal of Mohammad as not simply the physical vessel of Divine revelation, but as comprehending the revelation, and being charged by God with enacting it. It also is indicative of the Islamic modernist emphasis on the internal sensibilities and dispositions of the modern Muslim. Their reconstruction of the historical prophet was manifest in the content of modern Islam, which also had profound methodological implications.

The revelation fundamentally altered Mohammad, not just externally, by God compelling him to become a prophet, and somewhat later, a messenger, but internally as well. Mohammad was the recipient of Divine guidance (including 'knowledge of the unseen'), knowledge which trans-

---

[11] Curiously, Draper identifies Bahira as a Nestorian Christian. Accordingly, Mohammad and his travelling companions were 'entertained at the Nestorian convent of the town of Bozrah, south of Damascus'. This substantiates Draper's larger argument that Mohammad's religion was deeply inspired by Nestorianism: Mohammad's 'subsequent career shows how completely their [Nestorian] religious thoughts had taken possession of him, and repeated acts manifest his affectionate regard for them'. For Draper, Islam at its inception was essentially a Nestorian revolt against the idea of the Trinity. See Draper, *History of the Conflict Between Religion and Science*, 78–80.

[12] Ali, *Life and Teachings of Mohammed*, 28.

[13] Ali, *Life and Teachings of Mohammed*, 28.

[14] Ali, *Life and Teachings of Mohammed*, 155.

formed him from an individual who reflected pre-Islamic paganism, to an individual imbued with an elevated consciousness of Divine truth. Ali wrote that Mohammad enjoyed 'an expansive heart elevated by deep communion with the Soul of the Universe'.[15] Divine guidance enabled Mohammad to transcend his historical context and become the agent of God's intent.

Mohammad's heightened consciousness of Divine truth is apparent in Ali's extensive treatment of angels, devils and miracles. On the one hand, Ali suggested, citing Renan's historicisation of Jesus, that Mohammad 'could not have been . . . intellectually different from the people of his age'.[16] It is more than likely, Ali posited, that the Prophet, like his contemporaries, believed in angels and evil spirits. Ali noted, in explicit parallel with Jesus, that 'probably Mohammed, like Jesus and other great moral teachers of the world, believed in the existence of intermediate beings, celestial messengers from God to man'. 'What we, in modern times,' he explained, 'look upon as the principles of nature, they looked upon as angels, ministrants of heaven.'[17] Ali posited that 'Mohammad also like Jesus probably believed in the existence of the Principle of Evil as a personal entity'.[18] 'Early Christians', or 'the immediate disciples of Jesus', Ali explained, 'firmly believed the angels and devils to be personal entities, being slightly ethereal, but in every way human-like; and this belief, those disciples of Jesus must have received from the Master himself'.[19] This early Christian religious landscape, presumably captured and replicated in Christian tradition, Ali intimated, ran parallel to that of early Islam, since 'the Mahommedan patristic notion regarding angels and devils, is similar to the orthodox Christian belief'.[20]

On the other hand, Mohammad's heightened consciousness of the Divine meant that he was capable of perceiving a greater truth, one that lay beyond the limitations of his intellectual context: 'An analysis of [Mohammad's] words reveals a more rationalistic element, a subjective conception, clothed in words suited for the apprehension of his followers.'[21] In other words, Ali suggested, although Mohammad inherited contemporary religious conceptions, his greater consciousness of the Divine enabled him to transcend them. Nevertheless, despite the Prophet's divinely enabled aptitudes, he recognised that the majority of his followers could not attain a comparable level of Divine consciousness, and so continued to use familiar language in order to speak meaningfully to them. Mohammad spoke in idiom, even if his followers believed in the literal truth of his words. As Ali explained,

---

[15] Ali, *Life and Teachings of Mohammed*, 155.
[16] Ali, *Life and Teachings of Mohammed*, 86–7, citing Renan, *Vie de Jésus*, 267.
[17] Ali, *Life and Teachings of Mohammed*, xx.
[18] Ali, *Life and Teachings of Mohammed*, 86–7.
[19] Ali, *Life and Teachings of Mohammed*, 86–7.
[20] Ali, *Life and Teachings of Mohammed*, 86–7.
[21] Ali, *Life and Teachings of Mohammed*, 86–7.

Mohammad was addressing himself not only to the advanced minds of a few idealistic thinkers who happened to be then living, but to the wide world around him engrossed in materialism of every type. He had to adapt himself to the comprehensions of all.[22]

We see this tension between context and transcendence repeatedly emphasised in Ali's lengthy discussions of miracles. According to Ali, the tendency to associate Mohammad with the exercise of supernatural power was symptomatic of residual primitive conceptions of the Divine. In the following passage, Ali equated the idea that Mohammad should and could exercise supernatural power with pre-Islamic, pagan misconceptions of the Divine. In Ali's new rendering of Islamic history, when Mohammad first began to preach publicly (in AD 613), he called on his fellow Meccans to believe in God and His message of salvation:

> 'If you will accept what I bring you,' [Mohammad promised], 'there is happiness for you in this world and the next; if you reject my admonitions, I shall be patient, and leave God to judge between you and me.' They asked for miracles to prove his mission. Remark his reply. 'God has not sent me to you to work wonders. He has sent me to preach to you . . .' Disclaiming every power of wonderworking, Mohammad rests the truth of his divine commission entirely upon his teachings . . . 'I am but a man like you,' he says, 'but I bring you hopeful tidings.'[23]

In the passage above, Mohammad's refusal to perform miracles – or in Ali's derogatory language, 'wonderworking' – is glossed as evidence of Mohammad's greater grasp of the nature of the Divine. The Prophet attempted to focus his listeners' attention on the content of his message, stressing that the truth lay in the message itself, not in whether or not he was able to invoke supernatural powers.

Ali's treatment of miracles is symptomatic of his phenomenological and evolutionary understanding of religion. He employed contemporary criteria of religious evolutionary categories here, to cast 'wonderworking' and 'miracles' as the products of more primitive, pagan religious conceptions of the Divine, in the same category as Zeus' lightning bolt. Miracles as explanations of natural events were indicative of ignorance of natural law, of the tendency characteristic of pagan religions to attribute natural phenomena to Divine intervention and supernatural forces – to perceive God as immanent.

---

[22] Ali, *Life and Teachings of Mohammed*, 278.
[23] Ali, *Life and Teachings of Mohammed*, 49. Ali is citing the Quran, but does not specify which verse. There are seventy-three mentions of 'bringing hopeful/glad tidings' in the Quran. See for example Quran 2:213: 'Mankind was [of] one religion [before their deviation]; then Allah sent the prophets as bringers of good tidings and warners and sent down with them the Scripture in truth to judge between the people concerning that in which they differed.'

Miracles as the intersession of the Divine in the world were equally the result of more primitive conceptions of God's interaction with the world.

In Ali's rendering, Mohammad, in refusing to perform miracles, was rejecting conceptions of the Divine that centred on 'magic' as human attempts to invoke supernatural powers, instead insisting that his listeners adopt a greater degree of religious consciousness of the truth of the Divine – expressed as monotheism. By rendering miracles as expressive of an inherently 'primitive' religious consciousness, Ali argued that more evolved religious understandings abandoned belief in supernatural explanations of natural phenomena, in favour of greater consciousness and spirituality. In the passage cited above, Mohammad urged his listeners to accept a higher truth and to abandon belief in miracles as false expressions of Divine power.

In his discussion of miracles, Ali clearly distinguished between Mohammad's own and Mohammad's listeners' capacity to understand God. Those individuals who readily accepted Mohammad's message were described as enjoying a greater level of religious consciousness. Ali wrote that, gradually, Mohammad succeeded in attracting followers: 'In spite of all opposition, however, slowly but surely, the new teachings gained ground. The seeds of truth thus scattered could not fail to fructify.'[24] The truth of God's revelation was sufficient, in and of itself, to persuade people of its validity. God, he insisted, did not need miracles – 'truth has no need of trickery'.[25]

Mohammad's straddling of his own pagan context with a more evolved religious understanding is also apparent in Ali's account of the Battle of Badr which occurred in AD 624. The triumph of the Prophet's band of followers who had accompanied him in his migration from Mecca to Medina in 622 against the vastly superior military force of the Quraysh is portrayed in conventional Islamic historical accounts as the result of the intervention of angels. Ali proposed an alternative reading, suggesting that we understand the story allegorically, rather than literally:

> It seemed as if the angels of heaven were warring for the Moslems. Indeed, to the earnest minds of Mohammed and his followers, who, like the early Christians, saw God's Providence in all the gifts of nature, in every relation of life, at each turn of their affairs, individual or public – to them those blasts of wind and sand, the elements warring against the enemies of God, in that critical moment, appeared veritable succor sent from Heaven – as angels riding on the wings of the wind and driving the faithless Idolaters before them in confusion.[26]

---

[24] Ali, *Life and Teachings of Mohammed*, 50.
[25] Ali made a point of emphasising the difference between Christianity and Islam. 'Patristic Christianity held, and still holds, to the miracles as a proof of the divinity of Jesus', he noted. *Life and Teachings of Mohammed*, note on 103.
[26] Ali, *Life and Teachings of Mohammed*, 83.

Parsing this account, Ali proposed that 'what we, in modern times, look upon as the principles of nature, they looked upon as angels, ministrants of heaven'.[27] Times have changed, science has advanced, natural laws have taken the explanatory wind out of the wings of angels. God, he insisted, was less immanent. Natural laws accounted for the mechanics of nature – nature did not need God's constant sustenance – God remained the architect of natural laws, but not the day-to-day engineer. Nature and history obeyed immutable and eternal laws; they were comprehensible and predictable.

We must read these passages, Ali insisted, in their historical context. Primitive beliefs and the language used to express these beliefs must be historicised, not replicated as literal truth. Accounts of miracles need to be understood as primitive explanatory mechanisms. The angels of Badr must be relegated to idiom, not maintained as dogma – idioms attempting, however imperfectly, to express an essential truth – the triumph against all odds of the Muslims against their idolatrous foes. The problem was not the use of idiom *per se*, Ali explained, but that idiom, initially expressive of a primitive capacity of religious understanding, had become trapped in this primitive level and was no longer consonant with modern science or a more evolved religious consciousness. The understanding of truth cannot progress if it is not historicised – truth, in his view, was an eternal essence which needed to be removed from the husk of context.

In Ali's account of Badr there is a tension between Mohammad believing in angels alongside his contemporaries, and Mohammad deploying the idiom of 'angels' to express a higher truth; between Mohammad as a human embedded in his historical context, and Mohammad's God-given capacity to transcend the limitations of this context. Ali never fully resolved this inherent tension, instead stressing Mohammad's ability to tailor his message to the needs of his audience. In a separate passage, Ali described Mohammad's deliberate retention of the language of angels in order to speak meaningfully to his audience. Mohammad's expression of truth, therefore, must be read with this balancing act in mind. Mohammad was an agent of translation, deliberately employing language that his audience could comprehend, 'words suited for the apprehension of his followers'.[28]

Mohammad as the Agent of Translation

Mohammad's elevated consciousness of the Divine – his capacity to perceive Divine truth – enabled him to comprehend the essence of Islam as equivalent to God's intent for mankind. His consciousness of the Divine released him from the shackles of his context – intellectually and spiritually. Mohammad was freed by God and endowed with the necessary capacity to enact Divine will: the implementation of God's intent. After all, Mohammad was not

---

[27] Ali, *Life and Teachings of Mohammed*, 148.
[28] Ali, *Life and Teachings of Mohammed*, 86.

provided with a heightened consciousness of the Divine solely for his own benefit – he was charged by God with effecting the civilisational progress of humankind. His success in moving his own society from one civilisational level to the next was dependent on implementation, on the successful transformation of historical context itself.

Mohammad's genius, according to Syed Ameer Ali, was precisely his ability to successfully negotiate God's intent as the progress of mankind within the inherent limits of his historical context. Mohammad changed what he could change. He recognised his society's capacity for advancement, even as he appreciated the limitations of this capacity. Context, after all, was complex and multifaceted. It was comprised of customs, practices and institutions (cultural, economic, political), but also of intellectual, spiritual and religious conceptions. Intellectual landscape and customary practices were mutually interactive, mutually reflexive and mutually sustaining.

In order to effect civilisational change, to wrench his society from paganism and firmly embed it in the more progressive civilisational level of monotheism, Mohammad needed to alter existing practices, even as he needed to alter the existing mental and spiritual assumptions that sustained them. The leap from paganism to monotheism depended on the rejection of pagan conceptions of the Divine, as well as on the rejection of social customs and institutions sustained by paganism. Islam was as much about cultivating a new intellectual and spiritual habitus as it was about adopting more 'civilized' institutions and practices.

Mohammad's capacity to negotiate between essence and context, to translate God's intent into his own particular historical moment, was, in Ali's estimation, the source of his genius. This is apparent in several occasions in Ali's historical narrative when he recounted how Mohammad, despite his initial inclinations to adhere to existing customs and practices, was in the end able to harness his greater knowledge of God's intent and the intellectual transcendence that this afforded him. As a result, the Prophet made decisions to reject customary practices, consciously and deliberately, in contravention of his own innate inclinations. Mohammad was torn between his own intellectual and moral context, of which he was a product, and his recognition of the primitivism of this context. Only his spiritual consciousness, and the understanding of the Divine that this afforded him, enabled him to implement God's intent – to transcend his own historical context and move his society into a greater level of progress and civilisation.

We see this tension played out within Mohammad, between his acceptance of the assumptions and practices he was raised with, and the heightened awareness of the nature and intent of the Divine that God's guidance brought with it. An illustration of the conflict within Mohammad, and of the triumph of his recognition that God's intent was inconsistent with the maintenance of existing practices, is found in Ali's account of the treatment of enemy dead in the aftermath of the Battle of Uhud (AD 625). In this pivotal battle only one year after the Prophet's triumph at the Battle of Badr, the

Quraysh very nearly succeeded in defeating the Prophet's forces. The battle was particularly bloody, with many casualties on both sides. At a moment when it seemed that the Quraysh had triumphed over the Muslims, they engaged in the 'barbarous mutilation of slain [Moslem] enemies',[29] oftentimes members of their own tribe or even family. Hind, wife of the head of one of the prominent Qurayshi families and Mohammad's arch-enemy, Abu Sufyan, successfully sought to have Mohammad's uncle and close devotee, Hamza, killed on the field of battle. According to Ali, Hind and other Qurayshi women 'showed the greatest ferocity in this savage work of vengeance, tearing out and devouring the heart of Hamza, and making bracelets and necklaces of the ears and noses of the dead'.[30] In the context of the pre-Islamic pagan practice of disfiguring the dead of one's enemies, Ali argued that Mohammad showed exceptional 'lenience' towards the vanquished, in explicit contravention of the pre-Islamic 'barbarian' practices of the Quraysh. Ali recounts that the Prophet

> was at first so moved by grief and indignation as to declare that the dead of the Koreish [sic] should be treated in like manner . . . but his pitiful heart rebelled at his own thoughts, and in calmer moments he uttered the inspired words, 'Bear wrong patiently; verily best it will be for the patiently-enduring,' and from that day the horrible practice of mutilation which prevailed among all the nations of antiquity was inexorably forbidden to the Moslems.[31]

In this account of the Prophet's forbearance, it was God's guidance (via the Quran) that enabled him to divorce himself from the confines of his context and strive to implement God's intent. It is worth underscoring here that Ali emphasised Arabia as sharing civilisational context with other 'nations of antiquity'. In so doing, he rejected European scholarship's emphasis on the particularism of Arabia and the purely 'Semitic' nature of Islam, and cast Islam in universal terms. The Prophet was not a purely 'Arabian prophet', he was a prophet for all mankind.

The Prophet's ability to negotiate between paganism as a set of practices buttressed by religious conceptions, and Islam as necessitating a different set of practices sustained by monotheistic conceptions of the Divine, is nowhere more apparent than in Mohammad's complex position on polygamy and slavery. Ali forcefully argued that neither polygamy nor slavery were condoned by God or Mohammad.

Ali historicised the practice of polygamy in the context of late antiquity. 'Among all Eastern nations of antiquity, polygamy was a recognized institution,' he maintained, which included Persians, Medes, Babylonians,

---

[29] Ali, *Life and Teachings of Mohammed*, 95.
[30] Ali, *Life and Teachings of Mohammed*, 96.
[31] Ali, *Life and Teachings of Mohammed*, 96. Ali is citing the Quran 31:17.

Assyrians, Athenians, Thracians, Lydians, and Ancient Greeks.[32] Pre-Islamic pagan society was no different than the societies that surrounded it. Polygamy was practised 'among [the Prophet's] own people' and among 'the people of the neighboring countries (Persia, Byzantium, Arabs)'.[33] Ali historicised the institutions of polygamy and slavery, insisting that they could only be evaluated within the confines of their own context.

Not only was polygamy widely practised in antiquity, but it served specific social and economic functions. Ali explained that 'the fact must be borne in mind that the existence of polygamy depends on circumstances. Certain times, certain conditions of society make its practice absolutely needful for the preservation of women from starvation or utter destitution.'[34] Mohammad understood that the ideals of Islam demanded the abolishment of polygamy as a primitive practice at odds with God's intent. At the same time, he appreciated that polygamy was deeply embedded in context – and could not simply be prohibited, without a concomitant change in that context – both in terms of its systemic utility (providing sustenance and protection to single, especially widowed women), but also in terms of the prevalent cultural beliefs that legitimised it. Mohammad implemented change to the extent that his society could sustain it. He translated the imperative of abolishing polygamy, within the ongoing need to practise it:

> As the legislator of his own nation – the benefactor of the human race at large, it was Mohammed's mission to provide efficient remedies for all these accumulated evils. By limiting the maximum number of contemporaneous marriages, by giving rights and privileges to the wives as against their husbands; by making absolute equity towards all, obligatory on the man; by guarding against their being thrown helpless on the world at the willful caprice of a licentious individual, Mohammed struck at the root of the evil.[35]

God's intent was understood by Mohammad and enacted within the limits of possibility. Mohammad's own conduct was consonant with his preference for monogamy, as enjoined by God, and yet also his acknowledgment of the enduring positive social function of polygamy in his historical context. As long as Mohammad's first wife, Khadija, was alive, Ali noted, 'he never availed himself of the Arab custom of taking several wives. During her lifetime his love was unswerving.'[36] Khadija's death in AD 619 coincided with the increase in Qurayshi opposition and persecution of Mohammad and his followers. Mohammad's decision to take multiple wives needed to be understood in this context, Ali argued, as not only consistent with Arab custom, but

---

[32] Ali, *Life and Teachings of Mohammed*, 217.
[33] Ali, *Life and Teachings of Mohammed*, 224.
[34] Ali, *Life and Teachings of Mohammed*, 226.
[35] Ali, *Life and Teachings of Mohammed*, 225.
[36] Ali, *Life and Teachings of Mohammed*, 30.

more importantly, as a deliberate political strategy that enabled Mohammad to safeguard his beleaguered community of followers. Ali noted that every marriage contracted by Mohammad following the death of his first love, Khadija, was designed either to 'cement various rival families and powerful tribes together and bind them to himself by marriage ties' or to offer 'subsistence and protection' to widows of his followers: 'By taking [widows] into the bosom of his family Mohammad provided for them, in the only way which the circumstances of the age and the people rendered possible.'[37] Ali insisted that customs be historicised and evaluated for their meaning and function in context – rather than according to contemporary, modern norms. As he explained, 'Usages and customs depend on the progress of ideas; and are good or evil according to circumstances, or as they are or are not in accordance with the conscience – "the spirit" – of the time.'[38]

Ali proposed a similar interpretation of Mohammad's position on slavery. On the one hand, in line with his understanding of God's intent, Mohammad recognised that slavery was a primitive practice, inconsistent with the essence of Islam and not condoned by God. Yet to the extent that he could not achieve its abolition outright within the limitations of current conditions, Mohammad attempted to encourage its demise and regulate its practice. Mohammad 'looked upon the custom [of slavery] as temporary in its nature, and held that its extinction was sure to be achieved by the progress of ideas and change of circumstances'.[39] 'Islam did not "consecrate" slavery, as has been erroneously supposed', Ali explained, 'but provided in every way for its abolition and extinction.'[40] In the meantime, however, Mohammad successfully negotiated the abolition of slavery as God's intent within the capacity of his particular society to change. This was necessarily a long and complex process:

> It has been justly contended that, as the promulgation of the laws, precepts and teachings of Islam extended over twenty years; it is naturally to be expected, many of the pre-Islamite [sic] institutions which were eventually abolished, were at first either tacitly permitted or expressly recognized ... its [slavery's] extermination was only to be achieved by the continued agency of wise and humane laws, and not by the sudden and entire emancipation of the existing slaves, which was morally and economically impossible. Therefore numberless provisions ... were introduced in order to promote a gradual enfranchisement. A contrary policy would have produced an utter collapse of the infant commonwealth.[41]

---

[37] Ali, *Life and Teachings of Mohammed*, 234, 235.
[38] Ali, *Life and Teachings of Mohammed*, 236.
[39] Ali, *Life and Teachings of Mohammed*, 257–8.
[40] Ali, *Life and Teachings of Mohammed*, 260.
[41] Ali, *Life and Teachings of Mohammed*, 255.

Mohammad, charged with the civilisational progress of mankind, articulated laws. These laws, animated by Islamic ideals, operated in consonance with the 'circumstances of the age'. Islamic laws as promulgated by Mohammad must be historicised and read for their moral intentionality. Such a reading clearly demonstrates that the aspiration of the complete abolishment of slavery was embedded in Islamic law. According to Ali,

> the Islamic Code dealt a blow at the institution of slavery, which, had it not been for the deep root it had taken among the surrounding nations and the natural perversion and obliquity of the human mind, would have been completely extinguished, as soon as the generation which then practiced it, had passed away.

Ali provided two possible readings of the laws regarding slavery: 'The one showing that Islam completely abolished the system; the other, that by connecting the most onerous responsibilities with its practice, Mohammed's religion provided for its gradual but absolute extinction.'[42] In other words, if one read the law for embedded intentionality, it became apparent that the intention was to abolish slavery, not simply limit it. Its limitation was thus contextually necessary and should not be read as enjoined, or permitted, in Islam.

The same contextual reading held true for Islamic law concerning the status of women:

> It is the negative part of the law which shows the profound depth underlying it. The proviso we refer to is not only qualitative in its character, but serves in fact to nullify the permissive clause. Construed plainly, it means – No man shall have more than one wife, if he cannot deal 'justly' and equally with all (Quran chap iv, v. 3) . . . The conditional clause added to the permissive part being essentially obligatory in its nature . . . the law itself may be considered as prohibitive of a plurality of wives.[43]

The problem, Ali opined, was not that Mohammad failed to fully implement Islamic ideals in seventh-century Arabia – a project which would have been impossible and would have resulted in the failure to make any progress whatsoever. Mohammad recognised, correctly in Ali's opinion, that civilisational progress necessarily involved gradual evolution. One cannot skip civilisational stages, but must move sequentially from one to the next. Religion can serve as a motor of progress, but progress is inevitably relative and can only be judged in historical context.

The problem, Ali insisted, was our contemporary failure to historicise Mohammad's actions. Like other Islamic modernists, Ali maintained that

---

[42] Ali, *Life and Teachings of Mohammed*, 254–5.
[43] Ali, *Life and Teachings of Mohammed*, 225–6.

religious reform was imperative, and that such reform necessarily embodied not only content, but method. The quest for the historical prophet lay at the nexus of these dual objectives of Islamic modernist reform. This quest uncovered the 'truth' of the Prophet Mohammad, as distinct from the traditional rendition of him, and illuminated a new methodological path forwards.

Towards a Modern Methodology

Mohammad, in so far as he successfully translated essence into context, indicated a methodological approach to both the identification of Islamic essence as well as its implementation in historical context. It was in the historical prophet's art of translation that we find outlined a new, modern Islamic methodology – one based on the assumptions and implications of historicism.

The essence of Islam was located in the Quran, but the Quran, as the revelation to Mohammad by God, itself acknowledged its own historical context. According to Syed Ameer Ali, one can follow Mohammad's own spiritual development, the gradual expansion of his consciousness of the Divine and recognition of Divine intent, in the changing 'voice' of the Quran. Ali explained:

> A careful study of the Koran makes it evident that the mind of Mohammed went through the same process of development which marked the religious consciousness of Jesus . . . The various chapters of the Koran which contain the ornate descriptions of paradise, whether figurative or literal, were delivered wholly or in part at Mecca. Probably in the infancy of his religious consciousness Mohammad himself believed in some or other of the traditions which floated around him. But with a wider awakening of the soul, a deeper communion with the Spirit of the Universe, thoughts which bore a material aspect at first became spiritualized. The mind of the Teacher progressed not only with the march of time and the development of his Religious Consciousness, but also with the progress of his disciples in apprehending spiritual conceptions. Hence, in the later *suras*, we observe a complete merging of the material in the spiritual, of the body in the soul.[44]

In this passage, Ali clearly suggested that Mohammad's capacity for abstraction and rationalism developed alongside the expansion of his 'religious consciousness' which resulted from his 'communion with the Spirit of the Universe'. God gradually conveyed ideas and concepts to Mohammad according to his expanding capacity to comprehend them. As Mohammad moved from 'the infancy of his religious consciousness' to adulthood, the language of the Quran itself became increasingly 'spiritual' and 'abstract'. Interestingly, in this characterisation of the nature of the Quran, the Quran

---

[44] Ali, *Life and Teachings of Mohammed*, 281–2.

was not only responsive to Mohammad's spiritual development, but sensitive to the capacity of Mohammad's disciples. Ali suggested that the language of the Quran must be read with these complex registers in mind. As he explained, the 'poetic element in the conception of the angels [in the Quran] ... will not yield in beauty or sublimity to the most eloquent words of the Psalmist. Indeed, the same poetic character is visible in both of them.'[45] There are thus multiple layers of possible readings – depending on the varying capacity of the readers to comprehend the Divine. Some will read for the literal meaning of the 'angels' – as a confirmation of their existence, whereas others, more deeply conscious, more expansive spiritually, like Mohammad and to a lesser extent, his closest followers, will recognise the angels as poetic idiom.

The crucial methodological point that Ali was making here, was that one must read the Quran with these different layers of meaning in mind. Quranic hermeneutics must take into account that Quranic language, and ultimately concepts, responded to the capacity of its audiences – first and foremost Mohammad, but indirectly also his followers. The Quran has to be read as embodying God's intent, but also as expressing this intent consonant with its audience in their historical context. As Ali declared, 'the Koran is the most faithful index to the history of the times'.[46]

God's intent, correctly perceived by Mohammad, was refracted by the necessity of implementation and the limits of possibility that this imposed. God's intent is perceptible through the historicisation of the Prophet – to understand the Prophet's historical context, and its attendant limits, is to discern the intentionality in his actions and directives, and by extension, God's intent as imbedded in his own. The identification of God's intent therefore requires a dual translation – first of the Prophet's context, and secondarily, via his context, of the Quran. In other words, embedded in the Prophetic Hadith is the Prophet's intent, and embedded in the Prophet's intent is, ultimately, God's. Without the application of historicism, one cannot separate the wheat from the chaff, the essence from context. The result is a literal, rather than a contextual reading of the Quran, and of the Hadith.

Ali's deeply historicist methodology was animated by his conception of human civilisational evolution. Simply put, Mohammad's historical context is not our own. Law, essential for the regulation of human affairs, must be in harmony with the level of civilisation that it operates in. Law, as the expression of God's intent, must continually be rearticulated according to 'the circumstances of the age'. The maintenance of existing law is appropriate only when there is no fundamental shift in context. Failure to recognise a change in context and adapt law accordingly results in the perversion of law – both in its application and intent. As Ali explained,

---

[45] Ali, *Life and Teachings of Mohammed*, 86.
[46] Ali, *Life and Teachings of Mohammed*, note on 77.

the wonderful adaptability of the Islamic precepts for all ages and nations; their entire concordance with the light of Reason; the absence of all mysterious doctrines to cast a shade of sentimental ignorance round the primal truths implanted in the human breast, – all prove that Islam represents the latest development of the religious faculties of our being.[47]

Ali made this argument abundantly clear in his discussion of the laws regarding slavery and polygamy. The institution of slavery, Ali wrote, like polygamy, which was once 'prevalent universally among mankind at some stage or other of their growth, has – at least among the nations which claim to be civilized – outlived the necessities which induce its practice, and must sooner or later become extinct'.[48] He went onto elaborate that, 'with the progress of thought, with the change of conditions ever going on in this world, the necessity for polygamy, or more properly polygyny, disappears, and its practice is tacitly abandoned or expressly forbidden'.[49]

Mohammad understood the imperative of harmonising essence with context – and the imperative of implementing law. This, after all, was his genius, his greatest accomplishment, and what would forever distinguish him from Jesus who died before he could 'place his teachings on a more systematic basis'.[50] 'The compatibility of the laws promulgated by Mohammed with every stage of progress', Ali declared, 'shows their founder's wisdom. The elasticity of laws is the great test of their beneficence and usefulness, and this merit is eminently possessed by those of Islam.'[51]

Contemporary religious reform, therefore, must embrace this essential truth – of the existence not only of the essence, the eternal, immutable ideals of Islam – but also the recognition of the inevitability of historical change, of the movement from one context to another – the particular, historical and finite – the permanence of impermanence. Failure to recognise historical context was to conflate means and ends; to insist upon the replication of more primitive manifestations of essence, appropriate for more primitive contexts – in other words, the maintenance of tradition.

Tradition, in Muslim modernists' conception, was premised on the denial of context. Tradition comprised both content and, implicitly, method. In terms of content, tradition was un-historicised Hadith – Hadith that had not been threshed – that had not been historicised in order to isolate and identify Prophetic and ultimately, Divine intent. Methodologically, traditionalism was the commitment to the replication of precedent – the continual imitation and reproduction of earlier interpretations and expressions, the absence of

---

[47] Ali, *Life and Teachings of Mohammed*, 187.
[48] Ali, *Life and Teachings of Mohammed*, 260.
[49] Ali, *Life and Teachings of Mohammed*, 226–7.
[50] Ali, *Life and Teachings of Mohammed*, 185.
[51] Ali, *Life and Teachings of Mohammed*, 227.

critical distance, of rational evaluation of function in context, or appreciation of embedded intentionality.

The quest for the historical prophet was the pursuit of the truth of the Prophet, cleansed of the distortions of tradition. It was essential to rid the historical record of claims that Mohammad had performed miracles. Miracles, for Ali, had no place in modern Islam. In modern times, Ali believed, when we have advanced our understanding of natural law and evolved a greater conception of the Divine, miracles were nothing more than primitive (mis)perceptions of the world. Rescuing Mohammad from attributions of supernatural power was a battle Ali waged against the primitivism he believed was perpetuated by adherence to Islamic tradition. It was essential to the modernist project to distinguish the truth of Mohammad from the misperceptions ossified into tradition that continued to erase his agency as translator of God's intent. Mohammad embodied a transcendent truth, but this truth was expressed within the parameters of his historical context.

Mohammad as the Modern Muslim

Mohammad, cleansed of the tarnish of tradition, exemplified the ideal modern Muslim. He embodied the sensibilities and dispositions of modern Islam. As Syed Ameer Ali explained, directly quoting Milman's discussion of Christianity, Islam

> is not merely a system of positive moral rules, based on a true conception of Human Progress, but it is also 'the establishment of certain principles, the enforcement of certain dispositions, the cultivation of a certain temper of mind, which the conscience is to apply to the every-varying exigencies of time and place.'[52]

It was exactly these 'dispositions', this 'temper of mind', that Mohammad exemplified in Ali's reconstruction of him. He was the embodiment of the spiritual consciousness of the Divine, the translator par excellence of essence in context. Mohammad was the 'poetic idiom' of God's intent. Ali's rendition of Mohammad embodied the characteristics of modern Islam. Modern Islam consisted of a rationalised, internalised, ethical set of values – an intellectual and spiritual habitus. Mohammad, as the perfect exemplar of the sensibilities and dispositions of modern Islam, is illustrated in Ali's descriptions of him. Mohammad possessed 'an expansive heart elevated by deep communion with the Soul of the Universe, – he was gifted with the power of influencing equally the learned and the unlearned . . . he was gifted with mighty powers

---

[52] Ali, *Life and Teachings of Mohammed*, 186, quoting Henry Hart Milman, *History of Latin Christianity*, vol. I, 206.

of imagination, elevation of mind, delicacy and refinement of feeling'.[53] Ali described Mohammad as 'the most generous, his breast the most courageous, his tongue the most truthful'; 'modestly and kindness, patience, self-denial and generosity pervaded his conduct'.[54]

Mohammad expressed in heart, mind and actions, the perfect unity of moral progress and social regeneration. According to Ali, 'Mohammed was extremely simple in his habits. His eating and drinking, his dress and his furniture, retained to the very last a character of patriarchal simplicity.'[55] Ali, in stressing Mohammad's spirituality and rationality, the sensibilities and dispositions of a rational, modern Islam, was also careful to note that the manifestations of piety that Mohammad prescribed were a means to those ends. They were designed as practices to cultivate these very same sensibilities and dispositions, as avenues of enlightenment and paths to spiritual consciousness.

Ali described Mohammad's prescriptions of piety in terms of their utility. Accordingly, prayer, the 'yearning of the human soul to pour out its love . . . to God' was enjoined by Mohammad, who united individual spiritual needs with larger social needs without compromising the former. Mohammad preserved the 'true religious spirit' that animated the performance of piety. Yet pious rituals were intended only to facilitate the individuals' relationship to God, to encourage moral progress, and to develop individuals' capacity to 'purify their heart' and develop their consciousness of and emotional relationship to God.

Piety was essentially the construction of individual subjectivity – it did not derive meaning as transactional, formal worship. Piety was oriented toward the effect on the individual, not the act itself as pleasing to God. Faithfulness to God's intent entailed the cultivation of the interiority of the individual, not scripted performance or ritual sacrifice. Mohammad's prescribed forms of piety were avenues for spiritual development. Piety, while not eschewing performance, was animated by spiritual concerns: 'The Prophet of God declared that the most important purification is the cleansing of the heart from all blameable inclinations and frailties, and the mind from all vicious ideas, and from all thoughts which distract the human attention from God.'[56]

As Ali explained, 'prayers are only the utterances of the sentiments which fill the human heart . . . all religious systems . . . have recognized, in

---

[53] Ali, *Life and Teachings of Mohammed*, 155–6.
[54] Ali, *Life and Teachings of Mohammed*, 157.
[55] Ali, *Life and Teachings of Mohammed*, 158.
[56] Ali, *Life and Teachings of Mohammed*, 178–9. There are interesting parallels here with nineteenth-century Zoroastrian religious reform which called for a rationalised and internalised ethics and emphasised the internal effect of external practices. The mantra of 'Good Thoughts, Good Words, Good Deeds', rather than viewing external actions in and of themselves as efficacious, emphasised the effect of certain practices on the individual. See Ringer, *Pious Citizens*.

some shape or other, the efficacy of prayer. In most, however, the theurgic character predominates over the moral; in some the moral idea is entirely wanting.'[57] Mohammad recognised the imperative of manifesting Divine intent in laws and prescriptions of piety; yet unlike Christianity or Judaism, never made the mistake of conflating these goals with the formalisation of ritual or the authorisation of clerical intermediaries:

> In instituting prayers, Mohammed recognized the yearning of the human soul to pour out its love and gratitude to the God of Truth, and by making the practice of devotion periodic, he impressed that disciplinary character on the observance of prayer, which keeps the thought from wandering into the regions of the material. The formulae, consecrated by his example and practice, whilst sparing the Islamic world the evils of contests regarding liturgies, leave to the individual worshipper the amplest scope for the most heartfelt outpouring of devotion and humility before the Almighty Presence. The value of prayer, as the means of moral elevation, and the purification of the heart, has been clearly set forth by the Koran.[58]

Ali made this crucial distinction repeatedly, between performance as ritual, and performance as spiritual, often in explicit contrast with Christianity and other religions that he characterised as confusing means with ends. 'The practice of baptism in the Christian Church [and Egyptians, Jews, heathen religions in the East and West] ... show the peculiar sanctity which was attached to external purifications',[59] Ali wrote. Mohammad prescribed rituals, but only as a means to greater spiritual and moral ends:

> Mohammed conserved and consecrated this ancient and beneficent custom. He required frequent ablutions as proper preliminaries to the worship and adoration of the Pure God. At the same time he especially inculcated that mere external or rather physical purity was not the essence of devotion. He distinctly laid down that the all-pervading Soul of the Universe can only be approached in purity and humility of spirit.[60]

Ali defended Mohammad from any accusations of formalism, insisting that he instituted ritual performance in its ideal form in order to engender individual mindfulness of God as part of a larger project of the cultivation of a pious interiority. The descent down the slippery slope of justifying ritual as an end in and of itself, rather than a productive tool, was the consequence of tradition. Ali disassociated Mohammad from what would later become the maintenance of formalism, the insertion of clerical authority into the

---

[57] Ali, *Life and Teachings of Mohammed*, 171.
[58] Ali, *Life and Teachings of Mohammed*, 174–5.
[59] Ali, *Life and Teachings of Mohammed*, 178.
[60] Ali, *Life and Teachings of Mohammed*, 178.

interpretation of the Divine, and the relegation of ethics to the empty performance of ritual. Modern Islam was rational, individual and spiritual – a set of sensibilities and dispositions, embodied in, but not defined by, external expressions of piety.

The quest for the historical prophet was animated by Islamic modernist historicist methodology and the overarching objective of revivifying Islam. For modernists, the retrieval of the Prophet Mohammad from the detritus and distortions of tradition was the prerequisite to redeploying the Prophet as the eternal exemplar – the model of emulation for all Muslims. Islamic modernists recast the Prophet Mohammad as the ideal expression of modern Islam – of a rationalised, internalised and spiritualised expression of God's intent. As such, Mohammad could again serve as precedent, but precedent defined by his intentions and pious sensibilities, not by his specific actions in his historical context. Historicising the prophet enabled his resuscitation as an enduring model of emulation – the ideal modern Muslim.

Comparative Quests: Syed Ameer Ali's *Life of Mohammad* and Ernest Renan's *Life of Jesus*

Syed Ameer Ali's *Life of Mohammad* drew deeply on European historical scholarship of Christianity and Christian history, in addition to that of Islam and Islamic history. In particular, he employed explicit parallels between Jesus as reconstructed by Ernest Renan in *Life of Jesus*, and his own interpretations of Mohammad in *Life of Mohammad*. He also cited Renan's *Life of Jesus* to substantiate his refutation of European Christian exceptionalism and to support his counter argument for Islamic superiority. A closer examination of ways in which Renan's project of re-enchantment parallels and diverges from that of Ali's affords valuable insight into the similarities and differences between these two contemporaneous religious modernists.

In *Life of Jesus* (1863), Ernest Renan deployed historicism to free the essence of Christianity from the shackles of tradition and to construct a spiritual, personalised, and deeply aesthetic Christianity that allowed individual Catholics in his own nineteenth-century France to re-embrace their faith. Renan's disenchantment with tradition enabled his re-enchantment of a newly retrieved 'essence of Christianity'. The enduring meaning of religion was recast from being located in tradition, to being found in the individual's spiritual relationship to Christianity's essence.

For Renan, as for Islamic modernists, historicism both necessitated and permitted religious reform. Renan's *Life of Jesus* was premised first on the assumption of the existence of an essence of Christianity, and second, on the claim that this essence was retrievable via historicism and could be transplanted to effect a revivification of religion in the modern era. Methodologically, Renan deployed historicism as contextualisation to reject tradition and to recover the 'essence' of Christianity, an essence which he claimed resided in Jesus. Historicism permitted Renan to rescue Jesus from the distortions of Christian tradition and to recontextualise Jesus in contemporary France.

Renan insisted, as did Ali, that traditionalism, as the methodology of precedent, was incompatible with reason and the imperative of continual reinterpretation. As he explained:

> The great progress in critical thought has been to substitute the category of becoming for that of being, the conception of the relative for that of the absolute, movement for immobility. Previously, everything was considered as existing; one spoke in absolute terms about philosophy, law, politics, art, and poetry. Now everything is considered to be in the process of becoming.[61]

This 'process of becoming', and the associated rejection of absolutes, were corollaries in the triumph of historicism – defined as the recognition of the perpetual existence of humankind in historical context. If, indeed, one admitted to historicism, then one was likewise forced to accept the consequences – that all consciousness of truth was contextually contingent and that humanity was engaged in a continual process of becoming – an eternal process of spiritual enlightenment. Renan embraced the permanence of context and the continual need to revise, rewrite and re-imagine religious truth. As Renan eloquently argued, 'criticism knows no respect: it judges gods and men. As far as it is concerned there is neither standing nor mystery; it destroys all magic, disturbs every veil. It is the sole authority without bridle, for it is but reason itself.'[62]

According to Renan, Jesus's Christianity and, he insisted, the only true Christianity, was an internalised and spiritual faith, expressed in simple acts of piety. Akin to Ali's rendition of Mohammad's rationalised religion, Renan's true Christianity manifest in Jesus was characterised by the denunciation of ritual, clerical intermediaries, dogmatism and formalism. In Renan's rendition, Jesus's religion was 'a pure religion, a religion without priests and without external observances, resting entirely on the feelings of the heart, on the imitation of God, on the direct relation of the conscience with the heavenly Father'.[63] Renan insisted that 'Jesus was not a founder of dogma, a creator of symbols; he ushered a new spirit into the world'.[64] There were no religious practices to be found in Jesus' time, only simple prayer, no formalised rituals or performances, no religious hierarchy, in other words, no Church:[65] 'It was a pure religion, without practices, without temples, and without priests; it was the moral judgment of the world, entrusted to the

---

[61] Renan, *Averroes et l'Averroïsme*, 11.
[62] Renan, 'Les historiens critiques de Jésus', cited in Lee, *Ernest Renan: In the Shadow of Faith*, 98.
[63] Renan, *Vie de Jésus*, 41.
[64] Renan, *Vie de Jésus*, 149–50.
[65] Renan, *Vie de Jésus*, 141–2.

conscience of the just man and to the arms of the people.'⁶⁶ Renan redefined true Christianity – original Christianity manifest as Jesus – as one where individuals were free to develop their spiritual consciousness of God. Jesus' Christianity was rational, individual, and above all, spiritual:

> The true kingdom of God, the kingdom of the spirit, that makes each one of us king and priest; this kingdom which, like a grain of mustard seed that has grown into a tree which shades the entire world, and amidst whose branches the birds have their nests– Jesus understood this, he wanted it, he established it.⁶⁷

On Jesus' death, his disciples, unable to transcend the spiritual and scientific limitations of their Judaic context, misunderstood and misrepresented Jesus. Renan patiently explained that the frequent account of miracles in the Gospels resulted from a combination of peoples' incomprehension of natural law, together with the powerful inclination born of primitive religious consciousness to legitimise prophets by having them deploy supernatural powers.⁶⁸ Renan dismissed stories of the supernatural and claims to Jesus' Divine nature, as emanating from these intellectual and spiritual deficiencies. Jesus was mistakenly attributed with a supernatural birth and an equally supernatural resurrection from death, both of which convictions only increased in intensity and philosophical complexity over time.⁶⁹

Like Ali, Renan denounced accounts of miracles as symptomatic of a more primitive view of the Divine: 'The great modern achievement will be accomplished only when belief in the supernatural, in whatever form, is destroyed in the same way as belief in magic and witchcraft have been [abandoned]. All of this is of the same order.'⁷⁰ Renan and Ali were both committed to the humanity of their respective prophets. Renan insisted that Jesus' greatness lay in his humanity; Jesus was 'the incomparable man' – the epitome of religious consciousness, and an eternal example for all mankind. Jesus was a social revolutionary, the embodiment of pure consciousness of God.⁷¹ As such, he embodied the religious ideal for all mankind for all of time: 'Jesus was more than a reformer of an old religion, he was the creator of the eternal religion of humanity.'⁷²

Renan argued that Christianity had developed apart from, if not in contravention of, Jesus' teachings. Rituals, hierarchies and institutions crept in and distorted the pure teachings of Jesus himself. As Renan wrote, 'nothing is

---

⁶⁶ Renan, *Vie de Jésus*, 167.
⁶⁷ Renan, *Vie de Jésus*, 166. Renan is referring to the Parable of the Mustard Seed in the Gospel of Matthew 13:31–2.
⁶⁸ Renan, *Vie de Jésus*, 158–9. Renan asserted that all peoples in the ancient Near East believed in miracles, with the exception of the Greeks(!).
⁶⁹ Renan, *Vie de Jésus*, 153.
⁷⁰ Renan, *L'Avenir de la Science*, 766.
⁷¹ Renan, *Vie de Jésus*, xx.
⁷² Renan, *Vie de Jésus*, 18.

further from scholastic theology than the Gospel ... God, conceived simply as Father – this was the entirety of Jesus' theology'.[73] Christianity, therefore, from the death of Jesus, deviated from truth, a deviation which became embodied, solidified and propagated in Christian tradition. Tradition, as the perpetuation of one interpretation of truth despite changing historical context, led to the 'petrification', and ultimately the distortion, of true Christianity. By making the distinction between the Christianity of historical time and Jesus' Christianity, Renan redefined Christianity and called for its purification – the return to origins, the reclaiming of essence through historicisation and the associated shedding of historical detritus.

Renan's most profound criticism of the Catholic Church was that it sought to preserve dogma as truth, thus preventing the liberation of each individual soul to seek their own spiritual consciousness of God. It was the Church's role as intermediary between man and God, and the inhibition of individual spirituality that inevitably resulted, that Renan sought to overcome. In claiming that 'the true kingdom of God that everyone carries in their Heart' was the 'essence of Christianity', Renan sought to liberate Christianity from the Catholic Church.[74] He effectively contrasted Jesus' Christianity with the Christianity of his time, noting that 'the breath of God was free amongst them; with us, it is chained by the iron bonds of an impoverished society and condemned to an unmitigated mediocrity'.[75]

The similarities between Renan's *Life of Jesus* and Ali's *Life of Mohammad* are striking. For both Renan and Ali, religious history was the story of humanity's 'longing after the infinite', of greater and lesser degrees of consciousness and spirituality. The preservation and perpetuation of truth as tradition was inimical to the need for progress. Religion must be embraced as a shared human phenomenon, as human experience, a perpetual 'becoming' – not as a set of discreet unchanging doctrines that demanded obedience. Religious modernists, whether Catholic or Islamic, reconceived religion not as dogma or even tradition, but as a spiritual truth accessible through individual consciousness – a truth which could propel humankind on a path of civilisational progress. Renan described Jesus in very similar terms as Ali described Mohammad. Both figures were depicted as enjoying the Divinely bestowed capacity for consciousness of the Divine. For religious modernists, religion, redefined as individual consciousness of the Divine, was the motor of human progress visible through human history.

Renan and Ali claimed that the essence of their respective religions transcended time and place. These claims to recognise their respective transcendent essences were simultaneously claims to the eternality and universalism of these essences. For Ali, Mohammad's achievements were those of humanity, since 'the progress of the world, morally and intellectually,

---

[73] Renan, *Vie de Jésus*, 36.
[74] Renan, *Vie de Jésus*, 37.
[75] Renan, *Vie de Jésus*, 255.

is collective'.[76] Just as Ali depicted Mohammad's Divinely inspired genius as effectively loosening him from the fetters of his context, Renan argued that Jesus, too, was transcendent of time and place. While born a Jew, his embodiment of full consciousness of the Divine allowed him to transcend the limitations of his context, his contemporaries and of Judaism. Jesus began as a Jew, but eventually, as his religious consciousness developed and expanded, he rejected Judaism entirely. As Renan insisted, 'In other words, Jesus was no longer a Jew. He was a revolutionary of the highest order; he called all men to a religion founded solely on their being children of God.'[77] At the very moment of Jesus' rejection of and separation from Judaism, he was transformed into the 'origin' of Christianity. As such, he embodied the 'essence' of Christianity – the universal religion of mankind par excellence. Renan insisted on Jesus' rejection of the particular (Judaism) and embrace of the universal (Christianity): 'He proclaimed the rights of man, not the rights of Jews; the religion of man, not the religion of Jews; the deliverance of man, not the deliverance of Jews.'[78] Jesus was the origin of universal religion, 'he established the religion of humanity, a religion whose foundations were built not on blood, but on the heart'.[79] Renan's and Islamic modernists' assertions of universalism were competing claims of superiority that depended on the classification of their respective religious 'essences' as the most evolved in the hierarchical taxonomy of religions.

For both Renan and Ali, the retrieval of the 'essence' was the first step in its recontextualisation – its embedding in the present. The relocation of essence to the present hinged on essence being characterised as transcendent and universal, and thus applicable and relevant for the present. Renan argued that Jesus transcended the limitations of his own context, prefiguring his eventual embrace, as recontextualisation in the present. Jesus' Christianity was 'modern' – it embodied the sensibilities and disposition of modern rationalised religion characterised by the absence of ritual and dogma, and the freedom of individuals to pursue their journey towards greater spiritual consciousness of the Divine. Jesus' religion was not only 'pure' – absent tradition, dogma or clerical intermediaries – but eternal – the universal religion of humankind. Renan's religion was implicitly modern as well – only modern Christians, imbued with modern religious sensibilities, were capable of embracing Jesus, of becoming his disciples, and of finally manifesting the truth of Jesus that had never before been manifest in history. 'If Jesus were to return among us', Renan assured his readers, 'he would recognize as disciples, not those who claim to encompass him entirely with a few phrases of the catechism, but those who labor to carry on [his work].'[80]

[76] Ali, *Life and Teachings of Mohammed*, v.
[77] Renan, *Vie de Jésus*, 139.
[78] Renan, *Vie de Jésus*, 139.
[79] Renan, *Vie de Jésus*, 140.
[80] Renan, *Vie de Jésus*, 80.

Renan's insistence that Jesus was misconstrued by his disciples, and that 'true religion' was distorted by the institutionalisation of Christianity, enabled him to extract Jesus from historical Christianity and to posit a new definition and location of Christianity. In so doing, he cast true Christianity – the essence of Christianity that Jesus so perfectly embodied – in contemporary terms, as synonymous with 'purity of heart and fraternity of mankind'.[81] 'We are the true Christians', Renan promised, 'Christian tradition has little claim on the truth that was Jesus.'[82] This true Christianity, Renan explained, was truer to Jesus' own – a Christianity without rituals, without institutions, without a clerical hierarchy; one in which all barriers to the development of personal, individual consciousness of God were removed. Renan's emphasis on individual consciousness of God served to entice his pious reader to embrace this new Christianity, and in so doing, to embrace their own active participation in the advancement of their own spiritual life.

Renan issued a powerful call to his readers – to embrace the 'essence' of Christianity – one which Jesus' disciples were not sufficiently evolved to recognise, but one which Europe of the nineteenth century was finally prepared to comprehend. After eighteen centuries of history, the retrieval of true Christianity was finally possible. According to Renan, 'pure Christianity is again, after the passage of eighteen centuries, a universal and eternal religion'.[83] To renew itself, 'Christianity . . . only has to return to the Gospels . . . the spirit that Jesus introduced to the world is very much our own.'[84] Renan cast the 'essence of Christianity' and its retrieval from history as entailing the final embrace of Jesus by his readers.

In recreating Jesus' life, Renan claimed to achieve what no disciple of Jesus ever had – to fully understand Jesus – to fully grasp the essence of Christianity. Indeed, it was Renan's firm foothold in post-revolutionary France, his critical distance, which he claimed provided him with the scholarly and intellectual capacity to understand Jesus in ways that the writers of the Gospels could not – limited as they were by their more primitive civilisational context. Renan positioned himself as the first true disciple of Jesus. In so doing, he offered his readers the possibility of embracing the true Jesus and becoming Jesus' true disciples. Renan forged a direct link between the positivist historical time of human evolution and the eschatological time of Christianity. The revolution of Jesus was essential to the evolution of humanity. History became the evolution of religion, the continuous development of human consciousness of the Divine. *Life of Jesus* collapsed historical and theological utopias within Enlightenment humanism.

Renan, like his Muslim modernist counterparts, believed that historicism liberated the essence of Christianity from the Christianity of tradition, and in

---

[81] Renan, *Vie de Jésus*, 44.
[82] Renan, *Vie de Jésus*, 254.
[83] Renan, *Vie de Jésus*, 255.
[84] Renan, *Vie de Jésus*, 25.

so doing, enabled its re-embrace in the present. Renan was adamant that the revivification of religion – as rationalised, internalised and spiritualised consciousness of the Divine – was not only consistent with modernity, but essential to it. Man, he believed, needed religion as a motor of progress. Renan, like Ali, collapsed time, bridging the time of Jesus with that of contemporary France. Jesus' r/evolution was fulfilled by his embrace by contemporary Christianity – the fulfilment of human religious evolution expressed in civilisational revolution. For both Ali and Renan, their respective prophets were the origin of modernity, the fountainhead of *Liberté, Égalité, Fraternité*. Disenchantment was a means to re-enchantment – the rescue and embrace of the power of the true essence of Christianity, not its subjugation and imprisonment in tradition and dogma: 'Science, in complete freedom, without any other chains than that of reason, without any fixed symbols, without temples, without priests', Renan wrote, 'will flourish in what we call the profane world. This is the form of beliefs that alone, henceforth, will produce humanity.'[85]

Despite remarkable similarities between Renan's *Life of Jesus* and Ali's *Life of Mohammad*, there are also notable differences, particularly regarding the location and retrievability of truth, and the role of law. Renan's treatment of the Gospels contrasted markedly with Ali's treatment of the Quran and Hadith. Renan's *Life of Jesus* self-consciously hailed from the German Protestant tradition of biblical criticism, yet as the first Catholic contribution to the scholarly genre of what Albert Schweitzer would later call 'the quest of the historical Jesus',[86] Renan parted ways with the objectives of the long line of 'lives of Jesus' penned by German Protestant biblical critics.[87]

For Renan, the truth of Jesus simply was not retrievable from the Gospels. Renan treated the Gospels as profane sources, rejecting the Catholic imperative to believe in their Divine inspiration. Yet Renan also resisted the impulse of some of his German Protestant forerunners to succumb to an overempha-

---

[85] Renan, *L'Avenir de la Science*, 812.
[86] Schweitzer, *The Quest for the Historical Jesus*.
[87] Renan's *Life of Jesus* was characterised by 'historical and philological thought with a discernable German accent'. See Priest, *The Gospel According to Renan*, 38. Renan repeatedly invoked his indebtedness to Strauss' *Life of Jesus* (*Das Leben Jesu*) published in German in 1835, which, together with German Protestant biblical scholar Heinrich Ewald's *The History of Christ and his Time* (published in 1855), were the only two biographies of Jesus that he took along on his year's séjour in Palestine in 1860–1 where he penned *Vie de Jésus*. On Renan's indebtedness to Ewald's historical methodology, see Priest, *Gospel*, 55–6. Priest also notes that Renan asked the liberal Protestant theologian and exegete Edmond Henri Adophe Schérer (1815–89) to finish his *Life of Jesus* in the event that he died without completing it, something that came very close to actually happening. On Renan's serious study of German language, German philosophy, and eventually, German biblical criticism dating from his days at the St Sulpice seminary, see Priest, *Gospel*, 20–1, 56, 58. See also Psichari, *Renan d'après lui-même*, 195, 202.

sis on the literal text of the Gospels. Renan side-stepped the conventions of the 'quest of the historical Jesus' genre of exegesis, and paid little attention to reconciling the literary or linguistic details of the four Gospels with each other.[88] Renan insisted that the Gospels were merely a collection of contingent historical sources and should not be read for specific facts; their inconsistencies and corruptions simply could not be reconciled:

> The evangelists themselves, who have bequeathed us the image of Jesus, are so much beneath him about whom they speak, that they constantly disfigure him from their inability to attain to his height. Their writings are full of errors and incongruities. At every line, one feels a discourse of divine beauty, set down by narrators who do not understand it, and who substitute their own ideas for those which they have only half understood. On the whole, the character of Jesus, far from having been embellished by his biographies, has been diminished by them. [Textual] criticism, in order to recover him as he was, needs to discard a series of misconceptions, resulting from the mediocrity of spirit of his disciples. They painted him as they conceived of him, and often, fully believing that they were aggrandizing him, they have in reality diminished him.[89]

A critical reading of the Gospels thus should not attempt any reconciliation of the disparate 'facts' concerning Jesus, but must be read between the lines for the effect Jesus had on his disciples – the unconscious effects of being in his presence. Likening the Gospels to the verses of the Quran, Renan stated that 'the same inspiration penetrated them all and gave them unity'.[90] Renan likened this approach to interviewing witnesses under the presumption that each witness would have a mixture of perspectives, information and misunderstandings, which simply could not be reconciled with each other. The value of the witnesses should not be the extraction of 'fact' but the teasing out of what they had experienced, however fragmented, however imperfect.

In Renan's view, any attempt to reconcile the accounts of Jesus in the Gospels was not only impossible, but rendered irrelevant by the fact that the authors themselves had not grasped the essence of Jesus. Unable, unlike Jesus, to transcend the limitations of their historical context, the disciples, while profoundly affected by Jesus, were not capable of fundamentally comprehending his message. For Renan, therefore, the truth of Christianity, its inherent essence, was solely located in Jesus.

Ali concurred with Renan that the Gospels as sources offered little hope of retrieving the essence of Jesus, and argued that consequently there existed little possibility of identifying and resuscitating the essence of Christianity. One of the primary pillars of his claim for Islamic superiority to Christianity was the retrievability of Islamic essence, as opposed to the impossibility of

---

[88] Howard, *Religion and the Rise of Historicism*.
[89] Renan, *Vie de Jésus*, 256–7.
[90] Renan, *Vie de Jésus*, 98.

retrieving Christianity's essence. However, he fundamentally disagreed with Renan's suggestion of a hermeneutical equivalency between the Gospels and the Quran. Unlike the Gospels, he maintained, God's intent could be recovered from the Quran and Prophetic Hadith. The truth of Islam, Ali maintained, was located in the Quran, but also indirectly in Mohammad's comprehension and enactment of this eternal truth.

Whereas for Renan the essence of Jesus was equivalent to the essence of Christianity, for Ali, the essence of Islam was God's intent, located in the Quran, and correctly perceived and implemented by Mohammad. The Quran had to be read for God's intent, and the Hadith for the Prophet's comprehension and application of God's intent in historical context. Ali proposed a new, modern, historicist hermeneutics of the Quran. Context and essence needed to be distinguished in any reading of the Quran. Similarly, the Hadith could be read in order to distinguish the Prophet's understanding of God's intent, with its application within the limits of the possibility of context. In other words, both the Quran and the Hadith needed to be read for God's intent – and the texts themselves understood as navigating between authorial intent and audience context.

Renan and Ali's projects of recontextualisation also had different emphases. Renan's re-enchanted Christianity was entirely centred on individual spirituality. Spiritual progress, as man's ever greater consciousness of the Divine, was, he believed, the motor of civilisation and scientific progress, as it created possibilities of creativity, freedom of individual thought, and aesthetic sensibilities. Renan predicted:

> The world will ever be religious, and Christianity in a large sense is the last word in religion. Christianity is capable of indefinite [sic] transformations. All official organization of Christianity . . . is destined to disappear . . . The religious and utterly non-dogmatic principle proclaimed by Jesus will develop eternally, with infinite flexibility, bringing with it ever more advanced symbols and, in any case, creating forms of worship appropriate for the capacity of each according to the different stages of human culture.[91]

For Islamic modernists, modern religion had important spiritual dimensions but also served crucial institutional and social functions. Ali was deeply committed to individual spirituality – expressed in the cultivation of modern religious sensibilities and dispositions re-inscribed as Prophetic precedent. Unlike Renan, however, he also insisted on the necessity of reformulating Islamic law in harmony with modern values. For him, law, once it had been recontextualised, could serve as a crucial motor of progress. Ali's vision of social change was two pronged: it depended on institutional change as the manifestation of Islamic essence in harmony with 'circumstances of the age', working in concert with the construction of modern individuals imbued

---

[91] Renan, 'L'avenir religieux des sociétés modernes', 403.

with the sensibilities and dispositions of modern Islam. For Ali, it was the interdependence of institutions and individuals – the synergy produced by greater consciousness of the Divine manifest in both individual characters and institutions – that alone would enable progress into the modern.

As discussed in Chapter 3, one of the common arguments prevalent in nineteenth-century European Christian religious studies scholarship was that Christian superiority rested on the absence of law, in deliberate contradistinction to the Semitic religions of Judaism and Islam. Such arguments suggested that Christianity was less concrete, less particular, less context-dependent, and by extension, more spiritual, more abstract and more transcendent of historical particularism – in other words, the only religion capable of true universalism. Ali, as discussed in previous chapters, argued the opposite: that Jesus' failure to implement essence in context – in the form of law – led to the demise, and ultimately, the erasure of true Christianity from history. After all, Ali and other modernists insisted, religion must be practical. Religion needed to be a vehicle for progress as God's intent.

The differences between Renan's *Life of Jesus* and Ali's *Life of Mohammad* are symptomatic of their different religious contexts and understandings of the political, cultural and social needs of their respective audiences. Renan, operating in nineteenth-century France, offered a compelling alternative to Catholicism – not for those who remained deeply committed to the Church or those for whom religion itself was irretrievably irrational, but for those who remained profoundly ambivalent. As Robert Priest noted, *Life of Jesus* 'enraged and entranced generations of French men and women because it presented a new Jesus for the nineteenth century'.[92] *Life of Jesus* permitted the deliverance from dogma, from tradition as unchanging precedent and canonical, definitive truth; freedom to reimagine religion, to move it squarely out of institutional authority into the realm of the individual conscious agent. *Life of Jesus* replaced the performance of ritual obedience with spiritual 'becoming' as an alternative pious sensibility. *Life of Jesus* offered an imaginative possible Christianity, enabling a re-enchantment with religion through its definitive severing from history – this was a rationalised, individualised and spiritualised Christianity firmly divorced from Catholic history and tradition. Renan's 'essence' of Christianity, its beauty, its rejection of definition, existed only in the spiritual consciousness of his readers. It opened up individual agency; it made possible the redefinition of Christianity as faith and as practice. This alternative was deeply embedded in the tradition of Enlightenment humanism and rationalist anti-clericalism, and clearly struck a chord with the spiritual needs of the nineteenth-century French public.[93]

---

[92] Priest, *Gospel*, 3.
[93] Renan's *Life of Jesus*, first published in 1863, was widely denounced by both Protestant religious studies scholars and by Catholic defenders of tradition. Even so, it enjoyed enormous popular consumption and resonated deeply with large segments of the French public, going through eight editions in only three months.

Ali, primarily addressing an audience of Indian Muslims, but also imagining his audience to include all members of the Muslim *umma*, was equally committed to reconciling the disenchantment implicit in historicism, with the eternal relevance of religion. He, however, conceded that the very European expansionist powers that threatened Muslim countries were the very same powers that had become modern. His *Life of Mohammad*, thus, was a seminal component of his larger project of proposing a practical set of objectives that, if embraced, could enable India and other Muslim countries to similarly become modern and reassert sovereignty.

Despite clear differences in their audiences, religious traditions and political contexts, Renan's Catholic modernism and Ali's Islamic modernism were remarkably similar in their quest not to reconcile religion with modernity, but to unify the two. Modernists were committed to preserving a role for religion in modernity – in the necessity of religion's rational re-enchantment. Like Islamic modernists, Renan argued that dogma, tradition and orthodoxy were indefensible when subjected to the rational scrutiny enabled by historicism. 'The modern spirit is well-considered intellect', Renan declared. Moreover, the definitions and articulations of religion had to evolve in harmony with greater religious consciousness; religion had evolved, and the residue of earlier, more primitive conceptions needed to be revised. Renan stated that

> belief in revelation, in a supernatural order, is the antithesis of criticism, it is the remnant of the old anthropomorphic conception of the world, formed in an era when man had not yet arrived at a clear understanding of the laws of nature.[94]

Likewise, for Ali, Mohammad represented the unity of truth:

> To Mohammed the fundamental laws of Truth and Nature, which seem innate in the moral Consciousness of Humanity – are the essence of Divine ordinances. They are as much laws, in the strictest sense of the word, as the laws which regulate the movements of the celestial bodies.[95]

Religious modernists were propelled by the profound conviction that rationalism failed to accommodate the necessity and utility of religion beyond instrumentalist arguments concerning social function. They proposed a third way, between an unrelenting rationalism and the maintenance of ossified tradition. Religious modernists proposed to integrate religion and science – methodologically and conceptually. They advocated a rationalisation of religion, yet at the same time insisted that religious truth existed and

Eighteen months after its initial publication, it had sold 168,000 copies. See Priest, *Gospel*, 110.

[94] Renan, *L'Avenir de la Science*, 764.
[95] Ali, *Life and Teachings of Mohammed*, 299.

could be identified and retrieved from the inaccuracies of history. Religion must, they believed, continue to animate modern mankind. The desacralisation of tradition via historicism permitted the resacralisation of God's intent as manifest in human religious evolution.

Modernists were committed to the ongoing centrality of religion to man's nature. Man as *homo religiosus* could not dispense with religion. *Life of Jesus*, like *Life of Mohammad*, permitted the deliverance from dogma and from tradition as unchanging precedent and canonical, definitive truth. At the same time, these works both enabled the freedom to reimagine religion and to move religion squarely out of external institutional authority into the realm of the individual conscious agent. Renan and Ali replaced the performance of ritual obedience with the cultivation of modern sensibilities and dispositions as more evolved expressions of piety.

Renan painted a powerful, spiritually satisfying alternative to Catholicism, one which absorbed Catholic sensibilities, even as it promoted the liberation of the individual from the Catholic Church. This was Renan's objective in his *Life of Jesus*, the work that most fully embodied his religious project and which he considered his 'life's greatest work'.[96] Islamic modernists similarly liberated Muslims from the clutches of tradition and invited them to embrace true Islam as modern and universalist. For all religious modernists, deliverance from dogma and freedom to reinterpret religion thus went hand in hand. It is here, in this scientific project of reconstruction, of reconciliation, of the revivification of religion, that we need to locate nineteenth-century religious modernisms. Historicism permitted the destruction of accepted truths, even as it permitted the retrieval of the enduring essence of truth: 'the reconstitution of the sacred in the very act of its destruction'.[97]

---

[96] Renan attested to this in a letter to his wife dated 14 August 1861. Psichari, *Renan d'après lui-même*, 222.
[97] Lee, *Ernest Renan*, 106.

CONCLUSION:
GOD'S INTENT – THE RE-ENCHANTMENT OF THE SACRED IN THE AGE OF HISTORY

The break between science and religion, which is noticed from time to time in various peoples, belongs to a certain period of their development. It happens sometimes from a lack of knowledge, sometimes from a lack of understanding of religion. But the ultimate ideal toward which mankind is striving, and the ultimate goal of his development on Earth, is the merging of religion and science, of those highest regions of the spiritual world of man.[1]

Imam Bayezidof (1883)

Religions, by whatever names they are called, all resemble each other. No agreement and no reconciliation are possible between these religions and philosophy. Religion imposes on man its faith and its belief, whereas philosophy frees him of it totally or in part.[2]

Jamal al-Din al-Afghani (1883)

Modernity as Translation

Nineteenth-century religious modernists were committed to the centrality of religion to humankind, and believed that religious essence, once identified, could be recovered from the detritus of history and recontextualised in the present. Religious modernism was a project of the re-enchantment of the sacred in the age of history. Islamic modernists, in particular, were animated by the desire to revivify religion and in so doing, to claim modernity.

Religion, modernists believed, in its current form and practice, was incompatible with historicist conceptions of mankind and of history, and with new scientific truths and methods. For some 'secular' modernists, historicism demonstrated the fallacy of religion. For them, religion was disenchanted

---

[1] Baiazitov, 'A Refutation', 41.
[2] *Journal des débats politiques et littéraires*, Friday, 18 May 1883, 3.

and belonged to traditional, more primitive understandings of the world. For religious modernists, however, religious truth was not reducible to tradition, dogma or religious institutions. For religious modernists, religious reform was as inescapable as it was desirable. Historicism provided the means to retrieve the true essence of religion from the detritus of history. The project of religious modernism entailed identifying religious essence, cleansing it of the tarnish of tradition, and re-embedding it the present. Disenchantment as contextualisation was a means to re-enchantment as recontextualisation.

An exploration of Islamic modernists in comparative perspective teases apart the tangle of modernity and historicism and reveals their different, albeit interconnected, strands. Comparison also reveals similarities and differences among religious modernisms and forces us to account for them. Moreover, it suggests ways of conceptualising modernities, and modernity's complicated relationship with Europe, in new and fruitful ways.

By approaching modernity, historicism and the Enlightenment as distinct phenomena, their connections and causal relationships with each other become apparent. Historicism emerged out of the crucible of the Scientific Revolution and the Enlightenment, in a Europe utterly entangled in the world. The contours of historicism emerged and solidified over the course of the eighteenth century. The new landscape of historicism demanded that religion, science and history be recalibrated. Historicism, I argue, is not synonymous with modernity, but productive of it. Historicism was the soil in which modernity was cultivated. Modernity thus, is revealed to be a claim, or set of claims, produced by the adoption of historicism. Religion, through its passage through the landscape of historicism, was redefined and relocated.

As modernity self-defined vis-à-vis its constructed 'other' – tradition – it drew a metaphorical line in the sand. Clearly, this line, and the definitions that sustained it, was a claim that erased more complex realities. However, this claim did reflect a different truth – that to be 'modern' was to reject 'tradition'. Religion thus, to become modern – to cross the 'line in the sand' – needed to effect a rupture with tradition – methodologically and epistemologically. Religion, in order to become modern, underwent a process of translation.

Consider translation as having two principle pairs of components. The first pair consists of the from/to textual element – the text translated 'from' and the text translated 'to' – the raw material as it were and the finished product. The second pair consists of the translator as author and the intended audience. The author makes decisions about what and how to translate based on their understanding of the needs and comprehension of their audience, in other words, taking into account both the audience's historical context and their hermeneutic possibilities. The audience is ever-present in the decisions and strategies of the translator.

If we imagine translation to be a metaphor for religious modernism, the religious modernists are the translators/authors – the agents of translation. They translated 'traditional' religion into 'modern' religion via historicism in accordance with the needs and understanding of their audience. I underline this point as a way of insisting that translation – as religious modernism, or as modernisation more broadly conceived – is necessarily audience-dependent. This metaphor is useful for thinking about the relationship of religion to modernity. It is especially illuminating, however, when we consider modernisation, and religious modernism more specifically, outside of Europe.

Typically absent in accounts of modernisation outside Europe is agency. Modernisation is characterised as a process of replication of European models, and measured along a linear continuum ranging from imitation and adaptation to rejection. In this formula, modernity is produced in Europe and disseminated elsewhere. European modernity remains the yardstick against which all other modernities are measured according to degrees of deviation or fidelity to the European model. Considering modernisation as a process of translation, however, underscores the from/to element, as well as the agency of author and the relevance of audience. It suggests that 'from' and 'to' must necessarily be local, even as it allows for inspiration based on non-local models. In other words, modernity is necessarily a product of the translation from an indigenous 'traditional' to an indigenous 'modern', regardless of the models or inspirations deployed.

The exploration of translation must also be extended to the subject/object of translation itself. For example, the adoption of 'European' military technology or constitutionalism did not follow the same dynamics, imperatives, or relationship of author to audience as did the adoption of the novel as a genre, or western-style painting techniques. The adoption of military technology, while certainly imbued with its own attendant cultures of regularisation, of standardisation which extended beyond the technology itself to impact notions of organisation, was less subject to the necessity of translation than was the adoption of literary and artistic forms.[3] Military technology was considerably more independent of both author and audience; less culturally conditional. The same holds true for constitutionalism. Advocates conceived of constitutions as 'modern' but not inherently 'French' or 'European'. Constitutions were context-dependent, but this context was the civilisational level of 'modernity'. In their view, constitutionalism was a 'modern' institution, not a European institution. The universal nature of constitutionalism was further reinforced by the existence of indigenous Islamic precedents which enabled advocates to claim an Islamic genealogy of origins, independent of European models.

The adoption of the literary and artistic forms of the novel and paint-

---

[3] I am not arguing that there was no process of translation, since technologies did indeed require supporting cultural structures and attitudes. I am arguing, however, that this was a matter of degree, and that the adoption of military technology was not understood or experienced in the same way as more culturally specific forms, such as the novel or European-painting styles. On the cultural transformations attendant to shifts in time technology, see Wishnitzer, *Reading Clocks* 'Alla Turca'.

ing, by contrast, were much more dependent on authorial agency and the author's appreciation of audience. For instance, prominent Ottoman intellectual Ahmet Midhat Efendi's adoption of the novel as a genre was deeply linked to his intentions to foster new individual subjectivities in a growing Ottoman reading public. As he rifled through French novels and newspaper articles, searching for ideas and plots as inspiration for his own works, he negotiated his own didactic intentions within the terrain of his audiences' needs and capacities. Ahmet Midhat, in his 1875 novel *Felatun Bey and Rakım Efendi*, deployed strategies from Victorian literature to create agency in his readership, not only modelling citizenship through the content of the novel, but allowing the readers to participate and practice agency through the act of reading itself. As I have argued elsewhere, Ahmet Midhat was an 'agent of translation' and engaged in 'creative innovation'.[4] As he himself noted, his 'translations' of French novels were not intended to be literal renditions, so much as inspirations for his own, distinctly Ottoman project.

The adoption of certain techniques or technologies should not be reduced to a process of imitation or replication. Ahmet Midhat's deployment of the novel for his own purposes, many of which paralleled those of his European literary counterparts, does not in and of itself dictate the use that these forms were put to, or their intended products. One cannot, therefore, conceive of epistemologies as inert. Ahmet Midhat, while firmly committed to retaining the relevance of Islam, fundamentally recast it within a 'modern' historicist epistemology. So, if we assert that his framework remained 'Islamic', we must nevertheless be careful not to essentialise 'Islam' or assert its historical stability. Understanding Ahmet Midhat's project as one of translation, from the Ottoman traditional to the Ottoman modern, more aptly captures the imperatives and agency of his own intentionality and his relationship with his audience.

Taken more broadly, we need to see modernisation as a process of translation from the constructed 'traditional' to the constructed 'modern', not as a process of adapting European modernities into other, non-European contexts. Modernity was not a seed produced on a European plant and carried on the wind to germinate elsewhere. Rather, modernity was the product both of shared and different terrains. This rendition moves us away from a European story of modernity's diffusion to the rest of the world, allows us to abandon the irresolvable conundrum of finding a 'true' immutable definition of modernity, and frees us to investigate and compare modernities as clusters of claims in context. Recentring reform in its various contexts and meanings, rather than assuming they are pale approximations of European

---

[4] Ringer, 'Beyond Binaries: Ahmet Midhat Efendi's Prescriptive Modern'. For key works on Ahmet Midhat Efendi in English, see Levi and Ringer (trans.), *Felatun Bey and Rakım Efendi*. See also Demircioğlu, 'Translating Europe: The Case of Ahmet Midhat as an Ottoman Agent of Translation'; and Tufekçioğlu, 'The Islamic Epistemology in a Western Genre', 7–15.

reforms, allows us to recalibrate questions of causality, European influence, argumentation and intent. It also allows us to emphasise the variety of sources of models, possibilities and discourses available to reformers, rather than focusing solely on the European. In addition to Europe, reform programmes in other Middle Eastern and South Asian societies, together with intellectually rich indigenous traditions, provided many sources and models of reform.

The project of modernity, therefore, must be seen in comparative perspective. Translation is not imitation; parallel processes based on local relevance and imperatives are not acts of imitation. The fact that reformers were engaged with religious reform in many parts of the world suggests that reformers hailing from a wide geographic area all perceived certain needs similarly, even as they addressed those needs in context-dependent and audience-dependent ways. Reformers, and the reforms they spearheaded, should be understood as 'creative innovators' – as agents of translation.

Modernities and Difference

Commitments to the translation of religion into the modern were shared amongst religious modernisms in various religious traditions. This is not coincidental, but stems from the shared embrace of historicism as epistemology and method. At the same time, it is important not to diminish differences between religious modernisms – both between religious traditions, but equally, within religious traditions. Context cannot be viewed simplistically as denoting religious tradition, but must include diverse localised factors. It is not a binary of un/belonging, but rather one of multiple layers.

Despite the powerful similarities which characterised them, Islamic modernist responses to the challenges of historicism were not identical. It is crucial to explore varieties within the larger category of Islamic modernism as a function of the constellation of particular contexts that individual practitioners operated within. Contexts include the political and cultural, but also the oft-neglected Islamic. Islamic tradition, far from denoting a uniform set of beliefs, practices and theological discussions, represents a complex, at times even contradictory, set of ideas, approaches, problems, solutions and articulations – each of which operated within its particular field in time and space, but also differently over time and space. Islamic tradition was a house with many rooms. Islamic modernists operated within these overlapping Islams and Islamic traditions, drawing on common, as well as less-shared strains within Islamic thought. In addition to imagining 'Islams' and 'Islamic traditions' as fields with continually reshaping contours, we also must investigate ways in which Islamic modernisms participated in this reshaping. For example, many modernists referenced classical theologian and jurisprudent Hamid al-Ghazzali (d. 1111) as evidence of the long-standing centrality of rationalism within Islamic tradition. Quite apart from the discussion of Ghazzali's thought in his own intellectual context, our obligation as historians is to determine how Ghazzali's thought was variously represented and given meaning in the project of Islamic modernism. As argued by Said Özervarlı, Ghazzali was understood to demonstrate the existence of a strong rationalist tradition in Islam, but more particularly, represented the capacity of Islam to absorb different strains of thought – in other words, to synthesise and adapt.[5] Islamic modernist references to Ghazzali established an Islamic precedent of synthesis, providing the translation process with an indigenous genealogy.

The emergence of religious modernisms in the nineteenth century also shared significant intellectual overlap with religious fundamentalisms. Both were built on the bedrock of historicism and conceived of modernity as a rupture in time; both called for a rejection of tradition and concomitant 'return to the Quran' as the location of truth, the imperative of denouncing precedent as irrelevant, and of the 'opening the gates of *ijtihad*' as a means of 'identification and retrieval of Islamic truth' and its recontextualisation in the present. Fundamentalists may not have shared the same commitment to 'modern values' or the self-awareness of their project as 'modernising' as did Islamic modernists, but differences in values and self-ascribed identity within the tradition notwithstanding, fundamentalism too must be seen as a product of historicism.

Modernity's Complicated Relationship with Europe

The project of Islamic modernism was complicated by the region's relationship to Europe. On the one hand, the penetration of historicism meant that reformers accepted its epistemology and methodology as true. The landscape of historicism was not perceived by Islamic modernists as a foreign or imported one. Islamic modernists did not view their project of religious reform as a project of imitation or adaption of European models. Truth, they believed, was not culturally determined; it was not 'owned' by Europe, it had no 'author'. Instead, historicism as epistemology and methodology were inherently compatible with religious essence. Islamic modernists understood their project of religious reform as a rescue operation, not as one of destruction; modern Islam was true Islam, released from the falsity of tradition.

At the same time, Islamic modernists' relationship with Europe was effected by political and intellectual asymmetries. The power disparity between European great powers and Islamic lands in the Middle East and South Asia provided a powerful impetus to reform, and to reform quickly. Moreover, Europe was widely perceived as having achieved 'modernity'. European great powers served as empirical examples of the capacity of

---

[5] On the role of Ghazzali as exemplifying integration of ideas, see Özervarlı, 'Ottoman Perceptions of al-Ghazzali's Works', 260. For some scholars in the nineteenth century, Mu'tazila philosophy demonstrated Islam's capacity for rationalism, integration and synthesis. See Martin, *Defenders of Reason in Islam*, 2.

modernisation to generate power, and thus as examples of possible models of modernity. The Islamic modernist project, beyond occupying itself with the location of essence and the revivification of Islam in the modern, was deeply concerned with identifying prerequisites of modernity. Indeed, the whole purpose of religious reform was the generation of modernity. Islamic modernists' advocacy of the construction of modern Muslim subjectivities, therefore, was consciously intended to enable Islamic countries to become modern. They believed that the adoption of modern ideals and practices were generative of political and economic strength, and that Islam, reformed and reconceived as modern Islam, could and would serve as the causal agent of modernity.

The emphasis on the generative capacity of modern religion to facilitate the adoption of modern sensibilities and dispositions which would then lead to scientific progress and political and economic strength was a primary leitmotiv of Islamic modernist thought. Islamic modernists were firmly convinced that religious tradition as content, together with traditionalism as method, were inhibitors of progress and civilisation, and that only the redefinition and relocation of Islam could enable their societies to generate 'modern' progress and civilisation. Modernity hinged on the capacity to rid Islam of tradition and traditionalism.

The increasingly interconnected and interpenetrated world – which was experienced particularly intensely in the Middle East/South Asia/European realms – meant that participation as equal partners, versus subjugation as inferior partners, in the newly developing international systems of exchange and connectivity necessitated the competitive development of similar infrastructures and systems. Identifying the European 'secret of strength' therefore was a necessary and intrinsic part of determining the prerequisites for modernity: what were and were not essential? There was of course, a spectrum of thought, but also general agreement that certain features were necessary. These features included, but were not limited to: the rationalisation of bureaucracy and administration, the regularisation of financial and commercial spheres, the secularisation of education and law, and the development of a participatory citizenry. Modernising reformers, far from seeking to imitate Europe, therefore, sought to identify and develop institutions and ideas that would meet their own needs – needs which they had in common with many other modernising societies, in Europe and beyond. To the extent that they did borrow from Europe, such borrowing was conditional on its local relevance.

Institutions and the cultures that sustained them were advocated by reformers as necessary in order to meet new needs and to participate as equal partners on the world stage. Even as Europe was a model of the power of modern sensibilities, values and systems to generate economic and political power, it was an existential threat that undergirded the urgency that reformers felt to accommodate and compete in these new systems at the trans-local level. Not all reformers were committed to religious reform as essential to modernity. Some modernising reformers considered Islam to be inimical to modernity. For others, however, who believed that modern ideals were synonymous with the essence of Islam, it was the form and space of Islam, not the essence of Islam, that prevented progress.

In the intellectual realm, Islamic modernists had to navigate amongst the powerful established intellectual frameworks that emerged and solidified in Europe. The universal religious/civilisational taxonomy, together with the criteria of 'advanced' and 'primitive' religions/cultures were fully operational. The fact that these definitions and criteria were generated in a largely Protestant context, and that they not surprisingly were used to confirm Protestant claims to civilisational and religious superiority, made the project of deploying these intellectual frameworks more complicated.

European historical and religious studies scholarship, operating within a dominant Protestant paradigm, claimed that European modernity was the exclusive consequence of European Christian agency. European scholars claimed that Protestant Christianity was superior to other religions, and buttressed this by proffering an exclusively European genealogy of modernity, a genealogy which was justified as historically cum scientifically verifiable. Islamic modernists rejected European scholarly claims to exceptionalism and marshalled historical evidence to demonstrate its fundamental fallacy, according the very same criteria of civilisation.

The question remains, however, what the relationship is between religious modernisms and Protestantism. Was Protestantism the model for all other modern religions? Were other religious modernisms essentially replicas of Protestantism? The question is a difficult one. Leonora Batnitzky argues that 'religion is a modern German Protestant category that Judaism does not quite fit into'.[6] The same could be said for Catholic, Zoroastrian, Muslim and Hindu religious modernist projects. Yet while acknowledging that the criteria of modern religion were developed in scholarly realms dominated by Protestants, it does not necessarily follow that all nineteenth-century religious modernisms were replications of Protestantism. This assumption essentialises modern religion and accepts Protestant claims of ownership of modernity. The Enlightenment was not a Protestant enterprise. Historicism did not emerge in a uniquely Protestant context. Nor was Protestantism, despite the powerful authority of the European Protestant religious studies community by the nineteenth century, undisputedly the most modern religion.

One might instead suggest that if we disaggregate claims from facts, and historicism from modernity, then we are left with many religious traditions that were forced to recalibrate 'religion' in accordance with historicism. It would then be a matter of exploring the different relationships of these religious traditions to the possibilities and restrictions attendant in historicism. Sorkin argues persuasively for the religious multivalence of 'religious enlighteners' in the Enlightenment:

---

[6] Batnitzky, *How Judaism Became a Religion*, 13.

> The religious Enlightenment was not confined to any one denomination in one country or group of countries but crossed religious and national borders, encompassing Protestantism, Catholicism, and Judaism in a number of polities ... To account for the religious Enlightenment requires a comparative history of religion that, while respecting enduring differences, emphasizes shared developments.[7]

Protestantism may have been more easily rendered 'modern', but this might also be to ignore the long process of translation. Other religious traditions, whether Catholic, Hindu, Zoroastrian or Islamic, did not view their projects as replications of Protestantism; nor did they necessarily accept Protestant claims to superiority. Did this mean that modernists refused to admit that their projects were largely imitative? The question might be illuminated if we consider the issue of law. As Batnitzky elaborates, 'from the eighteenth century onward, modern Jewish thinkers have been concerned with the question of whether or not Judaism can fit into a modern, Protestant category of religion' given Judaism's traditional emphasis on law and practice.[8] Islam and Zoroastrianism faced similar challenges to the concept of law. In neither of these religious traditions did religious modernists view the existence of law as a fundamental barrier to the translation of religion into the modern. Zoroastrian modernists largely abandoned law, whereas Muslim modernists argued for its retention.[9] Syed Ameer Ali saw no irreconcilable tension between an internalised faith and the centrality of religious law, when he wrote:

> Our relations with our Creator are matters of conscience; our relations with our fellow beings must be matters of positive rules; and what higher sanction – to use a legal expression – can be attached for the enforcement of the relative duties of man to man, than the sanction of religion ... religion ought to mean the rule of life; its chief object ought to be the elevation of Humanity towards that perfection which is the end of our existence.[10]

Bayezidof expressed a similar sentiment, when he wrote:

> The task of modern science should consist of finding a starting point for the establishment of mutual understanding between science and religion for the collective reaching of truth ... Having established a tight mutual bond between these two regions of the spiritual world of man, religious feeling and reason, we will together be able to get rid of the fanaticism of religious fanatics and

---

[7] Sorkin, *Religious Enlightenment*, 5.
[8] Batnitzky, *How Judaism Became a Religion*, 1.
[9] On nineteenth-century Zoroastrian religious reform in India and Iran, see Ringer, *Pious Citizens*.
[10] Ali, *Life and Teachings of Mohammad*, 185.

the fanaticism of the fanatics of science, and then religion and science will harmoniously go on together on the road toward the acquisition of those truths, higher ideals of intelligent morality and virtue, that constitute the final goal of man on earth.[11]

It is not clear to me, therefore, that religious modernists were engaged with reconciling their religious traditions into an existing 'modern' so much as they were engaged in a process of translation and construction of their own modern. In other words, they were forced to navigate the landscape of historicism, but they chose their own route. To insist that modern religion is essentially Protestant is to ignore the varieties of modern religions, to privilege some over others as more 'modern', and to overlook the very long and arduous process of Protestantism's own translation into the modern.

Translation as the Redefinition and Relocation of Religion

Historicism made religious reform imperative and provided the intellectual framework that enabled both its deconstruction and reconstruction. Religious modernists engaged in a two-step process of redefining and relocating religion. The first was to identify and retrieve religious essence from historical context. The second was to recontextualise essence appropriate for the modern context. The necessary rejection of tradition was a civilisational rupture. Religious modernism involved the translation of religion into the modern; historicism was the method employed to cross modernity's 'line in the sand'.

Methodologically, Islamic modernists proposed a new hermeneutical approach to the Quran and Hadith. Islamic essence was conceived of as the transcendent values prescribed by God. Islamic modernists, deploying historicism, insisted that truth was not located in tradition. Tradition, imagined as the accumulation of past interpretations of the Quran and/or Prophetic Hadith, were replicated as true, but tradition assumed that history was 'flat' and without contextual ruptures. Islamic modernists fundamentally rejected the concept of tradition as enduring precedent, and traditionalism as a methodology of precedent. Islamic modernists did not argue that past interpretations were inherently false, only that they were permanently tethered to their own particular contexts. As context changed, tradition increasingly diverged from and became irrelevant to changed circumstances. The problem, as Islamic modernists perceived it, was not the existence of past interpretations themselves, but their trans-contextual perpetuation into the present. As Syed Ameer Ali explained, 'Islam is elastic and deliberately so. Laws should not be perpetuated as expressions of context, but must be continually re-expressed and re-contextualized.'[12]

---

[11] Baiazitov, 'A Refutation', 41.
[12] Ali, *Life and Teachings of Mohammad*, 227.

Historicism enabled Islamic essence to be identified, extracted from historical context and recontextualised in the present. The Quran had to be read as embodying eternal essence, even as it conveyed this essence in language designed for a particular audience. Likewise, the Hadith had to be threshed to separate the Prophet's understanding of God's intent from his translation of God's intent into his own particular historical context. As Ali explained, the Quran contained both God's words for all humankind for all eternity together with God's words directed at the Prophet's historical context. The Prophet, with the benefit of Divine guidance, understood God's intent and translated it into practice – he enacted God's intent within the limits of possibility of his own particular context.

Islamic modernists believed that only this two-step procedure – the identification and subsequent relocation of essence – would free Islam from tradition and enable it to serve again as a motor of progress. This project of disenchantment and re-enchantment was understood as one of recovery, not divergence – a realignment, not a departure. Modern Islam was cast as a return to truth, the rectification of the distortions of tradition and the reignition of Islam's essential progressive capacity.

The new, 'modern' Islamic methodology involved the juxtaposition of the particular (as specific historical context) with the universal (as the essence of Islam). By extracting the essence of Islam from history as a sequence of particular pasts, Islamic modernists restored the enduring meaning of Islam for the universal future. Particularism and universalism signified more than context versus essence. They also were the brightest stars in their respective constellations of attributes. These constellations can be rendered respectively as universalism, agency, essence, interiority, spirituality, 'becoming', individualism, future and critical inquiry, juxtaposed with particularism, passivity, context, formalism, ritual observance, obedience, societal constrictions, past and tradition. Looking at these attributes as they operate and reflect each other as a cluster illuminates the important connection between universalism and agency, the freedom to develop an interiorised individual consciousness and its dependence on ahistoricity. In other words, individual agency and ahistoricity, as the rejection of historical dependency (particularism), are embedded in the concept of universalism. Particularism, by contrast, is associated with the inability of the individual to transcend social norms, religious tradition or ritual obedience. In these conditions, the individual is prevented from acquiring agency and thus cannot serve as the motor of social progress. Societies with 'particularistic' religions were thus condemned to remain in the past, as artefacts of earlier, more primitive stages of evolution. Essence as ahistoricity is explicitly universalist, whereas context is inherently particular, historically bound. The competition to claim universalism by Christians and Muslims alike must be understood as operating within this web of meanings.

The definition of 'modern' Islam was inextricably bound to the relocation of Islam in time/place. Islam was defined as rational, ethical and based on the individual's consciousness of God. Modernists were committed to 'the unity of truth' – the notion that religious truth must be compatible with natural, scientific truth. Afghani stated this simply when he declared that 'the laws of nature, geometric proofs, and philosophical demonstrations are self-evident truths. Thus, someone who says, "My religion is inconsistent with self-evident truths," has inevitably passed judgment on the falsity of his religion.'[13] Despite their insistence on the social utility of prescriptive practices and law, modernists constructed Islam as primarily an ethical prompt. Practices were not important in and of themselves, but only for their capacity to regulate society and to encourage the development of individual pious sensibilities and dispositions. Intent, therefore, triumphed over practice – only insofar as practice embodied intent, was it considered valuable. External observances, in their view, were replaced with the development of modern subjectivities.

The individual was at the centre of modern Islam, as both the subject and object of progress and civilisation. Modern Islam was grounded on the individual's consciousness of the Divine. The internalisation of ethics rejected the performance of ritual as obedience, emphasising the imbuing of all actions with the recognition and embrace of God's intent as progress and civilisation. Obedience to God shifted from the observance of ritual practices, to the internalisation of ethics and the cultivation of the sensibilities and dispositions of the modern pious individual. For Bayezidof, this was a process of enlightenment. He wrote that 'just as the intellectual condition of people is varied, consequently the understanding of the divine and of the laws of nature is varied. God reveals Himself to man to the extent to which man is able to understand Him, and therefore it is necessary for everyone to develop his intellect.'[14]

The individual was imagined as participatory – conscious of and willing to accept the need for social and political reform. Modern pious individuals, as citizens, sustained and supported objectives of intellectual, political and social reform – and as such, were believed to be generative of modern society. Not surprisingly, nineteenth-century modernising reformers – whether religious or political– emphasised the fashioning of modern individuals as the indispensable component of constructing citizens and modern society.[15] The individual emerged as the subject and object of reform – both as the agent and the *raison d'être* of social change. The construction of the individual as citizen, as opposed to subject, was mirrored in shifting notions of individual agency. Citizens, unlike subjects, were their own agents in

---

[13] Afghani delivered this lecture on Thursday, 8 November 1882 in Albert Hall, Calcutta. Afghani, 'Lecture on Teaching and Learning', 108.

[14] Baiazitov, 'A Refutation', 41.

[15] Hadley, *Living Liberalism*. The emphasis on character formation as central to the construction of modern citizens is ubiquitous in Middle Eastern and South Asian social, political and religious reform in the nineteenth century. See Ringer, *Pious Citizens*.

the project of self-fashioning. Ali's notion of the interplay between society and the individual, between sensibilities and political institutions or, as he phrased it, between 'moral regeneration and social reform', were not simply related objectives, but mutually constitutive. Islamic modernists insisted that modern Islam embodied the attributes of modern citizens: pious individuals were thus the motor of modernity.

The individual moved firmly into the centre of the divine plan of human history – not only as the recipient of salvation but as the agent able to create the future. Individuals were sovereign in their political life – as participatory citizens – and sovereign in their religious life – as participatory souls. The individual was therefore both the subject and object of God's intent – the fulfilment of which was equivalent to the progress of humanity.

Locating modern religion within the moral consciousness of the individual redefined the idea of *jahiliyya*. Traditionally understood as a time period, the 'Age of Ignorance' which preceded the revelation of the Quran to the Prophet Mohammad, *jahiliyya* was a time of warfare, injustice and ignorance of religious truth. In the nineteenth century, *jahiliyya* also invoked the interior moral struggle in each individual's consciousness. The Prophet's struggle was universalised and interiorised as the perpetual Manichean battle between light and darkness, truth and falsehood, civilisational progress and backwardness. The centrality of the individual as both object and agent of progress also effected changes in the concept of the *umma* – the Muslim community. Older geographically specific concepts of *Dar al-Harb* and *Dar al-Islam* (the domains of War, and Islam, respectively) gave way to the 'Muslim World' as the sum total of all individual Muslims. Just as the *jahiliyya* was a battle divorced from chronological time, so too was the *umma*, as the new 'Muslim World', divorced from physical space and relocated in the interiorised consciousness of all Muslims.

Despite the adoption of historicism and notions of historical time as consonant with civilisational progress, progress itself was not voided of sacred content. Older notions of time as beginning and ending with Paradise, as past expulsion followed by future redemption, were folded into new historicist and evolutionary understandings of the progress of civilisation. Fulfilment of God's wishes moved away from being the performance of prescriptive ritual observances, towards an all-inclusive interiorised ethic whereby all behaviour was subsumed in the ethical imperative to express God's intent. The project of religious modernism, rather than entailing the marginalisation of religion, was in fact the opposite – the complete enveloping of all life into the sacred enactment of God's intent.

Secularism is religion redefined and relocated in the modern, not its rejection or absence. The spaces of pious practice may have shifted away from the public sphere even as piety assumed a larger role in the individual's relationship to society. For example, secularising programmes in the nineteenth-century Ottoman Empire and Iran sought to expand state control over law and education and, in the case of the Ottoman Empire, to equalise legal rights between Muslims and non-Muslim Ottomans. This did not mean the absence of 'religion' from law or education, or the end of religious sensibilities. In the Middle East and South Asia, the emphasis on public equality of rights and responsibilities was also sustained by the de-emphasis of expressions of religious difference in public. In other words, as the performance of piety moved from the public to the private sphere, thus constructing and defining them, piety itself was given further impetus through Islamic modernist emphasis on the pious citizen as fulfilling God's intent.[16] The emergence of secularism invites us to investigate religion's relocation, not to presume its absence.

Islamic modernists likened their project of religious modernism to the civilisational revolution effected by the Prophet Mohammad. For them, the Prophet grasped the torch of civilisation and, in so doing, crossed a civilisational threshold from paganism to monotheism. The Prophet's success hinged on his transcendence – his capacity to understand Divine intent and express it productively in context. Islamic modernists claimed the mantle of the Prophet for themselves, by enabling the civilisational leap into modernity via the construction of modern Islam. Because the essence of Islam was equivalent to 'modern' values, modern Islam was in greater harmony with the essence of Islam than it had ever been, even at the time of the Prophet. It is thus no coincidence that Renan insisted that *fraternité* was the 'essence of Christianity' and that the ideals of 1789 were explicitly claimed by Namık Kemal and Ali (and others) as the essence of Islam. Modernity was the realisation of God's intent. Nineteenth-century religious modernism articulated the theological foundations for modernity in the Islamic world and as such contributed to the intellectual conceptualisation of modernity. Modernity, however, is not a stable category. We should not assume that it 'is' but rather examine what it claims to be, over time, in different contexts.

In asserting that modern values constituted the essence of Islam, Islamic modernists forged a direct link between the positivist historical time of human evolution and the eschatological time of Islam. Historical time was divorced from chronological time and married to civilisational time. Civilisational progress entailed the crossing of a threshold – a rupture conceived of in historical terms. 'Backwardness' and 'modern' were thus claims of belonging to civilisational levels, and not consonant with contemporaneity measured chronologically. History became the story of religious evolution, the continuous development of human consciousness of the Divine expressed as universal civilisational progress. Historicism, which had forced the disenchantment of tradition's claim to truth, enabled the re-enchantment of the sacred in the progress of history itself. History retained its movement towards infinite perfection, the fulfilment of God's intent.

---

[16] On secularism as an attempt to construct and publicly perform equality of citizenship by restricting performance of religious difference, see Ringer, *Pious Citizens*.

Disenchantment, Revisited

In conclusion, let us return to where we began, with Weber, who insisted that modernity required the abandonment of magic and the embrace of 'the truth of science, which alone seizes not upon illusions and shadows but upon the true being'.[17] Renan expressed similar views when he wrote: 'Criticism knows no respect: It judges gods and men. As far as it is concerned, there is neither standing nor mystery; it destroys all magic, disturbs every veil. It is the sole authority without bridle, for it is but reason itself.'[18] Yet Renan and Islamic modernists failed to reconcile their commitment to historicism with their commitment to re-enchantment. It was not simply the magic of superstition that criticism necessarily destroyed – criticism destroyed all certainty, all claims to truth, leaving only a variety of possible truths. However profoundly religious modernist historians sought to re-establish a secure link with a sacred past, they ultimately had to contend with the methodological impossibility of certitude implicit in the positing of historical context. Historicism could be fruitfully employed to understand context, but the identification of context did not entail the concomitant location of essence – this remained a project of imagination and conviction, not scholarship.

Historicism was a useful tool in demolishing claims to definitive truth and claims to tradition as unerring precedent, but unwieldy in identifying and retrieving an acontextual and ahistorical essence. Historicism's utility was located solely in its destructive capacity: it problematised certainty, it could not recreate it. The conceit of religious modernists was the denial of their own context. Modern values, rather than being recognised as the products of their own context, were claimed as eternal – as consistent with God's intent for mankind. Modernists deployed their own values as yardsticks to identify and retrieve religious essence, but conflated them with essence itself. One could argue that religious modernists embraced the lack of certitude historicism demanded and merely constructed a possible historical narrative, a Prophet Mohammad (or a Jesus), who might have existed. Yet this humility is belied by their hubris in claiming to rediscover truth, the essence of Islam (or Christianity), and to claim the capacity to accurately interpret God's intent.

---

[17] Weber, 'The Disenchantment of Modern Life'.
[18] Renan, 'Les historiens critiques de Jésus', cited in Lee, *Ernest Renan: In the Shadow of Faith*, 98.

BIBLIOGRAPHY

Afghani, Jamal al-Din, 'Answer of Jamal ad-Din to Renan, *Journal des débats* May 18, 1883', trans. Nikki R. Keddie and Hamid Algar, in Nikki R. Keddie, *An Islamic Response to Imperialism: Political and Religious Writings of Jamal ad-Din 'al-Afghani'* (University of California Press, 1983), 181–7.
Afghani, Jamal al-Din, 'The Benefits of Philosophy', in Nikki R. Keddie, *An Islamic Response to Imperialism: Political and Religious Writings of Jamal ad-Din 'al-Afghani'* (University of California Press, 1983), 109–22.
Afghani, Jamal al-Din, 'Commentary on the Commentator', in Nikki R. Keddie, *An Islamic Response to Imperialism: Political and Religious Writings of Jamal ad-Din 'al-Afghani'* (University of California Press, 1983), 123–9.
Afghani, Jamal al-Din, 'Lecture on Teaching and Learning', in Nikki R. Keddie, *An Islamic Response to Imperialism: Political and Religious Writings of Jamal ad-Din 'al-Afghani'* (University of California Press, 1983), 101–8.
Afghani, Jamal al-Din, 'The Materialists in India', in Nikki R. Keddie, *An Islamic Response to Imperialism: Political and Religious Writings of Jamal ad-Din 'al-Afghani'* (University of California Press, 1983), 175–80.
Afghani, Jamal al-Din, 'Réponse à M. Renan', *Journal des débats politiques et littéraires*, 18 May 1883, 3, https://gallica.bnf.fr/ark:/12148/bpt6k462242j.
Afghani, Jamal al-Din, 'The Truth About the Neicheri Sect', in Nikki R. Keddie, *An Islamic Response to Imperialism: Political and Religious Writings of Jamal ad-Din 'al-Afghani'* (University of California Press, 1983), 130–74.
Ali, Syed Ameer, *A Critical Examination of the Life and Teachings of Mohammed* (Williams and Norgate, 1873).
Ali, Syed Ameer, *The Ethics of Islam* (Thacker, Spink & Co., 1893).
Ali, Syed Ameer, *The Legal Position of Women in Islam* (Hodder & Stoughton, 1912).
Ali, Syed Ameer, 'The Liberal Movement in Islam', *Indian Social Reformer*, 28 July 1901.
Ali, Syed Ameer, *The Life and Teachings of Mohammed; or, The Spirit of Islam* (W. H. Allen & Co., 1891).
Ali, Syed Ameer, *Memoirs and other Writings of Syed Ameer Ali*, ed. Syed Razi Wasti, 2 vols (Peoples Publishing House, 1968).
Ali, Syed Ameer, *The Personal Law of the Mahommedans, According to All the Schools:*

Together with a Comparative Sketch of the Law of Inheritance Among the Sunnis and the Shiahs (W. H. Allen & Co., 1880).

Ali, Syed Ameer, *A Short History of the Saracens: Being a Concise Account of the Rise and Decline of the Saracenic Power and of the Economic, Social and Intellectual Development of the Arab Nation from the Earliest Times to the Destruction of Bagdad, and the Expulsion of the Moors from Spain* (Macmillan & Co., 1898).

Ali-Karamali, Shaista P., and Fiona Dunne, 'The Ijtihad Controversy', *Arab Law Quarterly* 9: 3 (1994), 238–57.

Anderson, Benedict, *Imagined Communities: Reflections on the Origin and Spread of Nationalism* (Verso, 2006).

Ansari, Ali M., *The Politics of Nationalism in Modern Iran* (Cambridge University Press, 2012).

Arnold, Matthew, *Culture and Anarchy*, vol. 5 of *The Complete Prose Works of Matthew Arnold*, ed. R. H. Super (University of Michigan Press, 1965).

Asad, Talal, *Formations of the Secular: Christianity, Islam, Modernity* (Stanford University Press, 2003).

Ascher, Abraham, *P. A. Stolypin: The Search for Stability in Late Imperial Russia* (Stanford University Press, 2001).

Asil, Ercüment, 'The Tanzimat Novel in the Service of Science: Ahmet Midhat Efendi's *American Doctors*', in Monica M. Ringer and Etienne E. Charrière (eds), *Ottoman Culture and the Project of Modernity: Reform and the Tanzimat Novel* (I. B. Tauris, 2020), 103–16.

Aslanian, Sebouh, *From the Indian Ocean to the Mediterranean: The Global Trade Networks of Armenian Merchants from New Julfa* (University of California Press, 2014).

Auerbach, E., *Mimesis: The Representation of Reality in Western Literature*, trans. Willard R. Trask with a new introduction by Edward W. Said (Princeton University Press, 2003).

Aydin, Cemil, *The Politics of Anti-Westernism in Asia: Visions of World Order in Pan-Islamic and Pan-Asian Thought* (Columbia University Press, 2007).

Bachmann-Medick, Doris, 'Introduction: The Translational Turn', *Translation Studies* 2: 1 (2009), 2–16.

Baiazitov, Mökhemmedsafa Gataulla uli, 'A Refutation of Ernest Renan's Lecture on Islam and Science', translated from the Russian by James Quill, in Mökhemmedsafa Gataulla uli Baiazitov, *A Tatar Akhund's Refutation of Ernest Renan's Lecture on Islam & Science (1883)*, contributors James Quill, Monica M. Ringer, G. F. Marlier and Edward J. Lazzerini (Institute for the Study of Russia's Orient, 2019), 23–41.

Baiazitov, Mökhemmedsafa Gataulla uli, *A Tatar Akhund's Refutation of Ernest Renan's Lecture on Islam & Science (1883)*, contributors James Quill, Monica M. Ringer, G. F. Marlier and Edward J. Lazzerini (Institute for the Study of Russia's Orient, 2019).

Bakhos, Carol, and Michael Cook (eds), *Islam and Its Past: Jahiliyya, Late Antiquity, and the Qur'an* (Oxford University Press, 2017).

Bashir, Shahzad, 'Everlasting Doubt: Uncertainty in Islamic Representations of the Past', *Archiv für Religionsgeschichte* 20: 1 (March 2018), 25–44.

Batnitzky, Leora, *How Judaism Became a Religion: An Introduction to Modern Jewish Thought* (Princeton University Press, 2011).

Bayer, Thora Ilin, and Donald Phillip Verene (eds), *Giambattista Vico: Keys to the New Science* (Cornell University Press, 2009).

Bayezidof, Ataullah, *Islam ve Medeniyet (Islam and Civilization)*, ed. Ibrahim Ural (Türk Diyanet Vakfı Yayınları, 1993).

Bayezidof, Ataullah, 'Islam in Ilimlerle İlişkisi' (The Relationship of Islam and Science), in A. Bayezidof, *Islam ve Medeniyet* (Türkiye Diyanet Vakfı Yayınları, 1993), 42–126.

Bayezidof, Ataullah, *Redd-i Renan: Islamiyet ve Fünun*, trans. Olga de Lebedeva and Ahmet Cevdet (Tercüman-i Hakikat Matbaası, 1891).

Bayezidof, Ataullah, 'Renan-a Reddiye', in A. Bayezidof, *Islam ve Medeniyet* (Türkiye Diyanet Vakfı Yayınları, 1993), 5–40.

Bayly, Christopher A., *The Birth of the Modern World, 1780–1914: Global Connections and Comparisons* (Blackwell, 2009).

Benjamin, Walter, *Illuminations*, ed. Hannah Arendt, trans. Harry Zohn (Schocken Books, 1968).

Benjamin, Walter, 'The Translator's Task', trans. Steven Rendall, *Erudit.org*, 151–65, http://id.erudit.org/iderudit/037302ar.

Benningsen, Alexandre, and Chantal Lemercier-Quelquejay, *La presse et le mouvement national chez les musulmans de Russie avant 1920* (Mouton, 1964).

Berberian, Houri, *Roving Revolutionaries: Armenians and the Connected Revolutions in the Russian, Iranian, and Ottoman Worlds* (University of California Press, 2019).

Berkes, Niyazi, *The Development of Secularism in Turkey* (Routledge, 1998).

Bilgrami, Akeel, 'What is Enchantment?', in Michael Warner, Jonathan VanAntwerpen and Craig Calhoun (eds), *Varieties of Secularism in a Secular Age* (Harvard University Press, 2013), 145–65.

Blix, Göran, 'Charting the "Transitional period": The Emergence of Modern Time in the Nineteenth Century', *History and Theory* 45 (February 2006), 51–71.

Bod, Rens, 'Introduction', in Rens Bod, Jaap Maat and Thijs Weststeijn (eds), *The Making of the Humanities, Vol. 11: From Early Modern to Modern Disciplines* (Amsterdam University Press, 2012), 9–19.

Bod, Rens, Jaap Maat and Thijs Weststeijn (eds), *The Making of the Humanities, Vol. 11: From Early Modern to Modern Disciplines* (Amsterdam University Press, 2012).

Borrut, Antoine, *Entre mémoire et pouvoir: L'espace syrien soul les derniers Omeyyades et les premiers Abbassides* (Brill, 2011).

Borrut, Antoine, 'Vanishing Syria: Periodization and Power in Early Islam', *Der Islam* 91: 1 (2014), 37–68.

Bos, Jacques, 'Nineteenth-Century Historicism and its Predecessors: Historical Experience, Historical Ontology and Historical Method', in Rens Bod, Jaap Maat and Thijs Weststeijn (eds), *The Making of the Humanities, Vol. 11: From Early Modern to Modern Disciplines* (Amsterdam University Press, 2012), 131–47.

Brown, Jonathan, *The Canonization of al-Bukhari and Muslim: the formation of the Sunni Hadith Canon* (Brill, 2007).

Brown, Jonathan, *Hadith: Muhammad's Legacy in the Medieval and Modern World* (One World Press, 2009).

Bulliet, Richard, *Islam: The View from the Edge* (Columbia University Press, 1995).

Burnouf, Émile-Louis, 'La Science des Religions: sa méthode et ses limites', *Revue des Deux Mondes* 76: 4 (15 August1868), 864–90.

Campos, Michelle U., *Ottoman Brothers: Muslims, Christians, and Jews in Early Twentieth-Century Palestine* (Stanford University Press, 2011).

Carlisle, Janice, *John Stuart Mill and the Writing of Character* (University of Georgia Press, 2010).

Casanova, José, 'The Secular, Secularizations, Secularisms', in Craig J. Calhoun, Mark Jeuergensmeyer and Jonathan Van Antwerpen (eds), *Rethinking Secularism* (Oxford University Press, 2011), 54–74.

Çelik, Zeynep, *Displaying the Orient: Architecture of Islam at Nineteenth-Century World's Fairs* (University of California Press, 1992).
Çelik, Zeynep, Edhem Eldem and Bahattin Öztancay (eds), *Camera Ottomana: Photography and Modernity in the Ottoman Empire 1840–1914* (Koç University Press, 2015).
Cevdet, Ahmet Pasha, *Peygamberler ve Halifeler Tarihi* (Çelik, 2011).
Chakrabarty, Dipesh, *Provincializing Europe: Postcolonial Thought and Historical Difference* (Princeton University Press, 2008).
Charlton, D. G., *Secular Religions in France 1815–1870* (Oxford University Press, 1963).
Chateaubriand, François-René, *Le Génie du Christianisme*, 2 vols (Eugéne et Penaud frères, 1828).
Çıpa, H. Erdem, and Emine Fetvaci (eds), *Writing History at the Ottoman Court: Editing the Past, Fashioning the Future* (Indiana University Press, 2013).
Colani, Timothée, 'Examen de La *Vie de Jésus* de M. Renan', in *Revue de Théologie et de philosophie Chrétienne* (1864).
Conrad, Sebastian, 'Enlightenment in Global History: A Historiographical Critique', *American Historical Review* (October 2012), 999–1027.
Conrad, Sebastian, '"Nothing is the Way it Should Be": Global Transformations of the Time Regime in the Nineteenth Century', *Modern Intellectual History* 5: 3 (2018), 821–48.
Crews, Robert D., *For Prophet and Tsar: Islam and Empire in Russia and Central Asia* (Harvard University Press, 2009).
Cündioğlu, Dücane, 'Ernest Renan ve "reddiyeler" bağlaminda Islam-bilim tartişmalarina bibliografik birkatke', *Divan* 2 (1996), 1–94.
Dallal, Ahmad, 'The Origins and Objectives of Islamic Revivalist Thought, 1750–1850', *Journal of the American Oriental Society* 113: 3 (July–September 1993), 341–59.
Darmesteter, James, *The Life of Ernest Renan* (Houghton, Mifflin and Co., 1897).
Darwin, Charles, *The Origin of Species by Means of Natural Selection or the Preservation of Favored Races in the Struggle for Life* (D. Appleton and Co., [1859] 1897), vol. II.
Davis, Kathleen, *Periodization and Sovereignty: How Ideas of Feudalism and Secularization Govern the Politics of Time* (University of Philadelphia Press, 2008).
de Certeau, Michael, *The Practice of Everyday Life*, trans. Steven Rendall (University of California Press, 1984).
DeJean, Joan, *Ancients Against Moderns: Culture Wars and the Making of a Fin de Siècle* (University of Chicago Press, 1997).
Demichelis, Marco, 'Between Mu{AYN}tazilism and Syncretism: A Reappraisal of the Behavior of the Caliphate of al-Ma'mūn', *Journal of Near Eastern Studies* 71: 2 (2012), 257–74.
Demircioğlu, Cemal, 'Translating Europe: The Case of Ahmet Midhat as an Ottoman Agent of Translation', in John Milton and Paul Bandia (eds), *Agents of Translation* (John Benjamins Publishing Company, 2009).
Di-Capua, Yoav, *Gatekeepers of the Arab Past: Historians and History Writing in Twentieth-Century Egypt* (University of California Press, 2009).
Dizdaroğlu, Hikmet, *Namık Kemal, Hayatı, Sanatı, Eserleri* (Varlık Yayınevi, n.d.).
Donner, Fred M., *Narratives of Islamic Origins: The Beginnings of Islamic Historical Writing* (Darwin Press, 1998).
Dozy, Reinhart Pieter Anne, *Histoire des Musulmans d'Espagne*, 2 vols (1881).
Dozy, Reinhart, *The History of the Almodhades, Preceded by a Sketch of the History of Spain From the Times of the Conquest Till the Reign of Yu'sof Ibn-Te'shufi'n, and of the History of the Almoravides* (1847).

Draper, John William, *History of the Conflict Between Religion and Science* (D. Appleton and Co., [1874] 1892).
Drory, Rina, 'The Abbasid Construction of the Jahiliyya: Cultural Authority in the Making', *Studia Islamica* 83 (1996), 33–49.
Durkheim, Émile, *Les forms élémentaires de la vie réligieuse*, 4th edn (Presses Univérsitaires de France, 1980).
East, Katherine A., '*Superstitionis Malleus*: John Toland, Cicero, and the War on Priestcraft in Early Enlightenment England', *History of European Ideas* 40: 7 (2014), 965–83.
Efal, Adi, 'Philology and the History of Art', in Rens Bod, Jaap Maat and Thijs Weststeijn (eds), *The Making of the Humanities, Vol. 11: From Early Modern to Modern Disciplines* (Amsterdam University Press, 2012), 283–99.
Eldem, Edhem, 'Ottomans at the Alhambra, 1844–1914: An Investigation into the Perception of Al-Andalus by Ottoman Subjects in Times of Modernity', *Turcica* 49 (2018), 239–359.
El-Hibri, Tayeb, 'A Note on Biblical Narrative and Abbasid History', in Neguin Yavari, Lawrence G. Potter and Jean-Marc Ran Oppenheim (eds), *Views from the Edge: Essays in Honor of Richard W. Bulliet* (Columbia University Press, 2004).
El-Hibri, Tayeb, *Parable and Politics in Early Islamic History: The Rashidun Caliphs* (Columbia University Press, 2010).
El-Hibri, Tayeb, 'The Redemption of Umayyad Memory by the Abbasids', *Journal of Near Eastern Studies* 61: 4 (October 2002), 241–65.
El-Hibri, Tayeb, *Reinterpreting Islamic Historiography: Harun al-Rashid and the Narrative of the Abbasid Caliphate* (Cambridge University Press, 1999).
Eliot, T. S., 'Little Gidding', http://www.columbia.edu/itc/history/winter/w3206/edit/tseliotlittlegidding.html.
Elphinstone, Sir Mountstuart Grant Duff, *Ernest Renan, In Memoriam* (Macmillan, 1893).
Elshakry, Marwa, *Reading Darwin in Arabic, 1860–1950* (University of Chicago Press, 2013).
Emrence, Cem, *Remapping the Ottoman Middle East: Modernity, Imperial Bureaucracy, and the Islamic State* (I. B. Tauris, 2011).
Ess, Josef van, *The Flowering of Muslim Theology*, trans. Jane Marie Todd (Harvard University Press, 2006).
Ess, Josef van, 'La tradition dans la théologie mu`tazilite', in George Makdisi, Dominique Sourdel and Janine Sourdel-Thomine (eds), *La notion d'autorité au Moyen Age: Islam, Byzance, Occident* (Presses Universitaires de France, 1982), 211–26.
Ferdowsi, Abolqasem, *Shahnameh: The Persian Book of Kings*, trans. Dick Davis (Penguin, 1997).
Fetvaci, Emine, *Picturing History at the Ottoman Court* (Indiana University Press, 2013).
Feuerbach, Ludwig, *The Essence of Christianity* (Prometheus Books, [1841] 1989).
Flood, Finbarr Barry, *Objects of Translation: Material Culture and Medieval 'Hindu-Muslim' Encounter* (Princeton University Press, 2009).
Fortna, Benjamin C., *Imperial Classroom: Islam, the State, and Education in the Late Ottoman Empire* (Oxford University Press, 2002).
Fortna, Benjamin C., *Learning to Read in the Late Ottoman Empire and Early Turkish Republic* (Palgrave, 2012).
Forward, Martin, *The Failure of Islamic Modernism? Syed Ameer Ali's Interpretation of Islam* (Peter Lang Publishing, 1999).

Foucault, Michel, 'What is an Author?', in Paul Rabinow (ed.), *The Foucault Reader* (Pantheon Books, 1984), 101–20.
Fraser, Elisabeth, 'The Color of the Orient: On Ottoman Costume Albums, European Print Culture, and Cross-Cultural Exchange', in Tara Zanardi and Lynda Klich (eds), *Visual Typologies from the Early Modern to the Contemporary: Local Practices and Global Contexts* (Routledge, 2018), 45–59.
Fraser, Elisabeth A., 'Dressing Turks in the French Manner: Mouradgea d'Ohsson's Panorama of the Ottoman Empire', *Ars Orientalis* 39 (2010), 199–230.
Frazer, Sir James George, *The Golden Bough: A Study in Magic and Religion*, abridged edn (Palgrave Macmillan Ltd., 1922).
Frazer, Sir James George, *Sur Ernest Renan: precede d'un buste de l'auteur par Antoine Bourdelle* (C. Aveline, 1923).
Fuglum, Per, *Edward Gibbon: His View of Life and Conception of History* (Akademisk Forlag, 1953).
Gemici, Nurettin, 'Namık Kemal'in Ahmed Midhat Efendi'yle olan Fikri Ayrılıklarının Ortaya Çıkışı ve Sebebleri', *Türk Dünyası Araştırmalarık* 180 (Haziran 2009), 65–85.
Gencer, Bedri, *Islam'da Modernleşme: 1839–1939* (Doğu Batı Yayınları, 2017).
Geraci, Robert, 'Russian Orientalism at an Impasse: Tsarist Education Policy and the 1910 Conference on Islam', in Daniel Brower and Edward Lazzerini (eds), *Russia's Orient: Imperial Borderlands and Peoples, 1700–1917* (Indiana University Press, 1997), 138–67.
Gibbon, Edward, *The Decline and Fall of the Roman Empire* (with notes by the Rev. Henry Hart Milman), 12 vols (John Murray, [1776] 1838).
Gilbert, Felix, 'Historiography: What Ranke Meant', *The American Scholar* 56: 3 (Summer 1987), 393–7.
Gillespie, Michael Allen, *The Theological Origins of Modernity* (University of Chicago Press, 2009).
Gohrab, A. A. Seyed, and S. McGlinn (trans.), *One Word – Yek kalame: 19th-Century Persian Treatise Introducing Western Codified Law* (Leiden University Press, 2010).
Goldziher, Ignaz, *Muslim Studies*, ed. S. M. Stern, trans. C. R. Barber (Routledge, 2017).
Graham, William, 'Traditionalism in Islam: An Essay in Interpretation', *Journal of Interdisciplinary History* 23 (1993), 495–522.
Green, Nile, 'From Persianate Pasts to Aryan Antiquity: Transnationalism and Transformations in Afghan Intellectual History, c. 1800–1940,' *Afghanistan* 1: 1 (April 2018), 26–67.
Green, Nile, *Religious Economies of Global Islam* (Hurst & Co., 2015).
Green, Nile, 'Spacetime and the Muslim Journey West: Industrial Communications in the Making of the "Muslim World"', *American Historical Review* 118: 2 (April 2013), 401–29.
Green, Nile, 'The Waves of Heterotopia: Toward a Vernacular Intellectual History of the Indian Ocean', *American Historical Review* 123: 3 (June 2018), 846–74.
Green, Nile, and James L. Gelvin (eds), *Global Muslims in the Age of Steam and Print* (University of California Press, 2013).
Griffel, Frank (ed.), *Islam and Rationality: The Impact of al-Ghazali; Papers Collected on his 900th Anniversary*, vol. 2 (Brill, 2016).
Hadley, Elaine, *Living Liberalism: Practical Citizenship in mid-Victorian Britain* (University of Chicago, 2010).
Hallaq, Wael B., *Authority, Continuity and Change in Islamic Law* (Cambridge University Press, 2001).

Hallaq, Wael B., 'The Quest for Origins or Doctrine? Islamic Legal Studies as Colonialist Discourse', *UCLA Journal of Islamic and Near Eastern Law* (2002-3), 1-31.

Hallaq, Wael B., *Shari'a: Theory, Practice, Transformations* (Cambridge University Press, 2009).

Hamzah, Dyala (ed.), *The Making of the Arab Intellectual (1880-1960): Empire, Public Sphere and the Colonial Coordinates of Selfhood* (Routledge, 2012).

Hanioğlu, M. Şükrü, 'Blueprints for a Future Society: Late Ottoman Materialists on Science, Religion and Art', in Elizabeth Özdalga (ed.), *Late Ottoman Society: The Intellectual Legacy* (Routledge, 2005), 28-116.

Hirschler, Konrad, 'Narrating the Past: Social Contexts and Literary Structures of Arabic Historical Writing in the Seventh/Thirteenth Century', PhD dissertation, School of Oriental and African Studies, University of London (2003).

Hirschler, Konrad, 'Pre-Eighteenth-Century Traditions of Revivalism: Damascus in the Thirteenth Century', *Bulletin of the School of Oriental and African Studies* 68: 2 (2005), 195-214.

Hobsbawm, Eric, 'Introduction: Inventing Traditions', in Eric Hobsbawm and Terence Ranger (eds), *The Invention of Tradition* (Cambridge University Press, 1983).

Hourani, Albert, *Arabic Thought in the Liberal Age: 1798-1939* (Cambridge University Press, 1983).

Howard, Thomas Albert, *Religion and the Rise of Historicism: W. M. L. de Wette, Jacob Burckhardt, and the Theological Origins of Nineteenth-Century Historical Consciousness* (Cambridge University Press, 2000).

Howland, Douglas, 'The Predicament of Ideas in Culture: Translation and Historiography', *History and Theory* 42 (February 2003), 45-60.

Hoyland, Robert G., *The 'History of the Kings of the Persians' in Three Arabic Chronicles: The Transmission of the Iranian Past from Late Antiquity to Early Islam* (Liverpool University Press, 2018).

Hume, David, 'On Miracles', in *An Enquiry Concerning Human Understanding* (1748), https://www.bartleby.com/37/3/14.html.

Humphreys, R. Stephen, 'Qur'anic Myth and Narrative Structure in Early Islamic Historiography', in F. M. Clover and R. S. Humphreys (eds), *Tradition and Innovation in Late Antiquity* (University of Wisconsin Press, 1989), 271-90.

Hunt, Lynn, *Measuring Time, Making History* (Central European University Press, 2008).

Iggers, Georg G., 'Historicism: The History and Meaning of the Term', *Journal of the History of Ideas* 56: 1 (1995), 129-52.

Ishaq, Ibn, *The Life of Muhammad*, trans. A. Guillaume (1955).

Juynbol, G. H. A., 'Some New Ideas on the Development of *Sunna* as a Technical Term in Early Islam', *Jerusalem Studies in Arabic and Islam* 10 (1987), 97-118.

Karateke, Hakan T., 'The Challenge of Periodization: New Patterns in Nineteenth-Century Ottoman Historiography', in H. Erdem Çipa and Emine Fetvaci (eds), *Writing History at the Ottoman Court: Editing the Past, Fashioning the Future* (Indiana University Press, 2013), 129-54.

Katouzian, Homa, *The Persians: Ancient, Medieval and Modern Iran* (Yale University Press, 2010).

Keddie, Nikki R., *An Islamic Response to Imperialism: Political and Religious Writings of Jamal ad-Din 'al-Afghani'* (University of California Press, 1983).

Kedourie, Elie, *Afghani and {AYN}Abduh, An Essay on Religious Unbelief and Political Activism in Modern Islam* (Routledge, 1997).

Kedourie, Elie, 'Afghani in Paris: A Note', *Middle Eastern Studies* 8: 1 (1972), 103-5.

Kedourie, Elie, 'The Elusive Jamal-al-Din al-Afghani: A Comment', *The Muslim World* 59: 3–4 (1969), 315–16.
Kedourie, Elie, 'Further Light on Afghani', *Middle Eastern Studies* 1: 2 (1965), 187–202.
Kemal, Namik, *Büyük Islam Tarihi (A Complete History of Islam)* (Hürriyet Publishers, 1975).
Kemal, Namik, *'Renan Mudafaanamesi'*, trans. M. Fuad Köprülü (Güven Matbaası, 1962).
Khalid, Adeeb, *The Politics of Muslim Cultural Reform: Jadidism in Central Asia* (University of California Press, 1998).
Khalidi, Tarif, *Arabic Historical Thought in the Classical Period* (Cambridge University Press, 1994).
Knysh, Alexander, '"Orthodoxy" and "Heresy" in Medieval Islam: An Essay in Reassessment', *The Muslim World* 83: 1 (January 1993), 48–67.
Koselleck, Reinhart, *Futures Past: On the Semantics of Historical Time*, trans. Keith Tribe (MIT Press, 1985).
Koselleck, Reinhart, *The Practice of Conceptual History: Timing History, Spacing Concepts*, trans. Todd Samuel Presner (Stanford University Press, 2002).
Kuenen, Abraham, 'L'Islam offre-t-il les caractères de l'universalisme religieux', *Revue de l'histiore des Religions* 6 (1882), 1–40.
Kurzman, Charles (ed.), *Modernist Islam, 1840–1940: A Sourcebook* (Oxford University Press, 2002).
Kuttner, Thomas, 'Russian Jadīdism and the Islamic World: Ismail Gasprinskii in Cairo, 1908 (A Call to the Arabs for the Rejuvenation of the Islamic World)', *Cahiers Du Monde Russe et Soviétique* 16: 3/4 (1975), 383–424.
LaCapra, Dominick, *Emil Durkheim: Sociologist and Philosopher* (The Davies Group, 2001).
Lamennais, Felicité de, 'Essai sur l'indifference en matière de religion', vols 1–4 of *Œuvres complètes de F. de Lamennais*, 12 vols (1836–7).
Landy, Joshua, and Michael Saler (eds), *The Re-enchantment of the World: Secular Magic in a Rational Age* (Stanford University Press, 2009).
Lane-Poole, Stanley Edward, *The Story of the Moors in Spain* (1886).
Laplanche, Francois, *La Bible en France entre mythe et critique, VVI–XIS siècle* (A. Michel, 1994).
Larroque, Patrice, *Critique des Doctrines de La Religion Chretiènne*, eds A. Lacroix, Verboeckhoven, et cie., 3rd edn, 2 vols (Librarie Internationale, 1864).
Larroque, Patrice, *Opinion des Déistes Rationalistes sure la Vie de Jésus selon M Renan*, 2nd edn (E. Dentu, 1863).
Lassner, Jacob, *Islamic Revolution and Historical Memory*, American Oriental Society Series 66 (Yale University Press, 1986).
Layard, Sir Austen Henry, *The Condition of Turkey and her Dependencies: speech delivered in the House of Commons on Friday, May 29, 1863* (John Murray, 1863).
Lazzerini, Edward, 'Gadidism at the Turn of the Twentieth Century: A View from Within', *Cahiers du Monde Russe et Soviétique* 16: 2 (1975), 245–77.
Lazzerini, Edward, 'Gaspirali Ismail Bey's Perevodchik/Tercüman: A Clarion of Modernism', in Hasan B. Paksoy (ed.), *Central Asian Monuments* (Isis Press, 1992), 159–72.
Lazzerini, Edward, 'Ismail Bey Gasprinski and Muslim Modernism, 1878–1914', PhD dissertation, University of Washington, 1973.
Le Bon, Gustave, *La Civilisation des Arabes* (Firmin-Didot, 1884).
Lecky, William Edward Hartpole, *History of the Rise and Influence of the Spirit of Rationalism in Europe* (1865).

Lee, David C. J., *Ernest Renan: In the Shadow of Faith* (Duckworth Press, 1996).
Leerssen, Joep, 'The Rise of Philology: The Comparative Method, the Historicist Turn and the Surreptitious Influence of Giambattista Vico', in Rens Bod, Jaap Maat and Thijs Weststeijn (eds), *The Making of the Humanities, Vol. 11: From Early Modern to Modern Disciplines* (Amsterdam University Press, 2012), 23–35.
Levi, Melih, and Monica M. Ringer (trans.), *Felatun Bey and Rakım Efendi: An Ottoman Novel* (Syracuse University Press, 2016).
Levine, Joseph M., 'Ancients and Moderns Reconsidered', *Eighteenth-Century Studies* 15: 1 (Autumn 1981), 72–89.
Lewis, Bernard, *The Emergence of Modern Turkey* (Oxford University Press, 1968).
Lika, Foteini, 'Fact and Fancy in Nineteenth-Century Historiography and Fiction: The Case of Macaulay and Roidis', in Rens Bod, Jaap Maat and Thijs Weststeijn (eds), *The Making of the Humanities, Vol. 11: From Early Modern to Modern Disciplines* (Amsterdam University Press, 2012), 149–65.
Madelung, Wilferd, *The Succession to Muhammad: A Study of the Early Caliphate* (Cambridge University Press, 1997).
Makdisi, George, *The Rise of Colleges: Institutions of Learning in Islam and the West* (Edinburgh University Press, 1981).
Makdisi, George, Dominique Sourdel et Janine Sourdel-Thomine (eds), *La notion d'autorité au Moyen Age: Islam, Byzance, Occident* (Presses Universitaires de France, 1982).
Makdisi, Ussama, 'Ottoman Orientalism', *American Historical Review* 107: 2 (2002), 768–96.
Mango, Cyril, and Roger Scott (trans.), *The Chronicle of Theophanes Confessor* (Clarendon, 1997).
Marashi, Afshin, *Exile and the Nation: The Parsi Community of India and the Making of Modern Iran* (University of Texas Press, 2020).
Marashi, Afshin, *Nationalizing Iran: Culture, Power, and the State, 1870–1940* (University of Washington Press, 2008).
Marchand, Suzanne L., *German Orientalism in the Age of Empire: Religion, Race, and Scholarship* (Cambridge University Press, 2009).
Mardin, Şerif, *The Genesis of Young Ottoman Thought* (Princeton University Press, 1962).
Martin, Richard C., *Defenders of Reason in Islam: Mu'tazilism from Medieval School to Modern Symbol* (Oneworld Press, 1997).
Martin, Richard C. (ed.), *Encyclopedia of Islam and the Muslim World* (Macmillan Reference, 2004).
Massignon, Louis, '"La Lettre du Cadı de Mossoul à Layard" critique par Nameq Kemal d'une Source Citée par Renan', *Revue des études Islamiques* 1 (1927), 297–301.
Masuzawa, Tomoko, *In Search of Dreamtime: The Quest for the Origin of Religion* (University of Chicago Press, 1993).
Masuzawa, Tomoko, *The Invention of World Religions: or, How European Universalism was Preserved in the Language of Pluralism* (University of Chicago Press, 2005).
Mazumdar, Sucheta, Vasant Kaiwar and Thierry Labica (eds), *From Orientalism to Postcolonialism: Asia, Europe and the Lineages of Difference* (Routledge, 2009).
McAuliffe, Jane Dammen (ed.), *Encyclopedia of the Qur'an* (Brill, 2002).
McKeon, Michael, *The Origins of the English Novel, 1600–1740* (Johns Hopkins University Press, 2002).
Mehta, Uday Singh, *Liberalism and Empire: A Study in Nineteenth-Century British Liberal Thought* (University of Chicago Press, 1999).

Mill, Joseph S., *Nature, the Utility of Religion, and Theism* (Watts and Co., 1904).
Mills, Charles, *The History of the Crusades for the Recovery and Possession of the Holy Land* (1820).
Milman, Henry Hart, *History of Latin Christianity*, vol. 1 (John Murray, 1855).
Milman, Henry Hart, 'Preface', in Edward Gibbon, *The Decline and Fall of the Roman Empire* (1838).
Milton, John, and Paul Bandia (eds), *Agents of Translation* (John Benjamins, 2009).
Momigliano, Arnaldo, 'Gibbon's Contribution to Historical Method', *Historia: Zeitschrift für alte Geschichte* 2: 4 (1954), 450–63.
Momigliano, Arnaldo, 'Gibbon from an Italian Point of View', *Daedalus* 105: 3 (Summer 1976), 125–35.
Montesquieu, Charles de Secondat, *Considerations on the causes of the grandeur and decadence of the Romans: A New Translation* (D. Appleton and Co., [1734] 1882).
Montoya, Alicia C., 'Bourgeois versus Aristocratic Models of Scholarship: Medieval Studies at the Académie des Inscriptions, 1701–1751', in Rens Bod, Jaap Maat and Thijs Weststeijn (eds), *The Making of the Humanities, Vol. 11: From Early Modern to Modern Disciplines* (Amsterdam University Press, 2012), 303–19.
Morrow, Jeffery L., 'The Politics of Biblical Interpretation: A "Criticism of Criticism"', *New Blackfriars* 91: 1035 (September 2010), 528–45.
Muir, Sir William, *Annals of the Early Caliphate from Original Sources* (Smith, Elder and Co., 1883).
Muir, Sir William, *The Caliphate: Its Rise, Decline, and Fall* (Religious Tract Society, 1891).
Muir, Sir William, *The Life of Mahomet and History of Islam, to the Era of the Hegira. With introductory chapters on the original sources for the biography of Mahomet, and on the pre-Islamite History of Arabia*, vol. 1 (Smith, Elder and Co., 1858).
Muir, Sir William, *Mahomet and Islam: A Sketch of the Prophet's Life from Original Sources and a Brief Outline of His Religion* (Religious Tract Society, 1895).
Müller, Max, 'Lectures on the Science of Religion', in M. Müller, *Introduction to the Science of Religion* (Longmans, Green and Co., 1873), pp. 1–282.
Najmabadi, Afsaneh, *Women with Mustaches and Men Without Beards: Gender and Sexual Anxieties of Iranian Modernity* (University of California Press, 2005).
Nasr, Seyyed Hossein, *The Study Quran: A New Translation and Commentary* (Harper Collins, 2015).
Neuwirth, Angelika, 'Quran and History – a Disputed Relationship: Some Reflections on Qur'anic History and History in the Quran', *Journal of Qur'anic Studies* 5: 1 (2003), 1–18.
Norman, York A., 'Disputing the "Iron Circle": Renan, Afghani, and Kemal on Islam, Science, and Modernity', *Journal of World History* 22: 4 (December 2011), 693–714.
Nuri, Celal, 'İslamiyet Man-i Terakkimidir?', *Edebiyat-ı Umumiye Mecmuası* 5: 91 (1917), 1085–8.
Nussbaum, Felicity A. (ed.), *The Global Eighteenth Century* (Johns Hopkins University Press, 2003).
O'Brien, Karen, 'The Return of the Enlightenment', *American Historical Review* (December 2010), 1426–35.
Okay, Orhan, *Batı Medeniyeti Karşısında Ahmet Mithat Efendi* [Ahmet Midhat Efendi Confronts Western Civilization] (MEGSB, 1989).
Olender, Maurice, *The Languages of Paradise: Race, Religion and Philology in the Nineteenth Century*, trans. Arthur Goldhammer (Harvard University Press, 2008).

Otten, Terry, 'Macaulay's Critical Theory of Imagination and Reason', *Journal of Aesthetics and Art Criticism* 28: 1 (1969), 33–43.

Özervarlı, M. Said, 'Ottoman Perceptions of al-Ghazzali's Works and Discussions of his Historical Role in its Late Period', in Frank Griffel (ed.), *Islam and Rationality: The Impact of al-Ghazali. Papers Collected on his 900th Anniversary*, vol. 2 (Brill, 2016).

Pakdaman, Homa. *Djamal ed-Din Assad Abadi dit Afghani* (G. P. Maisonneuve et Larose, 1969).

Papaconstantinou, Arietta, 'Introduction', in Arietta Papaconstantinou, Neil McLynn and Daniel Schwartz (eds), *Conversion in late antique Christianity, Islam, and beyond: Papers from the Andrew W. Mellon Foundation Sawyer Seminar, University of Oxford, 2009–2010* (Ashgate, 2015).

Paul, Herman, 'The Scholarly Self: Ideals of Intellectual Virtue in Nineteenth-Century Leiden', in Rens Bod, Jaap Maat and Thijs Weststeijn (eds), *The Making of the Humanities, Vol. 11: From Early Modern to Modern Disciplines* (Amsterdam University Press, 2012), 397–411.

Peters, Rudolph, 'Idjtihad and Taqlid in 18th and 19th Century Islam', *Die Welt des Islams* 20: 3–4 (1980), 131–45.

Phillips, Mark Salber, 'Reconsiderations on History and Antiquarianism: Arnaldo Momigliano and the Historiography of Eighteenth-Century Britain', *Journal of the History of Ideas* 57: 2 (April 1996), 297–316.

Pholien, Georges, *Les Deux vie de Jésus de Renan* (Bibliotheque de la Faculté de Philosophie et Lettres de l'université de Liège, 1983).

Priest, Robert Daniel, *The Gospel According to Renan: Reading, Writing and Religion in Nineteenth-Century France* (Oxford University Press, 2015).

Priest, Robert Daniel, 'Reading, Writing and Religion in Nineteenth-Century France: The Popular Reception of Renan's *Life of Jesus*', *The Journal of Modern History* 86 (June 2014), 258–94.

Psichari, Henriette, *Renan d'après lui-même* (Librairie Plon, 1937).

Quadri, Junaid, 'Religion as Transcendence in Modern Islam: Tracking "Religious Matters" into a Secularizing Age', in Florian Zemmin (ed.), *Working with a Secular Age* (de Gruyter, 2017), 331–48.

Rahman, Fazlur, *Islam and Modernity: Transformation of an Intellectual Tradition* (University of Chicago Press, 1982).

Ranke, Leopold von, *History of the Latin and Teutonic Nations from 1494 to 1514*, trans. G. R. Dennis (George Bell & Sons, 1909).

Ranke, Leopold von, *Universal History* (1884).

Reardon, Bernard M. G., 'Ernest Renan and the Religion of Science', in David Jasper and T. R. Wright (eds), *The Critical Spirit and the Will to Believe: Essays in Nineteenth Century Literature and Religion* (St Martin's Press, 1989).

Reardon, Bernard M. G., *Liberalism and Tradition: Aspects of Catholic Thought in Nineteenth-Century France* (Cambridge University Press, 2010).

Reardon, Bernard M. G., *Religion in the Age of Romanticism: Studies in Early Nineteenth-Century Thought* (Cambridge University Press, 1985).

Renan, Ernest, *L'Avenir de la Science: Pensées de 1848* (Calmann-Lévy, 1890).

Renan, Ernest, 'L'avenir religieux des sociétés modernes', in *Questions Contemporaines* (Calmann-Lévy, 1912).

Renan, Ernest, '*Averroès et l'Averroïsm*', in H. Pischari (ed.), *Oeuvres Complètes d'Ernest Renan*, vol. 3 (Calmann-Lévy, 1947–61).

Renan, Ernest, 'Islam and Science', *Journal des débats politiques et littéraires*, 30 March

1883, http://blogs.histoireglobale.com/wp-content/uploads/2011/10/Renan-al-Afghani.pdf.

Renan, Ernest, 'Mélanges religieux et historiques', in H. Psichari (ed.), *Oeuvres Completes d'Ernest Renan*, vol. 8 (Calmann-Lévy, 1947–61).

Renan, Ernest, *Oeuvres Completes d'Ernest Renan*, ed. Henriette Psichari, 10 vols (Calmann-Lévy, 1947–61).

Renan, Ernest, *Vie de Jésus* (Calman-Lévy, 1863).

Rennie, Bryan (ed.), *Mircea Eliade: A Critical Reader* (Equinox, 2006).

Rétat, Laudyce, *Religion et imagination religieuse: leurs forms et leurs rapports dans l'œuvre d'Ernest Renan* (Klinckseick, 1977).

Réville, Albert, 'Ernest Renan,' *Revue de L'histoire des Religions* 26 (1892), 220–6.

Réville, Jean (ed.), *Actes du premier Congrès international d'histoire des religions réuni a Paris, du 3 au 8 septembre 1900 a l'occasion de l'Exposition Universelle*, 2 vols (Ernest Leroux, 1901–2).

Ringer, Monica M., 'Beyond Binaries: Ahmet Midhat Efendi's Prescriptive Modern', in Monica M. Ringer and Etienne E. Charrière (eds), *Ottoman Culture and the Project of Modernity: Reform and the Tanzimat Novel* (I. B. Tauris, 2020).

Ringer, Monica M., 'The Discourse on Modernization and the Problem of Cultural Integrity in Nineteenth-Century Iran', in Rudi Matthee and Beth Baron (eds), *Iran and Beyond: Essays in Middle Eastern History in Honor of Nikki R. Keddie* (Mazda, 2000).

Ringer, Monica M., *Education, Religion, and the Discourse of Cultural Reform in Qajar Iran* (Mazda, 2000).

Ringer, Monica M., 'Gataullah Baiazitov: An Islamic Modernist in Russia', in Mökhammad Safa Gataulla Baiazitov, *A Tatar Akhund's Refutation of Ernest Renan's Lecture on Islam and Science (1883)*, trans. James Quill (The Institute for the Study of Russia's Orient, University of Indiana, 2019).

Ringer, Monica M., 'Negotiating Modernity: Ulama and the Discourse of Modernity in Nineteenth-Century Iran', in Ramin Jahanbegloo (ed.), *Iran Between Tradition, Modernity and Postmodernity* (Lexington Books, 2004).

Ringer, Monica M., *Pious Citizens: Reforming Zoroastrianism in India and Iran* (Syracuse University Press, 2012).

Ringer, Monica M., 'The Quest for the Secret of Strength in Iranian Nineteenth-Century Travel Literature: Rethinking Tradition in the *Safarnameh*', in Nikki Keddie and Rudi Matthee (eds), *Iran and the Surrounding World 1501–2001: Interactions in Culture and Cultural Politics* (University of Washington Press, 2002).

Ringer, Monica M., and Etienne E. Charrière (eds), *Ottoman Culture and the Project of Modernity: Reform and the Tanzimat Novel* (I. B. Tauris, 2020).

Ringer, Monica M., and A. Holly Shissler, 'The Al-Afghani-Renan Debate, Reconsidered', *Iran Nameh* 30: 3 (Fall 2015), 28–45.

Robinson, Chase, *Islamic Historiography* (Cambridge University Press, 2004).

Rosenthal, Franz, 'The Influence of the Biblical Tradition on Muslim Historiography', in Bernard Lewis and P. M. Holt (eds), *Historians of the Middle East* (Oxford University Press, 1962), 35–45.

Rotger, Neus, 'Ancients, Moderns and the Gothic in Eighteenth-Century Historiography', in Rens Bod, Jaap Maat and Thijs Weststeijn (eds), *The Making of the Humanities, Vol. 11: From Early Modern to Modern Disciplines* (Amsterdam University Press, 2012), 322–37.

Rubiés, Joan-Pau, 'Comparing Cultures in the Early Modern World: Hierarchies, Genealogies and the Idea of European Modernity', in Renaud Gagné, Simon

Goldhill and Geoffrey E. R. Lloyd (eds), *Regimes of Comparatism: Frameworlds of Comparison in History, Religion and Anthropology* (Brill, 2019), 116–76.

Rubin, Uri, 'Prophets and Prophethood', in Andrew Rippin and Jawid Mojaddedi (eds), *The Wiley Blackwell Companion to the Qur'an*, 2nd edn (John Wiley & Sons, 2017), 248–61.

Rubin, Uri, 'The Seal of the Prophets and the Finality of Prophecy', *Zeitschrift der Deutschen Morgenländischen Gesellschaft* 164: 1 (2014), 65–96.

Sabra, A. I., 'The Appropriation and Subsequent Naturalization of Greek Science in Medieval Islam: A Preliminary Statement', *History of Science* XXV (1987), 223–43.

Saler, Michael, 'Modernity and Enchantment: A Historiographical Review', *The American Historical Review* (June 2006), 692–716.

Saliba, George, 'Greek Astronomy and the Medieval Arabic Tradition', *American Scientist* 90: 4 (July–August 2002), 360–7.

Sariyannis, Marinos, '"Temporal Modernization" in the Ottoman Pre-Tanzimat Context', *Études Balkaniques* 53: 2 (2017), 230–62.

Sartori, Paolo, 'Ijtihad in Bukhara: Central Asian Jadidism and Local Genealogies of Cultural Change', *Journal of the Economic and Social History of the Orient* 59: 1–2 (2016), 193–236.

Schact, Joseph, *The Origins of Muhammadan Jurisprudence* (Clarendon Press, 1979).

Schwab, Raymond, *La Renaissance Orientale* (Payot, 2014).

Schweitzer, Albert, *The Quest for the Historical Jesus: A Critical Study of its Progress from Reimarus to Wrede* (A. C. Black, [1906] 1926).

Sée, Henri, 'La Philosophie de l'histoire d'Ernest Renan', *Revue Historique* 170 (1932), 46–61.

Shaw, Wendy M. K., *Ottoman Painting: Reflections of Western Art from the Ottoman Empire to the Turkish Republic* (I. B. Tauris, 2011).

Shaw, Wendy M. K., *Possessors and Possessed: Museums, Archaeology, and the Visualization of History in the Late Ottoman Empire* (University of California Press, 2003).

Shayegh, Cyrus, *Who is Knowledgeable is Strong: Science, Class, and the Formation of Modern Iranian Society, 1900–1950* (University of California Press, 2009).

Sheehan, Jonathan, *The Enlightenment Bible: Translation, Scholarship, Culture* (Princeton University Press, 2007).

Sheehan, Jonathan, 'Enlightenment, Religion, and the Enigma of Secularization: A Review Essay', *The American Historical Review* 108: 4 (October 2003), 1061–80.

Sheehan, Jonathan, 'When was Disenchantment? History and the Secular Age', in Michael Warner, Jonathan Van Antwerpen and Craig Calhoun (eds), *Varieties of Secularism in a Secular Age* (Harvard University Press, 2013), 217–42.

Shissler, A. Holly, *Between Two Empires: Ahmet Agaoglu and the New Turkey* (I. B. Tauris, 2002).

Somel, Selçuk A., *The Modernization of Public Education in the Ottoman Empire, 1839–1908: Islamicization, Autocracy, and Discipline* (Brill, 2001).

Sorkin, David, *The Religious Enlightenment: Protestants, Jews, and Catholics from London to Vienna* (Princeton University Press, 2008).

Spannaus, Nathan, 'Formalism, Puritanicalism, Traditionalism: Approaches to Islamic Legal Reasoning in the 19th-century Russian Empire', *The Muslim World* 104: 3 (July 2014), 354–78.

Stone, Jon R. (ed.), *The Essential Max Müller: On Language, Mythology, and Religion* (Palgrave, 2002).

Strauss, David Friedrich, *The Life of Jesus Critically Examined*, trans. George Eliot (Swan Sonnenschein & Co., [1840] 1902).
Strauss, Johann, 'Le livre français d'Istanbul, 1730–1908', *Revue des mondes musulmans et de la Méditerranée* 87–8 (September 1999), 277–301.
Stroumsa, Guy G., 'Augustine and Books', in Mark Vessey (ed.), *A Companion to Augustine* (Blackwell, 2012), 151–7.
Stroumsa, Guy G., 'Early Christianity: A Religion of the Book?', in Margalit Finkelberg and Guy G. Stroumsa (eds), *Homer, The Bible and Beyond: Literary and Religious Canons in the Ancient World* (Brill, 2003), 153–73.
Stroumsa, Guy G., 'The End of Sacrifice: Religious Mutations of Late Antiquity', in Johann Arnason and Kurt Raaflaub (eds), *The Roman Empire in Context: Historical and Comparative Perspectives* (John Wiley, 2011), 134–47.
Stroumsa, Guy G., 'From Master of Wisdom to Spiritual Master in Late Antiquity', in David Brakke *et al.* (eds), *Religion and the Self in Antiquity* (Indiana University Press, 2005), 183–96.
Stroumsa, Guy G., 'History of Religions: The Comparative Moment', in Renaud Gagné, Simon Goldhill, Geoffrey E. R. Lloyd (eds), *Regimes of Comparatism: Frameworks of Comparison in History, Religion and Anthropology* (Brill, 2019), 318–42.
Stroumsa, Guy G., *A New Science: The Discovery of Religion in the Age of Reason* (Harvard University Press, 2010).
Stroumsa, Guy G., 'The New Self and Reading Practices in Late Antique Christianity', *Church History and Religious Culture* 95 (2015), 1–18.
Subrahmanyam, Sanjay, *Europe's India: Words, People, Empires, 1500–1800* (Harvard University Press, 2017).
Sullivan, Robert, *John Toland and the Deist Controversy: A Study in Adaptations* (Cambridge University Press, 1982).
al-Tabari, Abu Ja'far Muhammad ibn Jarir, *Tarikh al-rusul wa'l-moluk*, translated as *The History of al-Tabari*, ed. Ehsan Yarshater (State University of New York Press, 2007).
Tavakoli-Targhi, Mohammad, *Refashioning Iran: Orientalism, Occidentalism and Historiography* (Palgrave, 2001).
Taylor, Charles, 'Afterward: *Apologia pro Libro suo*', in Michael Warner, Jonathan VanAntwerpen and Craig Calhoun (eds), *Varieties of Secularism in a Secular Age* (Harvard University Press, 2013), 302–3.
Taylor, Charles, *A Secular Age* (Harvard University Press, 2007).
Toland, John, *John Toland's Letters to Serena*, ed. Ian Leask (Four Courts Press, 2013).
Tolz, Vera, *Russia's Own Orient: The Politics of Identity and Oriental Studies in the Late Imperial and Early Soviet Periods* (Oxford University Press, 2011).
Toulmin, Stephen, *Cosmopolis: The Hidden Agenda of Modernity* (University of Chicago Press, 1990).
Tufekcioğlu, Zeynep, 'The Islamic Epistemology in a Western Genre: Ahmet Mithat Efendi's *Esrar-i Cinayat*, the First Detective Novel of Turkish Literature', *CLUES* 29: 2 (Fall 2011), 7–15.
Tuna, Mustafa Özgür, 'Gaspirali v. Il'minskii: Two Identity Projects for the Muslims of the Russian Empire', *Nationalities Papers* 30: 2 (2002), 265–89.
Tylor, Edward B., *Primitive Culture: Researches into the Development of Mythology, Philosophy, Religion, Language, Art and Custom*, 3rd American edn, from the 2nd English edn in 2 vols (Henry Holt and Company, [1871] 1889).
Tyrrell, George, *Christianity at the Cross-roads*. 4th edn (Longmans, Green and Co., 1913).

Veer, Peter van der, *Imperial Encounters: Religion and Modernity in India and Britain* (Princeton University Press, 2001).
Voltaire, *Essai sur l'histoire Générale et sur les moeurs et l'esprit des nations, depuis Charlemagne jusqu'à nos jours*, 10 vols (1757).
Warner, Michael, Jonathan VanAntwerpen and Craig Calhoun (eds), *Varieties of Secularism in a Secular Age* (Harvard University Press, 2013).
Watt, Montgomery, 'The Closing of the Door of Ijtihad', in J. M. Barrai (ed.), *Orientalia Hispanica* 1 (Leiden, 1974), 675–8.
Weber, Eugene, *Peasants into Frenchmen: The Modernization of Rural France, 1870–1914* (Stanford University Press, 2005).
Weber, Eugene, 'Religion and Superstition in Nineteenth-Century France', *The Historical Journal* 31: 2 (1988), 399–423.
Weber, Max, 'The Disenchantment of Modern Life', lecture given in Germany, 1917, http://www.yorku.ca/lfoster/2006-07/sosi3830/lectures/MaxWeber_TheDisenchantmentofModernLife.html.
Weber, Max, 'Science as a Vocation', in H. H. Gerth and C. Wright Mills (eds), *From Max Weber: Essays in Sociology* (Oxford University Press, 1946), 129–56.
Wiseman, Nicholas, *Twelve Lectures on the Connection Between Science and Revealed Religion, Delivered in Rome* (1836).
Wishnitzer, Avner, *Reading Clocks 'Alla Turca': Time and Society in the Late Ottoman Empire* (University of Chicago Press, 2015).
Wright, Terrence R., 'The Letter and the Spirit: Deconstructing Renan's *Life of Jesus* and the Assumptions of Modernity', *Religion & Literature* 26: 2 (Summer 1994), 55–71.
Yalçinkaya, M. Alper, *Learned Patriots: Debating Science, State, and Society in the Nineteenth-Century Ottoman Empire* (University of Chicago Press, 2015).
Yalçinkaya, M. Alper, 'Science as an Ally of Religion: A Muslim Appropriation of the Conflict Thesis', *British Journal for the History of Science* 44: 2 (June 2011), 161–81.
Zachhuber, Johannes, 'The Historical Turn', in Joel Rasmussen, Judith Wolfe and Johannes Zachhuber (eds), *The Oxford Handbook of Nineteenth Century Christian Thought* (Oxford University Press, 2019).
Zachhuber, Johannes, *Theology as Science in Nineteenth-Century Germany: From F. C. Baur to Ernst Troeltsch* (Oxford University Press, 2013).
Zammito, John, 'Koselleck's Philosophy of Historical Time(s) and the Practice of History,' *History and Theory* 43: 1 (February 2004), 124–35.
Zemmin, Florian, *Modernity in Islamic Traditions: The Concept of 'Society' in the Journal al-Manar (Cairo, 1898–1940)* (de Gruyter, 2018).
Zemmin, Florian, 'A Secular Age and Islamic Modernism', in Florian Zemmin (ed.), *Working with a Secular Age* (de Gruyter, 2017), 307–29.
Zemmin, Florian (ed.), *Working with a Secular Age* (de Gruyter, 2017).

INDEX

Abbasid period, 41, 42, 47, 116–17
  and conversion, 59
  and decline, 68, 113, 115
  and Golden Age, 91–3, 109, 123–33, 134
  and history, 95–9, 100–1
  and precedent, 104–5, 106–7
  and Umayyads, 89, 90
Abduh, Mohamed, 3
Abrahamic texts, 19
Abu Bakr, 78–9, 81, 82, 83, 107, 109
Abu Sufyan, Mu'awiya ibn, 82, 84, 85–6, 90, 150
Abu Ubayda, 83
Adam, 19, 103
al-Afghani, Jamal al-Din, 1–3, 25, 37, 38–40
  and Abbasids, 124, 130
  and comparison, 120–1
  and dogmatism, 118–19
  and essence, 115
  and history, 69–71
  and law, 62–3
  and locating Islam, 51–4
  and progress, 67, 114
  and Quran, 75
  and religious taxonomy, 47, 49
  and self-evident truths, 183
Afghanistan, 27
Age of Discovery, 6–7
Ahmet Midhat Efendi

Felatun Bey and Rakım Efendi, 175
Alexander the Great, 70
Ali, Syed Ameer, 3, 10, 12, 37, 38–40
  and Abbasids, 91–3, 124, 130–3
  and antiquity, 121–2
  and Christianity, 60–1
  and essence, 115
  and European scholars, 137–8
  and *fraternité*, 185
  and individuals, 184
  and law, 61–3, 155–6, 180, 181
  and *The Life and Teachings of Mohammad*, 71–4, 160–71
  and locating Islam, 50–1
  and modernity, 133–4
  and pre-Islamic Arabia, 75–7
  and Prophet Mohammad, 142–8, 149–55, 157–9
  and the Quran, 182
  and Rashidun, 78–85
  and religious taxonomy, 47–8, 49
  and *A Short History of the Saracens*, 68–9, 71
  and 'true' Islam, 116–18
  and Umayyads, 85–7
Ali b. Abu Taleb, 78, 82, 83, 84, 109, 116
angels, 145, 148
animism, 45
Ansar, 83
anti-intellectualism, 114–15

Index

antiquity, 121–3
Arabia, 54–5, 59, 73, 74–7, 142–3, 150; see also Mecca; Medina
archaeology, 19
art, 32
Aryans, 72
astrology, 101–2

backwardness, 8, 24, 28, 109, 112, 115, 125
  and Mecca/Medina, 84–5, 86–7
Badr, Battle of, 147–8, 149
Bahira, 143–4
Banu Hashem, 91
Batnitzky, Leonora, 179, 180
al-Baydawi, 99
Bayezidof, Ataullah, 3, 37, 38–40, 137–8
  and Abbasids, 124, 127–8, 129–30, 133
  and God, 183
  and Islam, 74–5
  and Renan, 120
  and science, 180–1
belief, 52–3
Berberian, Houri, 39
Bible, the, 18–19, 26, 97
Bopp, Franz, 14
Bos, Jacques, 7
Bournouf, Émile-Louis, 15
British Empire, 80, 89
Byzantium, 80, 81, 85, 86

caliphs see Rashidun
Campos, Michelle, 29
Catholicism, 9, 57, 63–4, 179–80
  and Renan, 160, 163, 169, 171
Caussin de Percival, Armand-Pierre, 114
Central Asia, 27
Chakrabarty, Dipesh, 10–11
Chaldeans, 51, 69
Chengiz Khan, 92
Christianity, 9, 10, 15, 18–19, 24
  and Abbasids, 92
  and al-Afghani, 52, 53
  and Ali, 72–4, 138
  and Arabia, 75–6
  and comparison, 120–1, 122–3
  and essence, 46
  and European scholarship, 54–60

and Islam, 40–1, 60–1, 80–1
and location, 50–1
and modernity, 130–3, 134
and Prophet Mohammad, 143–4
and revelation, 65
and Spain, 88, 89–90
see also Jesus; Protestantism
civilisation, 13–18, 22–3, 69–71
  and Abbasids, 91–2
  and antiquity, 121–2
  and dissonance, 112, 113
  and law, 155–6
  and modernity, 134–7
  and progress, 67–8, 127–8
  and Prophet Mohammad, 149, 185
  and religion, 44–6
colonialism, 27, 28
comparativism, 23, 120–33, 160–71, 173
Conrad, Sebastian, 33
constitutionalism, 27, 30, 33–4, 174
context, 11–12, 17, 20, 95
conversation, 36
conversion, 59, 97
Creation, 19, 102–3
Cromer, Lord, 10
Crusades, 92
culture, 13–18, 44–5, 124

Damascus, 85, 90
Dar al-Harb (Lands of War), 22, 184
Dar al-Islam (Lands of Islam), 22, 184
Darwin, Charles, 14, 25
devils, 145
disenchantment, 3–10, 20, 172–3, 186
dissonance, 111–12, 113–14, 115, 134
Divine, the see God
dogmatism, 117, 118–19, 163, 170
al-Dowleh, Mirza Yusuf Khan Mostashir
  Yek Kalameh (One Word), 33–4

education, 27
Egypt, 27, 36, 51–2, 69
El-Hibri, Tayeb, 96–7, 98, 100, 101–2, 105
Eliot, T. S., 22
empathy, 12–13
enemy dead, 149–50
Enlightenment, 4–7, 9, 10, 21, 173, 179–80

equality, 53, 126, 91–2; *see also* inequality
erasure, 26–31
essence, 13–14, 17, 46–7, 65–6, 67–8
   and Christianity, 164, 165
   and dissonance, 111–13, 114
   and history, 94–5, 181–2
   and Prophet Mohammad, 108, 140–1
ethics, 58, 183
eunuchs, 86
Europe, 2–3, 9–11, 17, 19–27, 32–3
   and comparison, 120–1
   and Dark Ages, 123–33
   and historicism, 137–8
   and Middle East, 36
Europe (cont.)
   and modernity, 113, 115, 133–4, 174–6, 177–81
   see also Christianity
evolution, 19, 22–3, 41, 47–8, 60–1, 64

faith, 52–3
Fatima, 83
Ferdowsi, 102
   Shahnameh, 80
Ferruh, Ali, 3
Feuerbach, Ludwig, 14
fitna (rebellion, strife), 107
France, 1–2, 34, 160–1, 169
French Revolution, 9, 88, 126, 133
fundamentalism, 177

gender, 32–3; *see also* women
Germany, 26
al-Ghazzali, Hamid, 25, 176–7
Gibbon, Edward, 114
   The Decline and Fall of the Roman Empire, 8, 81
God, 43, 48, 49
   and Christianity, 163, 164
   and intent, 108–10
   and Prophet Mohammad, 65, 76–7, 144–7, 148–9, 150, 154–5
   and *Sunna*, 98–102, 103–6
Gospels, 122–3, 162–3, 165–8
Goths, 87, 88
Greeks, 51–2, 71, 124, 129
Green, Nile, 21–2, 39
Grimm, Jacob and Wilhelm, 14, 15

Hadith, 42–3, 94, 97–8, 128, 141
   and Ali, 121, 168
Hamza, 150
harems, 86
harmony, 111–12, 113, 115
hierarchy, 53, 68
Hind, 150
Hinduism, 9, 24, 51, 179–80
historicism, 7–18, 23, 41 112–13, 186
   and al-Afghani, 69–71
   and Ali, 71–4
   and civilisation, 134–5
   and Europe, 137–8
   and Islam, 24–5, 67–9, 93–110
   and modernity, 172–3
   and religion, 18–21, 179–80
   and Renan, 160–1, 165–6
   and science, 126
   and time, 184, 185
historiography, 26–31, 94
Hobbes, Thomas, 14, 62
Hume, David, 11, 18–19, 20

Ibn Athir, 121
Ibn Ishaq, 97, 121
   Life of the Prophet (*Sirat rasul Allah*), 102–3
Ibn Sa'd, 121
idolatry, 51, 56, 74–5, 76, 127
ijtihad, 25
imperialism, 27, 28
India, 29, 36, 38, 72, 80, 170
individuals, 183–4
inequality, 53, 86, 90
institutionalism, 27–8, 114, 116–18, 119, 178–9
Iran, 27, 28, 29, 32–4, 36, 184–5; *see also* Persians
Islam, 9, 10, 11
   and Ahmet Midhat, 175
   and al-Afghani, 51–4, 118–19
   and Ali, 50–1, 71–4, 116–18
   and comparison, 120–1, 122–3
   and essence, 46, 67–8
   and Europe, 21–2, 54–6, 57–9, 177–9
   and historicism, 24–5, 68–9, 93–110, 112–13, 181–2
   and individuals, 183–4
   and intellectuals, 37–40

and location, 40–1, 65–6, 182–3
and modernism, 37, 41–2, 60–3, 64–5, 140–1
and progress, 111–12
and Protestantism, 179–80
and Rashidun, 78–85
and reforms, 27–31, 63–4
and Renan, 125–6
and science, 1–3, 126–7, 129
and taxonomy, 48
and tradition, 113–16, 176–7
and translation, 35
and Umayyads, 85–90
and universalising, 133–9
see also Abbasid period; Prophet Mohammad; Quran

Jadid movement, 36
jahiliyya, 108–9, 127, 184
Jesus Christ, 15, 18–19, 50–1, 145, 160–71
and Ali, 71, 73–4, 122–3
and truth, 60, 61
Journal des débats politiques et littéraires, 1–3
Judaism, 9, 10, 15, 24, 50–1
and Ali, 72–3, 122
and Arabia, 75–6
and Islam, 54–5
and Jesus, 164
and Protestantism, 179, 180
and revelation, 65
and Spain, 88
Juynboll, 105

Kaaba, 142
Kemal, Namık, 3, 37–40, 74, 185
and Abbasids, 124, 127, 128–9, 133
and *The Complete History of Islam* (*Büyük Islam Tarihi*), 68–9, 120
Khadija, 142, 151, 152
Khalidi, Tarif, 96, 97–8, 99, 100, 105–6, 107
Khan, Sir Syed Ahmed, 38
kingship, 102, 104
Koran *see* Quran
Koselleck, Reinhardt, 11, 17, 135
Kuenen, Abraham, 54–5, 56, 57–8, 59, 60
Kurzman, Charles
Modernist Islam, 37

language, 13–15, 17, 125, 155
Lassner, Jacob, 95–6
law, 10, 54–6, 61–3, 153, 155–6, 168–9
laws of progress, 67–8, 72–4, 86
Le Bon, Gustav, 114
Levine, Joseph, 7
Liberté, Égalité, Fraternité, 88, 89, 91, 126, 133

Macaulay, Thomas Babington
History of England (1848–61), 12–13
Ma'mun, 116–17, 128
Marashi, Afshin, 39
Mas'udi, 102
Mecca, 84–5, 86, 90
media, 27
Medina, 84–5, 86, 90
messengers, 99, 103
Middle East, 21–2, 23, 26–7, 32–4
and reforms, 28, 29, 30, 36–7
see also Arabia
military technology, 174
Milman, Henry Hart, 8, 122–3
miracles, 18–19, 20, 145, 146–8, 162
modernity, 3–10, 20–1
and characteristics, 126
and Christianity, 130–1, 164–5
and civilisation, 134–7
and difference, 176–7
and Europe, 113, 115, 120, 177–81
and Islam, 24, 37, 39–40, 41–2, 93–110, 133–4, 140–1, 182–3
and origin, 31–2
and Prophet Mohammad, 157–60
and reforms, 27–31
and religion, 26–7, 170–1, 172–3
and translation, 173–6
Mohammad *see* Prophet Mohammad
Momigliano, Arnaldo, 8
Mongols, 68, 92, 113
monotheism, 16, 45, 48, 121–2, 127
and Prophet Mohammad, 76–7, 149, 150
see also Christianity; Islam
Montesquieu, 11, 34
morality, 58, 76–7, 143–4
Moses, 54, 65, 73, 84, 122
Muir, William, 55, 56, 60, 114
Müller, Max, 14, 20, 47

Muslims *see* Islam
Mu'tazilites, 116

Nahda movement, 36
Najmabadi, Afsaneh, 32–3
nationalism, 29
natural law, 18–19
Nihavand, battle of, 80
Nizam-e Jadid movement, 36
North Africa, 27, 87
novels, 174–5
Nuri, Celal, 3
Nussbaum, Felicity, 23

obedience, 48, 51, 53, 55, 104, 119, 182–3
  and Renan, 163, 169, 171
O'Brien, Karen, 6
Orientalists, 114–15
origin, 13–14, 31–2, 94–5
Orthodox Christianity, 57
orthodoxy, 119
ossification, 113–19
Ottoman Empire, 27, 32, 36, 37–8, 175, 184–5
Özervarlı, Said, 177

paganism, 45, 121–2, 127, 149, 150
painting, 174–5
Papaconstantinou, Arietta, 58–9
parables, 96–8, 100–1, 104–7
Paradise, 14
particularism, 182
pastiche, 95, 96
Persians, 51–2, 71, 79–80, 81, 85, 86
philology, 14–15, 17, 125
philosophy, 70
Phoenicians, 51, 70
piety, 73, 90, 99, 184–5
  and Prophet Mohammad, 123, 127, 141, 158–9
politics, 27–30, 126
polygamy, 85, 121, 126, 150–2, 156
polytheism, 16, 45
prayer, 49, 158–9
precedent, 104–7, 108
Priest, Robert, 169
primitivism, 16–17, 18, 27, 84, 86–7
  and religion, 44, 45–6, 47–9
print, 21

Prophet Mohammad, 41, 42–3, 57, 59
  and Abbasids, 91, 93
  and Ali, 71, 122, 123, 160–71
  and Christianity, 81
  and civilisation, 185
  and death, 104
  and God's laws, 76–7
  and historicisation, 141, 156–7
  and history, 68, 102, 103
  and 'incomparable man', 142–8
  and law, 156
  and modernity, 138–9, 157–60
  and parables, 97, 101
  and the Quran, 154–5
  and Rashidun, 78–9, 83–4
  and revelation, 65
  and *Sunna*, 104–6
  and translation, 148–54
  and Umayyads, 90
prophets, 99, 100, 102–4
Protestantism, 9, 17, 166–7, 179–81
  and superiority, 56–7, 59, 63–4

'Quarrel of the Ancients and the Moderns', 7–8
Quran, the, 41, 42–3
  and al-Afghani, 51, 52, 75
  and Ali, 121, 168
  and civilisation, 128
  and God, 99, 100
  and parables, 97, 98, 101
  and Prophet Mohammad, 103, 141, 154–5
  and translation, 181–2
Qurayshi, 83, 147, 150

Ranke, Leopold van, 13
Rashidun, 25, 41, 68, 78–85
  and precedent, 105, 106–7
  and Prophet Mohammad, 108–9
rationalism, 52–3, 116–17, 118
re-enchantment, 20–1, 43; *see also* disenchantment
reforms, 27–30, 33–4, 35, 36–7, 175–6
  and modernity, 177–9
  and Prophet Mohammad, 141, 153–4
religion, 2–6, 7, 8–10
  and al-Afghani, 70–1
  and Ali, 72–4

Index

and essence, 46–7
and historicism, 13–14, 15, 16, 17, 18–21
and modernity, 26–7, 170–1, 172–3
and progress, 44–6, 62–3, 68
and taxonomy, 47–9
and tolerance, 126, 130
and translation, 173–4, 181–5
and universal phenomenon, 40–1
see also Christianity; Islam; Judaism
Renan, Ernest, 17, 25, 39, 40, 114, 186
and Christianity, 57, 122
and *fraternité*, 185
and Islam, 55–6, 60, 135–6
and 'Islam and Science' lecture, 1–3, 37, 119, 120, 124–6, 128–9
and *Life of Jesus*, 160–71
and reform, 63–4
'Republic of Islam' *see* Rashidun
revelation, 31, 52, 54, 71–4
and Prophet Mohammad, 41, 65, 142, 144–5
rituals, 48–9, 50, 159–60, 183
Robinson, Chase, 95, 104
Rousseau, Jean-Jacques, 11, 14
Rubiés, Joan-Pau, 19
Rubin, Uri, 99, 103
Russia, 37

sacred texts, 18–19
Sa'd, 79
Saladin, 92
Saracens, 79–80
Sasanians, 102
science, 1–3, 7, 8–9, 20
and Abbasids, 124, 126, 131–3
and al-Afghani, 69–70
and Bayezidof, 180–1
and Islam, 30, 119, 126–7, 129
and tradition, 115
Scientific Revolution, 6–7, 21
sectarianism, 107
secularism, 4–5, 6, 9, 27–31, 184–5
Sédillot, Louis-Amélie, 114
Semitism, 54–5, 56
Shah, Wendy, 32
Shahrestani, 121
Sheehan, Jonathan, 4, 6

Shiite Islam, 91
Shissler, Holly, 39
slavery, 13, 77, 121, 126, 156
and Prophet Mohammad, 152, 153
Sorkin, David, 4–5, 8–9, 10, 179–80
South Asia, 21, 23, 26–7, 28, 32–3
space, 21–2
Spain, 87–90
Spinoza, Baruch, 11
'straight path', 99–100, 103–4, 107
Strauss, David Friedrich, 20
Stroumsa, Guy, 23
Sunna, 42, 98–102, 103–7, 141
Sunni Islam, 104
supernatural *see* miracles

al-Tabari, Muhammad ibn Jarir, 105, 121, 142, 143–4
The History of Prophets and Kings (Tarikh al-rusul wa'l-moluk), 94, 97–8, 102–3
Tanzimat reforms, 27, 34, 35, 36
Tatars, 37
Tavakoli-Targhi, Mohamad, 39
Taylor, Charles, 4
technology, 21
Tercuman-i Hakikat (The Translation of Truth) (journal), 37
time, 17–18, 22–3, 134–5, 184, 185
tradition, 113–14, 115–16, 117–19, 156–7
and Christianity, 163, 165
and Islam, 176–7, 181–2
and modernity, 134, 136, 137
translation, 35, 173–6, 181–5
and Prophet Mohammad, 141, 148–54
transportation, 21
travel, 21–3
tribalism, 76, 82, 85, 86, 89
Turkey, 28; *see also* Ottoman Empire
Tylor, Edward, 19
Primitive Culture, 16–17, 18, 44–5

Uhud, Battle of, 149–50
ulama, 27–8, 29, 30
Umar, 78–9, 81–2, 83, 84, 109
Umayyad period, 59, 68, 85–90, 109
umma, 170, 184
universalism, 23, 57–60, 182
Uthman, 78, 81–2, 83, 109

Van der Veer, Peter, 39
Vico, Gianbattista, 11
Voltaire, 11

Weber, Max, 3–4, 8, 186
women, 13, 27, 30, 126, 130
  and Abbasids, 92
  and polygamy, 151, 152, 153
  and Umayyads, 86, 87
World War I, 28–9

Ya'qubi, 102, 105
Yazdegird III, Emperor (Yezdjard), 79, 102

Zachhuber, Johannes, 10, 19, 26
Zemmin, Florian, 6
Zoroaster, 121, 122
Zoroastrianism, 24, 29, 50, 72, 179–80

EU representative:
Easy Access System Europe
Mustamäe tee 50, 10621 Tallinn, Estonia
Gpsr.requests@easproject.com

www.ingramcontent.com/pod-product-compliance
Lightning Source LLC
Chambersburg PA
CBHW070354240426
43671CB00013BA/2498